Equality and Non-discrimination

Equality and Non-discrimination
Catholic Roots, Current Challenges

EDITED BY
Jane F. Adolphe
Robert L. Fastiggi
AND
Michael A. Vacca

FOREWORD BY
Robert F. Gorman

☙PICKWICK *Publications* · Eugene, Oregon

EQUALITY AND NON-DISCRIMINATION
Catholic Roots, Current Challenges

Copyright © 2019 Wipf and Stock Publishers. All rights reserved. Except for brief quotations in critical publications or reviews, no part of this book may be reproduced in any manner without prior written permission from the publisher. Write: Permissions, Wipf and Stock Publishers, 199 W. 8th Ave., Suite 3, Eugene, OR 97401.

Pickwick Publications
An Imprint of Wipf and Stock Publishers
199 W. 8th Ave., Suite 3
Eugene, OR 97401

www.wipfandstock.com

PAPERBACK ISBN: 978-1-5326-3721-6
HARDCOVER ISBN: 978-1-5326-4641-6
EBOOK ISBN: 978-1-5326-4642-3

Cataloguing-in-Publication data:

Names: Adolphe, Jane, 1963–, editor. | Fastiggi, Robert L., editor. | Vacca, Michael, 1985–, editor. | Gorman, Robert F., foreword.

Title: Equality and non-discrimination : Catholic roots, current challenges / edited by Jane F. Adolphe, Robert L. Fastiggi, and Michael A. Vacca.

Description: Eugene, OR : Pickwick Publications, 2019 | Includes bibliographical references and index.

Identifiers: ISBN 978-1-5326-3721-6 (paperback) | ISBN 978-1-5326-4641-6 (hardcover) | ISBN 978-1-5326-4642-3 (ebook)

Subjects: LCSH: Christianity and politics—Catholic Church. | Liberalism—United States. | Freedom of religion. | Religion and state. | Marriage—Government policy. | Marriage—Religious aspects.

Classification: BX1753 .E68 2019 (print) | BX1753 .E68 (ebook)

Manufactured in the U.S.A. 04/09/19

To Hazel and Edward Adolphe, who raised four girls and three boys in the Catholic faith, teaching them about their common origin, dignity, and destiny, appreciating their differences, acknowledging their strengths, correcting their faults, and ever urging them to be good and to do good.

Contents

Authors | ix
Foreword | ROBERT F. GORMAN | xvii
Acknowledgments | xxi
Introduction | JANE F. ADOLPHE | xxiii

1. Human Equality and Non-discrimination in Light of Catholic Theology and Magisterial Teachings | ROBERT L. FASTIGGI | 1
2. Sacramental Roots of Canon Law: Fundamental Equality and Functional Difference | ERNEST CAPARROS | 12
3. The Principles of Equality and Non-discrimination | DANIEL B. GALLAGHER | 29
4. How to Think about Sexual Orientation and Gender Identity (SOGI) Policies and Religious Freedom | RYAN T. ANDERSON | 42
5. The Necessity for a Contextual Analysis for Equality and Non-Discrimination | IAIN T. BENSON | 63
6. Non-discrimination Policy in the Context of the European Union | MONSIGNOR PIOTR MAZURKIEWICZ | 76
7. Human Rights as Ideology: The Meaning of Equality and Non-discrimination in European Litigation within the Context of Religious Freedom | PAUL DIAMOND | 104
8. The Inter-American System: Sexual Orientation as a Category and/or Ground of Non-discrimination | CARMEN DOMÍNGUEZ HIDALGO | 133
9. Equality and Non-discrimination: The Peculiar Approach of the American Convention on Human Rights | URSULA C. BASSET | 149

10 ASEAN's Declaration of Human Rights (ADHR): Clashing Cultural and Regional Values | D. BRIAN SCARNECCHIA | 163

11 Religious Freedom and Christianity in the Middle East and North Africa (MENA) in the Context of the Papal Trip to Turkey | GEOFFREY STRICKLAND | 190

Index of Names and Subjects | 205

Scripture Index | 213

Authors

Ryan T. Anderson

Dr. Anderson is the William E. Simon Senior Research Fellow at The Heritage Foundation, and the founder and editor of *Public Discourse*, the online journal of the Witherspoon Institute of Princeton, New Jersey. He is the author of *Truth Overruled: The Future of Marriage and Religious Freedom* and the co-author with Princeton's Robert P. George and Sherif Girgis of *What Is Marriage? Man and Woman: A Defense*. Anderson's research has been cited by two U.S. Supreme Court justices, Justice Samuel Alito and Justice Clarence Thomas, in two Supreme Court cases. Anderson received his bachelor of arts degree from Princeton University, graduating *Phi Beta Kappa* and *magna cum laude*, and he received his doctoral degree in political philosophy from the University of Notre Dame. His dissertation was titled: "Neither Liberal Nor Libertarian: A Natural Law Approach to Social Justice and Economic Rights." Anderson has made appearances on ABC, CNN, CNBC, MSNBC, and Fox News. His work has appeared in the *New York Times*, the *Washington Post*, the *Wall Street Journal*, the *Harvard Journal of Law and Public Policy*, the *Harvard Health Policy Review*, the *Weekly Standard*, and *National Review*. In spring 2017, Oxford University Press released Anderson's latest book, *Debating Religious Liberty and Discrimination*, co-authored with Sherif Girgis and John Corvino. Also in spring 2017, the University of Notre Dame Press released a book of collected essays, *A Liberalism Safe for Catholicism? Perspectives from "The Review of Politics,"* which he edited with Dan Philpott. Anderson is currently at work on a book titled, *When Harry Became Sally: Responding to the Transgender Moment*. Follow him on Twitter: @

RyanTAnd For his latest essays and videos, follow his public Facebook page: https://www.facebook.com/RyanTAndersonPhD

Ursula C. Basset

Ursula C. Basset is a lawyer with a PhD in Juridical Sciences. She is also a Professor and Researcher at the *Pontificia Universidad Catòlica, Universidad Nacional de Buenos Aires* and a Director of the Postgraduate Career in Family Law at the *Universidad Catòlica de Salta*. She is also a member of many prestigious institutions: Board of Directors of the International Academy for the Study of the Jurisprudence in Family; Executive Board of the International Society of Family Law; Institute of Bioethics of the National Academy of Moral and Political Sciences (Buenos Aires, Argentina); Subcommission of Reform of the Civil Code (Argentina). Professor Basset is also an author of several publications on family law and bioethics.

Iain T. Benson

Born in Edinburgh, Scotland and raised in Western Canada, Iain Benson is a Professor of Law at the School of Law, University of Notre Dame, Sydney Australia and Extraordinary Professor, Faculty of Law, at the University of the Free State, Bloemfontein, South Africa. He holds degrees from the Universities of the Witwatersrand (PhD, Law); Cambridge (Law, MA); Windsor (JD); and Queens (BA, Hons.). He has been a visiting professor at the University of Western Ontario (2013) and Senior Visiting Scholar at Massey College, University of Toronto (2014). His work towards an understanding of secular and secularism has been cited by the Supreme Court of Canada and the Constitutional Court of South Africa. He was a member of the draft committee for the *South African Charter of Religious Rights and Freedoms* (2010), a document signed by all the religions in that country and an advisor to the South African Council for the Promotion of Religious Freedoms that advances understanding of the Charter. Retained by the Government of Canada, he authored material concerning *Religion and Public Policy as an aspect of Federal Multi-Culturalism Policy* (2008) and was the first Executive Director of the Centre for Cultural Renewal (1993–2009). He was an expert advisor to the Ontario Human Rights Commission's re-working of its understanding of "creed" and "competing rights" (2012–2014) and appointed by the Canadian government as one of ten inaugural directors of the Global Centre for Pluralism along with Kofi Annan and 8 others chaired by His Highness the Aga Khan IV (2010–present). In addition, Dr. Benson was the invited rapporteur on Law and Religious Diversity in Canada and South Africa to a conference organized by the Pontifical Academy of Social Sciences, Vatican City (2012). Dr. Benson has written and lectured extensively in the area of ethics, virtues/values and pluralism, and acted as an advisor in the fields of medical ethics and bioethics across Canada, Saudi Arabia, Eastern Europe, South Africa, Australia and New Zealand. He was called to the Bars of British Columbia and Ontario and practised law for over 30 years at all level of courts in Canada. He is a Knight of Magistral Grace of the Order of Malta and father of seven children.

Ernest Caparros

Ernest Caparros was Professor Emeritus at the University of Ottawa, with civil laws degrees from the University of Zaragoza, Spain (LL.L.), including a Doctor of Law from University of Laval, (LL.D.) and canon law degrees, including a Doctor of Canon Law from the University of Navarra, Spain (J.C.L., J.C.D.) and other degrees from the University of Granada, Spain (BA) and the University of Laval (D.E.S.D.). He taught civil law, comparative law, and canon law (1966 to 1980) at the University of Laval, where he was the director of *les Cahiers de Droit* (1965–1970), and until 2002, at the University of Ottawa, where he was the director of the *la Revue générale de droit* (1981 to 2002) and *la Collection Bleue* (1982–2002). He was the Director of the *Collection Gratianus Series*, a visiting Professor in canon law at the Pontifical University of the Holy Cross (Rome), and a Professor in the Department of Canon Law at the Institute for Theological Formation, in Montréal, where he acted as its first Director (2011–2013). He was the author and editor of many works (among them Code of Canon Law Annotated and Exegetical Commentary to the Code of Canon Law) as well as numerous articles and has spoken at various conferences on comparative religious law (general rapporteur for the International Academy of Comparative Law Congresses at Athens and Bristol) and canon law (International Congresses in Budapest, Mexico, Rome). He was a consultant to a number of organizations, and has given expert testimony in matters relating to the Parish of *l'Ange Gardien*. He was a member of the Royal Society of Canada, an associated member of the International Academy of Comparative Law, and a Knight of Magistral Grace of the Order of Malta.

Paul Diamond

After completing legal education and pupillage, Paul became Barrister to the Keep Sunday Special Campaign in 1988. In 1991, Paul was granted an audience with the Pope. He has authored various legal articles, including one in which Lord Denning supported his critique of interim relief pending a European Court of Justice ruling. Paul practiced in Administrative, Constitutional and European law. In 1996 Paul gained the first injunction against an abortion under the 1967 Act which was front page news. Subsequent to that case, he also took the 1997 banning of the Pro-Life Alliance Party Election Broadcast to the European Court. The Pro-Life Alliance was denied a Public Electoral Broadcast as the showing of an abortion would be distressing' to women who had had an abortion. He is one of a handful of individuals who understands the law of religious liberty in the legal framework of the Common Law, European Law and International Law. This rare combination of knowledge means that Paul is regularly sought after. He has an understanding of the law and of socio-cultural developments in society that underpin the law. Paul provides a consultancy on strategic responses to societal developments, both to public policy bodies and to religious leaders. Paul's analytical expertise, sense of humor and blunt eloquence make him an exceptionally dynamic speaker. Paul has a growing practice and has argued a number of groundbreaking cases on religious rights: many of his cases are front page of the newspapers. Paul is counsel of choice in high profile strategic cases and has represented many influential and significant individuals from the former Archbishop of Canterbury to the famous Soviet dissident, Vladimir Bukovsky.

Carmen Domínguez Hidalgo

Carmen Domínguez Hidalgo is a Professor of Civil Law at the *Pontificia Universidad Católica de Chile*. She is a graduate of the University of Concepción-Chile and a lawyer with a Masters in Comparative Law and Ph.D in Law from the Computense University of Madrid. She is a Professor of Civil Law, a member of the board of the Law School of the Catholic University of Chile and its Law Review. In addition, she is the director of the "Family Center of Catholic University of Chile." She has published three books and numerous articles on civil liability, legal theory, family law and bioethics and developed several research projects and domestic and foreign sources. She permanently teaches seminars lectures and conferences in Chile and abroad. She is a referee of the Chamber of Commerce and former Alternate

Judge at the Court of Appeal of Santiago, Chile. She is a consultant and expert in family law and bioethics for the Chilean Congress. She has also been a member of the Juridical Counsel of the Episcopal Conference of Chile, since 2004. Lastly she is the former President of REDIFAM (Network of Latino-American Catholic Centers on the Family) and a member of the board of the Latino-American Consortium of Religious Freedom as well as various networks concerned with family, bioethics and religious freedom issues. She is a member of the board of the bar Association of Chile A.G.

Robert L. Fastiggi

Dr. Robert Fastiggi is Professor of Systematic Theology at Sacred Heart Major Seminary in Detroit, where he has taught since 1999. Prior to coming to Sacred Heart, he taught at St. Edward's University in Austin, Texas from 1985–1999. Dr. Fastiggi received an AB in Religion (*summa cum laude*) from Dartmouth College in 1974; a MA in Theology from Fordham University in 1976; and a PhD in Historical Theology from Fordham in 1987. In addition, he has done private research in Paris and Montréal, and he took part in a study-tour of Saudi Arabia and Bahrain sponsored by the National Council for US-Arab relations. During his time at Sacred Heart, Dr. Fastiggi has taught a wide variety of courses, including Ecclesiology, Christology, Mariology, Moral Theology, and the Sacramental Life of the Church. He is a member of the Society for Catholic Liturgy and a former president of the Mariological Society of America. He has served as the executive editor of the 2009–2013 supplements to the *New Catholic Encyclopedia* and the co-editor of the English translation of the 43rd edition of the Denzinger-Hünermann *Compendium* published by Ignatius Press in 2012.

Daniel B. Gallagher

Daniel B. Gallagher is the Ralph and Jeanne Kanders Professor in the Practice of Latin at Cornell University in Ithaca, New York. He holds degrees from the University of Michigan (BS and MA), the Catholic University of America (MA in Philosophy), and the Pontifical Gregorian University (S.T.L.). He has also taught philosophy and Latin at Sacred Heart Major Seminary, Saint Mary's College, Aquinas College, and the University of Notre Dame. His articles have appeared in such journals as the *Postgraduate Journal of Aesthetics, Josephinum Journal of Theology, Sacred Architecture Journal, Journal for Christian Theological Research, Fellowship of Catholic Scholars Quarterly, Maritain Studies, The Latin Americanist,* and *Social*

Justice Review, in addition to various collected volumes. He is the translator of Vittorio Possenti's *Nihilism and Metaphysics*, the editor of the *Values in Italian Philosophy* Series, and a regular contributor to the *Philosophy and Popular Culture* series. His current research involves the relationship between "self-evidence" and "wisdom" in Aquinas and other medieval authors.

Monsignor Piotr Mazurkiewicz

Monsignor Piotr Mazurkiewicz is a Catholic priest ordained for the diocese of Warsaw in 1988. Then he work for seven years as a parish priest. He is an engineer in electricity, doctor in sociology, professor in political science and Catholic social doctrine. Since 1997 he is working at Cardinal Stefan Wyszynski University in Warsaw, Poland, delivering lectures in political ethics and philosophy, religion and politics, Church-state relations, Catholic social doctrine and European studies. He has been (2002–2008) a member of the Board of the European Society on Research in Ethics, Societas Ethica. Since 2002, he is a member of the Board of the Institute of Political Studies of the Polish Academy of Science. From 2008–2012 he served as the Secretary General of the Commission of the Bishops' of the European Community COMECE. From 2013–2014, he was a collaborator of the Pontifical Council for the Family. His main scientific publications are *Church and democracy, Europeanization of Europe, Violence in Politics*, and his other publications include *The Wind is Blowing in Prayers, In the Land of celibacy, Europe as a kinder surprise, Two towers and a minaret*, and *Totalitarianism in the postmodern age*.

D. Brian Scarnecchia

D. Brian Scarnecchia, M.Div., JD is a Professor of Law at Ave Maria School of Law in Naples, Florida where he teaches Jurisprudence, Bioethics and the Law and Catholic Social Teaching and the Law. He also served as the Chair of the Department of Catholic Social Thought and the Director of Human Life Studies at Franciscan University of Steubenville in Steubenville, Ohio. In addition, he has also worked as an Assistant County Prosecutor in Jefferson County, Ohio. He is the CEO and president of International Solidarity and Human Rights Institute (ISHRI), a non-governmental organization (NGO) in consultative status with the United Nations and the Organization of American States. He serves on the Board of Directors for the Society of Catholic Social Scientists (SCSS) and is their main NGO representative to the United Nations. He also serves on the Board of Directors of Population

Research Institute (PRI) that monitors coercive population control programs worldwide. He is the director of the Southeastern Asian Human Rights System for the International Center on Law, Life, Faith and Family (ICOLF). Professor Scarnecchia is the author of *Bioethics, Law and Human Life Issues: A Catholic Perspective on Marriage, Family, Contraception, Abortion, Reproductive Technology, and Death and Dying* and numerous scholarly and popular articles. He serves instead of services as an expert on family and social issues for the Catholic Inspired NGOs Rome Forum (CINGO) that works in close association with the Pontifical Council for the Family and the Office of the Secretary of State for the Holy See. He lectures nationally and internationally on life issues, marriage and family and human rights.

Geoffrey Strickland

Geoffrey Strickland, J.D., J.C.L., serves as Director of the Middle East and North Africa (MENA) Region for the International Center for Law, Life, Faith and Family (ICOLF). As the MENA Regional Director for ICOLF, he provides analysis upon themes related to the rights of life and religious freedom, particularly with regard to the persecution of Christians in the region.

Mr. Strickland has served the Holy See and related institutions in various capacities. He formerly served as an internal legal analyst for the Pontifical Council for the Family, facilitating as well the translation and interpretation of Spanish, Portuguese, French, Italian, and Arabic. Currently, Mr. Strickland works as Secretary of the Forum of Catholic Inspired Non-Governmental Organizations, while assisting Gospel of Life Ministries in their canonical and international growth.

Editors

Jane F. Adolphe

Jane Adolphe is Professor of Law at Ave Maria School of Law, in Naples, Florida, (2001–present). She also works as an expert with the Holy See, Secretariat of State, Section for Relations with States (2011–present). She has a Licentiate and a Doctorate in Canon law (J.C.L/J.C.D) from the Pontifical University of the Holy Cross, Rome; Common Law and Civil Law degrees (LL.B/B.C.L.) from University of McGill, Montreal; and a Bachelor of Arts (BA) from the University of Calgary. She is the co-editor with Ron Rychlak of *Persecution and Genocide of Christians: Prevention, Prohibition and Prosecution* (Angelico Press: 2017) and co-editor with Robert Fastiggi and

Michael Vacca, *St. Paul, the Natural Law and Contemporary Legal Theory* (Lexington: 2012). She is a member of the Bar of New York and the Bar of Alberta, and continues to serve as a member of the Editorial Board of the Canon Law: "Gratianus Series." She began her legal career clerking for the Alberta Court of Appeal and Court of Queen's Bench, after practicing with the Law Firm of "Bennett Jones Verchere." She served as a prosecutor with the Alberta Crown Prosecutor's Office, then later as a legal consultant for a law firm in Rome, Italy and as a legal advisor to the Holy See (2003 to 2011) which included her participation on various delegations of the Holy See at Conferences and meetings within the United Nations system. Her courses have included International Law and the Holy See, International Law, International Human Rights and Canon Law.

Robert L. Fastiggi (see *supra*)

Michael Arthur Vacca

Michael Arthur Vacca holds a JD from Ave Maria School of Law (2010) where he concentrated on laws and policies affecting the human person and the family as well as Catholic social teaching. He holds a BA from Hillsdale College in Political Science and English literature. From October 2010 Through October 2012, he worked for the Holy See in Rome, Italy as a legal advisor defending human life and the family. He is the author of an article published in an international bioethics journal *Medicina e Morale* entitled, "A Reexamination of Conscience Protections in Healthcare;" the co-author of an article published in the Ave Maria School of Law International Law Journal entitled, "Best Practices: Laws Protecting Human Life and the Family Around the Globe;" the author of an article published in the *Ave Maria International Law Journal* entitled "Talk About a Human Rights Violation: How Heterologous Assisted Reproduction Harms Children and Violates International Human Rights Law;" the author of an article in *Baku State University Law Review* entitled: "Natural Law as Guardian of the Human Person," and the co-editor of a book entitled *St. Paul, the Natural Law, and Contemporary Legal Theory* published by Lexington Books. He has appeared as a guest speaker on various Catholic programs discussing the topic of natural law and Catholic social teaching. He is regular contributor to *The Catholic Journal*, https://www.catholicjournal.us/author/michael-vacca/. Michael and his wife Sarah reside in Royal Oak MI, and are parishioners of the National Shrine of the Little Flower Basilica.

Foreword

Robert F. Gorman

In an age increasingly marked by exaggerated subjectivism and the denial of fundamental truths rooted in reality, this book is a breath of fresh air and a victory for common sense. Its chief theme concerns the relationship of two concepts of enduring moral significance: equality and non-discrimination. In modern terms, these two ideals are now almost obsessive preoccupations. But they also have been matter for philosophical reflection and discourse since ancient times. How one defines and thus discriminates these terms is an important matter for the health and wellbeing of both individual persons and of the society as a whole. Moreover, some inequalities are natural while some discrimination is necessary for the wellbeing and good order of society. For example, anyone invoking the value of 'diversity' is implicitly recognizing that inequality is part of social reality. Anyone with a 'discriminating' intellect is aware that not all ideas and opinions are equally important or equally true. It is crucial to get the definitions of equality and inequality and the distinction between non-discrimination and necessary discrimination right.

Equality is an important human value. But exactly what does it mean? We know that part of the dignity of persons is the uniqueness of person with diverse talents, capacities, and personalities. We also know that the unequal distribution of these talents leads to natural inequalities of outcome. In moral thought from the most ancient times versions of the golden rule and the silver rule recognize the essential dignity of persons as reasonable beings. In divine revelation, the biblical teaching that all human beings are made in the divine image and likeness of their creator offers further deep meditation on the fundamental dignity and equality of all. Everyone deserves to have their dignity respected and not discriminated against. But the behavior of persons is and always has been the subject of discrimination, because not all human acts are good, or right, or in keeping with even the dignity of persons.

This volume, rooted in reality, logic and common sense, speaks to a world confused about how to think about and define equality and non-discrimination. Jane Adolphe and her colleagues have assembled here a much-needed and timely critique of the fallacious ways in which the concepts of equality and non-discrimination have been applied in the modern constitutional law of states and in international law. Drawing on the timeless logic of realist philosophy and that of Catholic moral and social teaching, the contributions to this volume take a discriminating reader through the maze of modern confusion to a place of intellectual clarity.

The contributors are lawyers, philosophers and theologians who offer rich insights into the modern crisis of social thought. They examine the global assault on human life and dignity, on the dignity of family life and marriage, even on the natural dignity of masculinity and femininity, as the essential foundations of reality and basis for the attainment of the common good. Here contributors move beyond the positivist mentality to evaluate the first principles of natural law in which all human law is imbedded and which human law ignores to the peril of genuine human dignity and achievement of the common good.

Another contribution to these essays was a lengthy and magisterial treatment by Father Robert Araujo, SJ, recently deceased. Father Araujo adroitly dissected the modern misconceptions concerning equality and non-discrimination in U.S. constitutional law and practice. Due to the length of his piece, however, the editors have decided to publish the article separately. His wisdom, speaking to us beyond the grave, appeals to human reason and conscience, logic and the basic nature of reality as applied to legal and philosophical developments in American practice. Other chapters evaluate developments in the application of theories of equality and non-discrimination in the history of Western thought (Fastiggi and Gallagher), in modern European practice (Diamond and Mazurkiewicz), in contemporary inter-American practice (Basset and Domínguez), in the Asian setting (Scarnecchia), in the Middle East and North Africa (Strickland); and in the canon law tradition of the Catholic Church (Caparros). Other chapters deal with the contemporary debates about sexual orientation, gender identity policies, religious freedom and non-discrimination (Anderson) and the very meaning of equality (Benson). Thus in addition to the effort to restore a universally valid conception of equality and non-discrimination, this volume also offers a global snapshot of the developments in positive law of various regions. The authors describe disturbing trends but also consider regional strategies for affirming basic human goods.

In the struggle for genuine human dignity, this volume is a sober corrective to the errors of our time—a sign of contradiction to many disturbing contemporary trends, but also a sign of hope in the midst of so much confusion.

Acknowledgments

THE EDITORS ARE GRATEFUL to Ave Maria School of Law, Naples, Florida, and Sacred Heart Major Seminary, Detroit, Michigan for their generous support for the publication of this volume. They are likewise grateful to Mr. Matthew Wimer, Brian Palmer, Calvin Jaffarian, and Dr. Charlie Collier of Wipf and Stock for their assistance with production and editing. Finally, the editors wish to thank Mrs. Maria Montagnani for her careful formatting of the text and Maria Lynch for her work on the index.

Introduction

JANE F. ADOLPHE

THE IDEA FOR THIS book was born some years ago, when I was attending a Seminar for Advanced Studies in Public and Private International Law on the Protection of Children, at *L'Academie de Droit International de La Haye*, Netherlands, in 2009. At that Seminar, a former member of the Committee on the Rights of the Child, a treaty body set up under the Convention on the Rights of the Child, claimed that all rights could be virtually reduced to a discussion about equality and non-discrimination. It was a surprising contention when one considers the sheer number of human rights recognized in core international human rights instruments, ranging from civil and political to economic, cultural, and social. I wondered what this could mean for the Holy See, knowing that it was a State Party to five separate international human rights' instruments, and like other States Parties, was obliged to submit periodic reports to the monitoring bodies established under the said treaties.

On this point, the importance of equality and non-discrimination for international human rights treaties is evident in the 2006 revised set of Harmonized Guidelines for preparation of States parties' Reports under the core treaties negotiated and drafted within the United Nations system.[1] The Harmonized Guidelines divide the State report into two basic parts:

1. *Harmonized Guidelines on Reporting under the International Human Rights Treaties, including Guidelines on a Common Core Document (CCD) and Treaty-Specific Documents*, HRI/MC/2006/3, May 10, 2006 and Corr.1, adopted at the Fifth Inter-Committee Meeting of the Human Rights Treaty Bodies and Eighteenth Meeting of Treaty Body Chairpersons; See also the Report of the Secretary General, *Compilation of Guidelines on the Form and Content of Reports to be Submitted by States Parties to the International Human Rights Treaties*, HRI/GEN/2/Rev.6, June 3, 2006.

the Common Core Document (CCD) and the Treaty-Specific Document, which together constitutes each State's Report. It is noteworthy that in 2002, the United Nations' bureaucracy had pushed for one State report under all of the treaties in the UN Secretary-General's call for a single report that would have permitted States Parties to report on implementation as regards all of the applicable treaties, but the recommendation was rejected.[2] As the time was not yet right to produce a new way of reporting that would have reduced the discussion of human rights to equality and non-discrimination, the Harmonized Guidelines were revised in a way that significantly expanded the content and importance of the CCD.[3] It is now considered the backbone of the reporting procedure because it must include general information about the reporting State, from demographics to the creation of implementation mechanisms.[4] In addition, the CCD must include specific information on treaty provisions that are congruent with several treaties, in particular, provisions regarding equality and non-discrimination. The specific-treaty State report, on the other hand, which has historically been the focus of attention by States Parties, treaty-bodies, UN institutions, and non-governmental organizations (NGOs), has been narrowed in its scope, reduced to information about provisions specific to the respective treaty.

Section III of the CCD must include information about equality and non-discrimination and effective remedies. Indeed, equality and non-discrimination are key components of the CCD; they have become the prism through which international human rights are discussed and analyzed by treaty bodies. Consider for example, the following information that must be provided by States Parties:

- *equality before the law and equal protection of the law* for everyone within the State's jurisdiction;

2. Report of the Secretary General, *Strengthening the United Nations: An Agenda for Further Change:* A/57/387 September 9, 2002.

3 Navanethem Pillay, *Strengthening the United Nations Human Rights Treaty System: A Report by the United Nations High Commissioner for Human Rights*, June 2012, p. 51.

4. Report of the Secretary General, *Compilation of Guidelines on the Form and Content of Reports to be Submitted by States Parties to the International Human Rights Treaties*, HRI/GEN/2/Rev.6, June 3, 2006 (see the following headings and subheadings of the Common Core Document: I. General information about the reporting State: demographic, economic, social and cultural characteristics; constitutional, political and legal structure; II. General framework for the protection and promotion of human rights: acceptance of international human rights norms; legal framework for protection of human rights at the national level; framework for the promotion of human rights at the national level; reporting process at the national level; other related human rights information; III. Equality and non-discrimination and remedies.).

- *elimination of discrimination* in all its forms and on all grounds, including multiple discrimination, and promotion of formal and substantive equality for everyone;
- the *principle of non-discrimination* as a general binding principle in law and special measures to guarantee full and equal enjoyment of human rights;
- *prevention of discrimination* in all its forms and on all grounds and related provisions of existing penal laws, as applied by the courts;
- the human rights situation of persons belonging to *specific vulnerable groups* in the population;
- measures adopted to reduce economic, social and geographical disparities and to *prevent discrimination* against the persons belonging to the most disadvantaged groups;
- educational and public information campaigns to prevent and *eliminate negative attitudes to, and prejudice* against, individuals and groups which prevent them from fully enjoying their human rights;
- *guarantees to equality before the law and equal protection of the law* for everyone within the State's jurisdiction, in accordance with international human rights instruments
- temporary *special measures to accelerate progress towards equality*, and in such cases, the expected timeframe for the attainment of the goal of *equality of opportunity and treatment* and the withdrawal of such measures;
- *remedies and effective access to remedies* in domestic legislation for victims of human rights violations.[5]

Such requests presuppose a common understanding of certain notions, such as "equality," "non-discrimination," and "human rights," all complex concepts that have provoked considerable debate not only about their meanings, but also their justifications, and the relationships between them. The resolution of such issues, in turn, depends upon one's view of the human person, human nature, the nature of law, and the role of the State. In addition, one must appreciate the specific provisions of the relevant treaties as well as the international legal context, in which they are embedded. In particular regard to the Holy See and its reporting obligations, all of the aforementioned concerns must be considered in light of its unique nature.

5. Ibid., nos. 50 to 59.

To appreciate the complexity of the subject matter within the European region, one need only consider the 2009 Report prepared for the European Commission, entitled "Concepts of Equality and Non-Discrimination in Europe: A Practical Approach," (hereinafter "the 2009 Report"). [6] This report focused on various national legal systems and the meanings of a range of legal concepts that use the key terms: equality and discrimination (e.g., "formal equality," "substantive equality," "*de facto* equality," "equal treatment," "equal opportunities," "non-discrimination," "direct discrimination," and "indirect discrimination"). In addition, the 2009 Report studied the relationship between equality and discrimination in the same systems,[7] and considered a number of legal sources.[8] They, then, grouped different understandings of equality and discrimination into four main categories:

- *Viewing equality as rationality (like cases should be treated alike, and different cases should be treated differently).* [9]
- *Protecting key public goods such as human rights.*[10]
- *Protecting persons from discrimination based on particular characteristics and grounds.* [11]

---

6. Christopher McCrudden and Sacha Prechal, Members of the European Network of Legal Experts in the field of Gender Equality, *Concepts of Equality and Non-Discrimination in Europe: A Practical Approach*, November, 2009 [hereinafter 2009 Report], (financed by and prepared for the use of the European Commission, Directorate-General for Employment, Social Affairs and Equal Opportunities, although not necessarily representative of the Commission's official position).

7. Ibid., 9–10.

8. Ibid., 2 (The Report considered the constitutional traditions and domestic laws of the individual Member States and of the European Economic Area (EEA) countries as interpreted by national courts; European Community Law; and the European Convention on Human Rights.).

9. Ibid., 11 ("Equality, in this first meaning, requires that, save where there is an adequate justification, like cases must not be treated differently, and different cases must not be treated in the same way. This implies that where two categories are treated differently, the first issue is whether the categories involved are similar or not. If they are not, there is nothing wrong with treating them differently. If they are, the question is whether the difference in treatment can be justified. In this first meaning of equality, the justification that is required in order to be accepted may often be highly deferential to decisions taken by public bodies: if the action taken is 'rational', that may be enough.")

10. Ibid., 17 ("In the second meaning, the non-discrimination principle becomes an adjunct to the protection of particularly prized 'public goods'. Such 'prized public goods' should in principle be distributed to everyone without distinction. In the distribution of the 'public good', equals should be treated on a nondiscriminatory basis, except where differences can be justified. The justification standard to be satisfied is often stricter in this context than is the case where 'equality as rationality' is concerned.")

11. Ibid., 23. ("According to the third meaning of equality, it is not permitted to

- *Concerning positive duties to promote equality of opportunity and de facto equality.*[12]

It is noteworthy that one of the authors of the 2009 Report, in a paper written a few years early, had underlined several caveats with respect to the four categories. An important one was that the categories had been devised to simplify the rather "bewildering range of legal material" in the European legal context.[13] Accordingly, the categories were not to be considered as watertight compartments, since developments in one category could influence changes in other categories and the principles in one category could be in tension with each other.[14] Along these lines, the authors of the 2009 Report underlined possible conflicts between understandings of equality and non-discrimination, which could contribute to "dilemmas for states."[15]

In light of the above, the International Center on Law, Life, Faith and Family (ICOLF) organized an international meeting of experts who gathered in February 19-21, 2015 at Ave Maria School of Law, in Naples, Florida. Some experts considered equality, non-discrimination, and human rights in different regional human rights systems as well as the United Nations system, while others were asked to study the Catholic roots of equality and non-discrimination. Professor Robert Araujo S.J., who has

---

make a distinction on the basis of a group characteristic that is considered to be irrelevant or otherwise unacceptable, unless there is a justification. In this type of case, the group characteristics that may not lead to a distinction, such as nationality, race and sex, have often been set out in the text of the legal instrument, such as the Treaty, a Constitution, or other legislation. In this context, the justification of the difference in treatment will, in general, be scrutinized with considerable thoroughness, and the standard to be satisfied will often be high, but that standard may differ depending on the group characteristic under consideration."); *See also* the related question whether equality and non-discrimination laws should be applied to the area of goods and services Gudrun Kugler, *From Equality to Privilege: The Late Austrian Equal Treatment Bill*, Zeszyty Prawnicze (2013) 13/2, 203-215.

12. Ibid., 41 ("In the fourth meaning of equality, certain public authorities (and some private actors) are placed under a duty actively to take steps to promote greater equality of opportunity (the legal meaning of which are yet to be fully articulated) for particular groups. In that sense, it is a further development of the third ('status-based') meaning. However, the concept of 'equality of opportunity' goes beyond any of the concepts of discrimination characteristic of the previous meanings, and the duty shifts from being essentially negative, to become a positive duty. This positive duty may include a duty to engage in positive action, unlike under the third meaning where it is often permitted to engage in positive action but not required.").

13. Christopher McCrudden and Haris Kountouros, "Human Rights and European Equality Law," University of Oxford Faculty of Law Legal Studies Research Paper Series, Working Paper No. 8/2006, April 2006, 1-2.

14. Ibid.

15. The 2009 Report, *supra* note 9, p. 11.

since passed away, took up the herculean mission of analyzing the American legal context from the Catholic perspective, for which I am very grateful. His paper is not included in this publication, but will be published separately due to its length and depth.

The meeting was divided into various panel discussions. The first panel discussion was devoted to foundational principles pertaining to equality and discrimination within the Catholic intellectual tradition. Professor Robert Araujo, S.J. submitted his paper, but due to his failing health, Professor Richard Myers of Ave Maria School of Law delivered the paper on Father's behalf. Professor Robert Fastiggi spoke on human equality and non-discrimination in light of Catholic moral theology and magisterial teaching. In **Chapter I**, he states that because all human beings are equal in terms of origin, dignity, and destiny certain fundamental human rights must be affirmed, understanding that each individual person is born with particular natural differences (e.g., biological sex, talents) and into different particular circumstances. All of which underlines the interdependence of humanity whereby each person should benefit from the gifts of the others and all should strive together for fairer and more human conditions in cases of "sinful inequalities." (CCC, 1938). Professor Emeritus Ernest Caparros, who has since passed away, spoke about the sacramental roots of canon law, fundamental equality and functional difference. In **Chapter II**, he explains that seeking the canonical roots means "discovering the deep influence of Christian thought and of canon law in the life of interpersonal and societal relationships" whereby the message of the gospel transformed hearts and minds, humanized persons and when deeply rooted was reflected in the canonical juridical order, which, in turn, translated theological and ecclesiological concepts. Beginning with the equality of human beings created in the image and likeness of God, as well as natural differences to be male and female, called to be "two in one flesh" as they unite themselves in natural marriage, Christ elevated equality/difference to the sacramental level. Professor Daniel B. Gallagher presented on equality and non-discrimination from a natural law perspective. In **Chapter III**, he offers the tools for analysis which are needed to rightly think and make the proper distinctions associated with the complex issues of equality and non-discrimination laws. By instructing us to distinguish ends in things from purposes, the Chapter touches on "our capacity for truth; more specifically, our capacity to perceive the natural ends of things—and consequently, our supernatural ends as human beings destined for God,—by initially distinguishing them from purposes." Professor Kevin Flannery, S.J. from the Gregorian University in Rome also contributed to the group discussion on the virtue of religion.

As additional issues required consideration, Dr. Ryan was approached after the meeting to contribute a previously published paper on sexual orientation and gender identity as related to religious freedom. In **Chapter IV**, he considers public policy proposals to create new LGBT (lesbian, gay, bisexual and transgender) protections with certain religious exemptions and concludes that the same do not result in fairness for all but "penalizes many Americans who believe that we are created male and female and that male and female are created for each other—convictions that the court has recognized are held 'in good faith by reasonable and sincere people here and throughout the world'". He offers a better way to think about the concerns of all involved and offers solutions. Professor Iain Benson was requested to contribute a paper on the various concepts of equality. In **Chapter V**, he examines the various meanings and applications of the term "equality," and the effects of each for the treatment of religious associations. He concludes that any talk of "equality" or "inclusion" requires an authentic respect for and commitment to difference and "the forms of civil society within which variety is at home."

The second panel discussion at the expert meeting took up the issue of equality and non-discrimination within the European system. In **Chapter VI**, Monsignor Piotr Mazurkiewicz discusses the document "Developing Fair Non-Discrimination EU Legislation," produced by the Commission of the Bishops' Conferences of the European Community (COMECE) when he held the position of Secretary General of COMECE. Before offering a detailed discussion of the law, he commences with a definition of the notion of discrimination underlining that it is associated with making distinctions and suggesting that one needs a healthy balance between respecting what is the same in each person (inherent dignity) and what is different or unique in each person (strengths and weaknesses). His explanation for the lack of respect for both equality and difference, in conjunction with other weaknesses or flaws in the EU policy, brings the reader back to certain points raised in Chapters III about making distinctions, in Chapter IV on religious exemptions, and in Chapter V on terminology. In **Chapter VII**, Paul Diamond, Esq.,—a practicing lawyer in the United Kingdom, who brilliantly moderated the expert meeting—describes four stages in which the freedom of religion and religious belief have been minimized in society *per se*: 1) ridicule and open disrespect; 2) denial or limitation of a government favor (e.g., grants); 3) imposition of a detriment or denial of recognition (e.g., Christian club at a public school); and 4) criminal sanctions imposed for expressing a religious belief (e.g., certain hate crimes). With attention to the cases he has litigated in defense of Christians regarding equality and non-discrimination law, he takes the reader through the various stages in presenting his thesis that some of the greatest threats to religious freedom now stem from antidiscrimination and equality law with its highly ideological content that has undermined the rule of law. Monsignor Florian Kolfhaus, desk officer of the Holy See, Secretariat of State, Relations with States, as he then was, spoke about religious freedom in Europe and Mr. Jakob Cornides, Esq., a European trained lawyer, contributed to this theme as well. Both joined the group via technology.

The third panel discussion studied other human rights systems. In **Chapter VIII**, Chilean Professor Carmen Domínguez Hidalgo discusses the recent inclusion of sexual orientation as a suspect category in the Inter-American region, through juridical and legislative methods, which in at least one case, undercut the best interests of the child principle, when it was treated as a "super-category" by the court. In **Chapter IX**, Argentinian Professor Ursula Cristina Basset also discusses the Inter-American system but focuses on the unique character of this system and its equality and non-discrimination provisions, with reference to: the universal recognition of the personhood of every human being; the right to life from the moment of conception; the great value ascribed to the family, the protection of the family and the rights of the family; and the concept of "protective distinctions" for the vulnerable. She, then, contrasts these standards with judicial application of them in two recent court decisions involving questions of reproductive technology and sexual orientation respectively. She laments that the juridical decisions under consideration broke with "longstanding traditions and the very identity of Latin America." In **Chapter X**, Professor Brian Scarnecchia examines the Association of Southeastern Asian Nations and its Declaration of Human Rights (ADHR) with reference to the terms "Asian values," "religion", "national sovereignty," and "public morality," criticized by some as threatening the core principles of human rights, but justified by others for blocking disvalues or "new rights." He recommends that the public trust doctrine in environmental law be extended to include the whole ecological *res*, both natural and human, along the lines of Pope Francis in his 2015 Encyclical Letter *Laudato Si'* (On Care of Our Common Home). In **Chapter XI**, Mr. Geoffrey Strickland studies the expressions "Islamophoia" and Christianophobia" used by Pope Francis within the context of his Apostolic Visit to Turkey. Strickland offers working definitions of the terms and explores issues related to Islamophobia in the West and Christianophobia in the Middle East and North Africa (MENA) system, concluding that authentic non-discrimination requires treating them as related phenomena with an eye on renewal. Doctor Theresa Okafor, from Nigeria, also presented a paper on the meaning of gender and gender equality within the African Union. She was followed by Mr. Stefano Gennarini, who discussed the United Nations System and the issue of "sexual orientation" and "gender identity" as categories and/or grounds of non-discrimination in international law. The ideas in my presentation, regarding the principles of equality and non-discrimination in core human rights treaties have been included above in this introduction.

My hope is that this book encourages further study on equality and non-discrimination policies and law, especially within the United Nations System, understanding that a 2005 publication found that the human rights treaty bodies "exhibit[ed] quite divergent practices."[16]

Finally, the meeting would not have been possible without the moral support of Mr. Leonard Leo and his ability to raise the necessary financial support for the project. In addition, I am grateful for the financial donation and personal participation of Mr. Luca Volontè of the "Fondazione Novae Terrae," and also the support of Dean and President Kevin Cieply of Ave Maria School of Law (AMSL), who permitted ICOLF to hold the meeting at the AMSL Florida campus. On this point, I am particularly grateful for the organizational assistance of Professor Ligia De Jesus of AMSL, and staff members, who worked so hard to make the meeting a success. In regard to the publication of this book, I am indebted to Professor Brian Scarnecchia of AMSL for suggesting that Professor Robert Gorman prepare the preface. Finally, I am deeply grateful for the precious contributions of Fr. Robert Araujo S.J (1948–2015) and Prof. Ernest Caparros (1938–2018), who both passed away before the publication of this volume.

Bibliography

Camp, I.F and M. R. Gonzalez, "The Philosophical Notion of Equality." *Ave Maria Law Review* 8:1 (2009): 153–165.

Glendon, Mary Ann. "Knowing the Universal Declaration of Human Rights." *Notre Dame Law Review* 73:5 (1998)1153–1190.

———. *A World Made New: Eleanor Roosevelt and the Universal Declaration of Human Rights.* New York: Random House, 2002.

McCrudden, Christopher and Haris Kountouros, "Human Rights and European Equality Law," University of Oxford Faculty of Law Legal Studies Research Paper Series, Working Paper No. 8/2006, April, 2006. https://ssrn.com/abstract=899682 or http://dx.doi.org/10.2139/ssrn.899682

McCrudden, Christopher and Sacha Prechal, *Concepts of Equality and Non-Discrimination in Europe: A Practical Approach.* Brussels. European Commission, Directorate-General for Employment, Social Affairs and equal Opportunities 2009. file:///C:/

---

16. Wouter Vandenhole, *Non-discrimination and Equality in the View of the UN Human Rights Treaty Bodies*, Antwerpen-Oxford: Intersentia, 2005.

Users/Robert/Downloads/ConceptsofEqualityDRAFT18November2009%20(3).pdf.

Pillay, Navanethem *Strengthening the United Nations Human Rights Treaty System: A Report by the United Nations High Commissioner for Human Rights*, June 2012. http://www2.ohchr.org/english/bodies/HRTD/docs/HCReportTBStrengthening.pdf.

Vandenhole, Wouter *Non-discrimination and Equality in the View of the UN Human Rights Treaty Bodies*, Antwerpen-Oxford: Intersentia, 2005.

Chapter 1

Human Equality and Non-discrimination in Light of Catholic Theology and Magisterial Teachings

Robert L. Fastiggi

IN TODAY'S WORLD, THERE is great interest in equality and non-discrimination. Many social and political controversies revolve around the issues of equality, justice, and non-discrimination. Some of this is a reaction to the evils of slavery, racism, genocide, and ethnic cleansing displayed with graphic cruelty during the nineteenth and twentieth centuries. New forms of discrimination have also emerged as seen in the oppression of women, children, the elderly, and the unborn. This essay hopes to provide a survey of Catholic teaching on the topics of equality and non-discrimination. Its methodology is more theological and philosophical rather than political or social. The goal is to explore the foundations and principles of Catholic doctrine on equality and non-discrimination and show how these apply to some contemporary issues.

The Scriptural Roots of Human Dignity and Equality

Testimony is given to human equality in the very first chapters of the Bible. God creates man in his image and likeness (Gen 1:26–27), and he creates man as male and female (Gen 1:27). All men and women, therefore, share a common origin and dignity because all are created in the image and likeness of God. When St. Paul speaks to the Athenians in Acts 17:26 he reminds them that, "God made from one the whole human race to dwell on the surface of the earth."[1] All human beings, therefore, share a fundamental equality because of a common origin. All human beings are also directed toward a common destiny, manifested in a common search for God. St. Paul tells the Athenians that the order of creation is designed "so that people might seek God, even perhaps grope for him and find him, though indeed he is not far from any of us" (Acts 17:27).

The incarnation is the supreme manifestation of God to the world. Christ's death and resurrection constitute God's plan of salvation for the entire human race. This plan includes all human beings for he "wills everyone to be saved and come to the knowledge of the truth" (1 Tim 2:4). Christ's saving death and resurrection was not for one select group. Rather, his sacrifice was expiation "not for our sins only but for those of the whole world" (1 John 2:2). The Gospel of Jesus Christ is not meant merely for certain nations or ethnic groups but for all people. This is clear from the great commission of Christ to "make disciples of all nations" (Matt 28:19). It is likewise clear from the outpouring of the Holy Spirit at Pentecost, which enabled the disciples to speak in different tongues (Acts 2:4). This showed that the Gospel of Jesus Christ is to be shared with people of every language and culture. All human beings are equally deserving of the message of salvation.

The gospel initially spread in a Greco-Roman culture characterized by a social structure that regarded some groups as superior to other groups. The Christian faith challenged such social inequalities because in the Christian order "there is neither Jew nor Greek, there is neither slave nor free person, there is not male or female; for you are all one in Christ Jesus" (Gal 3:28). In a culture in which men tended to treat their wives as possessions, the Christian faith commanded husbands to love their wives "as their own bodies" (Eph 5:28), and to love their spouses "as Christ loved the church" (Eph 5:25).

In the church established by Christ, "there are a variety of ministries, which work for the good of the whole body."[2] The bishops in communion with the Roman Pontiff are "servants of Christ and stewards of the mysteries of God" (1 Cor 4:1). Even though there is a hierarchy of order and authority in the church, there is nevertheless a fundamental equality among all the members. This is why Jesus told his disciples not to model themselves after the Gentile rulers who lord it over others and "make their authority over them felt" (Mark 10:42). Instead, bishops, who succeed the apostles, must become the servants of those they govern and model themselves after the

---

1. All scriptural quotations are taken from *The New American Bible* (1986).
2. Vatican II, *Lumen Gentium*, 18.

Son of Man who "did not come to be served but to serve and to give his life as a ransom for many" (Mark 10:45).

Even though Scripture does not directly challenge the ancient institution of slavery, St. Paul's Letter to Philemon provides a strong argument against it. While in prison, Paul leads an escaped slave named Onesimus to Christ—becoming his father in the faith (Phlm 10). He sends Onesimus back to his master, Philemon, urging that he be received "no longer as a slave but more than a slave, a brother, beloved ... as a man and in the Lord" (Phlm 16). St. Paul further pleads to Philemon to welcome Onesimus just as he would welcome him [Paul] (Phlm 17). This brief letter of Paul shows how the Gospel of Christ affirms the equal dignity of all human beings regardless of social status. It also provides a basis for the eventual rejection of slavery.

Catholic Philosophical and Theological Foundations for Human Equality and Dignity

The Catholic Church affirms the equality of all human beings in terms of origin, dignity, and destiny. The *Catechism of the Catholic Church* explains the basis for this equality:

> Created in the image of the one God and equally endowed with rational souls, all men have the same nature and the same origin. Redeemed by the sacrifice of Christ, all are called to participate in the same divine beatitude: all therefore enjoy an equal dignity.[3]

The creation of all human beings in the image and likeness of God is a truth revealed in Scripture (Gen 1:26–27). Catholic philosophical reflection builds on this biblical truth by locating the image of God in the rational nature shared by all human beings. The Greek philosopher Aristotle (385–322 BC) saw the "rational principle" as the distinctive attribute of human nature.[4] The early Christian philosopher, Boethius (c. AD 480–525) pointed to rationality as one of the constitutive elements of personhood, for a person is "an individual substance of a rational nature."[5] St. Thomas Aquinas (c. 1225–1274) accepted Boethius' definition of a person

---

3. *Catechism of the Catholic Church* [CCC], 1934.

4. See especially Aristotle's *Nicomachean Ethics*, Book 1, chs. 13, 15–29 (1102b).

5. Boethius, "Liber de Persona et Duabus Naturis," ch. 3: *"Persona est rationalis naturae individua substantia."*

and noted that only intellectual creatures—angels and human beings—are persons made in God's image.[6]

According to Catholic theology, human beings are persons because the rational soul, which is the form of the human body, provides the rational nature, which is constitutive of personhood. Indeed, "it is because of its spiritual soul that the body made of matter becomes a living, human body; spirit and matter, in man, are not two natures united, but rather their union forms a single nature."[7] All human beings share in the image of God because the rational spiritual soul is what makes them truly human. In responding to the question whether the image of God is found in every man, St. Thomas Aquinas states:

> Since man is said to be the image of God by reason of his intellectual nature, he is the most perfectly like God according to that in which he can best imitate God in his intellectual nature. Now the intellectual nature imitates God chiefly in this, that God understands and loves Himself. Wherefore we see that the image of God is in man in three ways.
>
> First, inasmuch as man possesses a natural aptitude for understanding and loving God; and this aptitude consists in the very nature of the mind, which is common to all men.
>
> Secondly, inasmuch as man actually and habitually knows and loves God, though imperfectly; and this image consists in the conformity of grace.
>
> Thirdly, inasmuch as man knows and loves God perfectly; and this image consists in the likeness of glory. Wherefore on the words, "The light of Thy countenance, O Lord, is signed upon us" (Psalm 4:7), the gloss distinguishes a threefold image of "creation," of "re-creation," and of "likeness." The first is found in all men, the second only in the just, the third only in the blessed.[8]

This insight of Aquinas is extremely important because it helps us understand how a newly conceived child is to be accorded the same right to life as any other human person. This is because the rational soul, present from

---

6. Aquinas, *Summa theologica* I q. 93. a. 2. It should be noted, though, that Aquinas saw the need to modify Boethius's definition in reference to the three Persons of the Holy Trinity. Since there cannot be three substances in God, it is necessary to speak of three "subsistences" or hypostases in God. See Aquinas, *Summa theologica* I q. 29. a. 2. ad. 2.

7. *CCC*, 365.

8. Aquinas, *Summa theologica* I q. 93 a. 4.

the time of conception, makes the newly conceived child a human *person*, viz., an individual substance of a rational nature. Even if the functions of the rational nature take time to develop, the rational soul, animating the newly conceived human body, enables us to recognize the true existence of a full human person. From the moment of conception, there is present the rational soul that provides the natural aptitude for knowing and loving God and neighbor. This is why the church teaches that "human life must be respected and protected absolutely from the moment of conception."[9] Indeed, "from the first moment of his existence, a human being must be recognized as having the rights of a person—among which is the inviolate right of every innocent being to life."[10]

The rational nature, present in all human beings, provides the foundation for the fundamental equality of all people. Even human persons who are brain-damaged, senile, or otherwise handicapped retain their full humanity and are equal in dignity to fully healthy human persons. Some argue that human dignity can be lost when people pursue evil. Evil actions can certainly obscure human dignity, but the people who do evil still retain the rational nature and the image of God. In his 1963 encyclical, *Pacem in terris*, St. John XXIII makes this important observation:

> It is always perfectly justifiable to distinguish between error as such and the person who falls into error—even in the case of men who err regarding the truth or are led astray as a result of their inadequate knowledge, in matters either of religion or of the highest ethical standards. A man who has fallen into error does not cease to be a man. He never forfeits his personal dignity; and that is something that must always be taken into account. Besides, there exists in man's very nature an undying capacity to break through the barriers of error and seek the road to truth. God, in His great providence, is ever present with His aid. Today, maybe, a man lacks faith and turns aside into error; tomorrow, perhaps, illumined by God's light, he may indeed embrace the truth.[11]

Even those who commit murder retain their basic human dignity. In addressing the issue of capital punishment, Pope Francis writes: "Life, human life above all, belongs to God alone. Not even a murderer loses his personal dignity, and God himself pledges to guarantee this. As St Ambrose

---

9. *CCC*, 2270.

10. Ibid., 2270. Cf. "Congregation for the Doctrine of the Faith," *Donum vitae* (1987), I. 1.

11. John XXIII, *Pacem in terris*, 158.

taught, God did not want to punish Cain with homicide, for He wants the sinner to repent more than to die (cf. *Evangelium Vitae*, n. 9)."[12]

The equal dignity of all human beings from conception until natural death, therefore, is grounded in the common rational nature shared by all human beings. As Vatican II's *Gaudium et Spes* teaches: "Man judges rightly that by his intellect he surpasses the material universe, for he shares in the light of the divine mind"[13] The rational nature also enables human beings to know and love others and enter into communion with God.[14] Because of the rational nature, human beings likewise possess freedom and the dignity of conscience.[15]

Human Equality, Human Dignity, and Human Rights

Because all human beings are equal in terms of origin, dignity, and destiny, certain basic human rights must be affirmed. In spite of the failures of her members, the Catholic Church has consistently upheld certain fundamental rights that are grounded in human dignity. For example, the church has always taught that no one should be forced to enter into the Catholic Church against his or her will. This is why Pope St. Gregory I wrote to the Bishop of Naples in 602 to make it clear that the Jews of that city "should have complete freedom to observe and celebrate all their feasts and holy days as up till now . . . they have possessed."[16] Pope Alexander II reaffirmed this teaching in his letter of AD 1065 to Prince Landalfo of Benevento, and he condemned the practice of bringing Jews into the faith by violence.[17] In the late Middle Ages, the Rector of the Academy of Cracow, Paulus Vladimiri (1370–1435), upheld the natural rights of non-Christians and taught that they should never be converted by force.[18] At Vatican II, the right to religious freedom was expressed in very clear terms by the *Declaration on Religious Liberty, Dignitatis humanae*. The Council taught that "the right to religious freedom has its foundation in the very

---

12. Francis, *Letter to the President of the International Commission against the Death Penalty* (March 20, 2015); see also the *Acta Apostolicae Sedis 107*, 363.

13. Vatican II, *Gaudium et Spes*, 15, in Denzinger and Hünermann (henceforth D-H), *Compendium of Creeds*, 4315.

14. See Vatican II *Gaudium et Spes*, 12, 24; D-H, *Compendium of Creeds*, 4312, 4324.

15. See Ibid., 16–17; ibid., 4316–4317.

16. D-H, *Compendium of Creeds*, 480.

17. Ibid., 698.

18. See Belch, *Paulus Vladimiri and His Doctrine*, and Wielgus, *Medieval Polish Doctrine*.

dignity of the human person as this dignity is known through the revealed Word of God and by reason itself."[19]

In the sixteenth and seventeenth centuries, Catholic thinkers such as Francisco de Vitoria, O.P. (c. 1483–1546) and Francisco Suárez, S.J. (1548–1617) recognized the unity of the human race as the basis for human rights and international law. It was during this time that the church began to speak out more forcefully against slavery, especially as it was being practiced in the Americas. In his 1537 Brief, *Pastorale officium*, Paul III condemned the enslavement of the American Indians, and he taught that they cannot be deprived of their freedom and the ownership of their goods because "they are men and, therefore, capable of faith and salvation."[20] Since the time of Paul III, the church has consistently condemned not only the slave trade but the very institution of slavery itself. The church also has condemned the racism used as a justification for slavery. In his 1839 constitution, *In supremo apostolatus fastigio*, Gregory XVI condemned enslaving Blacks and treating them "as if they were not human but pure and simple animals."[21] In more recent times, the church has rejected "as foreign to the mind of Christ, any discrimination (*discriminationem*) against human beings or harassment of them because of their race, color, condition of life or religion . . . ."[22]

Human Equality, Differences, and Non-discrimination

As we have seen, the church condemns discrimination against human beings because of their race, color, condition of life or religion. What, though, is meant by discrimination? The concept of discrimination is based on the Latin, *discrimen* (distinction, difference). Taking into account differences is not the same as unjust discrimination. According to distributive justice, it is proper to regulate matters based on differences of needs and contributions.[23] It is likewise just to take note of differences when making decisions based on different talents or abilities when these are relevant. For example, it is perfectly just to distinguish between good and bad musicians when selecting members of an orchestra or between good and bad basketball players when selecting members of a basketball team. Justice is the virtue "that consists in the constant and firm will to

---

19. Vatican II, *Dignitatis humane*, 2; D-H, *Compendium of Creeds*, 4240.

20. D-H, *Compendium of Creeds*, 1495. For a good overview of the church's teachings against slavery, see Panzer, *Popes and Slavery*.

21. D-H, *Compendium of Creeds*, 2746.

22. Vatican II, *Nostra Aetate*, 5; D-H, *Compendium of Creeds*, 4199.

23. *CCC*, 2411.

give their due to God and neighbor."[24] People have the right to be treated equally, and in the public order no one should be discriminated against because of "race, color, condition of life or religion."[25]

Right reason, of course, is needed to distinguish between taking note of differences when they are relevant and unjust discrimination. For example, if a Catholic university were to advertise for a priest to serve as campus chaplain, it would not be unjust discrimination to favor a priest over a rabbi, an imam, or Protestant minister for the position. It would, though, be unjust to favor a Caucasian Catholic priest over a Black or Asian Catholic priest simply on the basis of race. In the public order, discrimination against people because of their religion is indeed unjust just as it is unjust to discriminate against people because of their race, sex, age, or personal condition. In terms of evaluating people for different positions, the key question should be whether the individual is able to do the specified job not whether the person is of a certain race, religion, sex, age, or condition.

The principles of equality and non-discrimination have become more complex in recent years because they are being extended to behaviors and lifestyles and not merely to persons. Not all forms of behavior are equal. Right reason helps us distinguish between honesty and dishonesty between violence and peacefulness and between respectful behavior and disrespectful behavior. While there are many issues that could be discussed in this regard, probably the most volatile today are those that involve sexual behavior and marriage. As is well-known, there are strong movements arguing for "marriage equality" that would grant equal legal status to same-sex "marriages" as to those of one man and one woman.

The first question that needs to be asked is whether homosexual actions can be understood as equivalent to the acts of sexual union that take place between husbands and wives. The Catholic Church teaches that there is no equivalence between the two:

> Basing itself on Sacred Scripture, which presents homosexual acts as acts of grave depravity, tradition has always declared that "homosexual acts are intrinsically disordered." They are contrary to the natural law. They close the sexual act to the gift of life. They do not proceed from a genuine affective and sexual complementarity. Under no circumstances can they be approved.[26]

---

24. Ibid., 1807.
25. Vatican II, *Nostra aetate*, 5.
26. CCC, 2357.

Although people with homosexual tendencies have personal dignity equal to heterosexual men and women, there can be no equivalence between homosexual unions and marital unions. The difference between the two is rooted in biology and natural law as well as the constant witness of cultures and religions throughout human history. The Congregation for the Doctrine of the Faith in 2003 taught:

> There are absolutely no grounds for considering homosexual unions to be in any way similar or even remotely analogous to God's plan for marriage and family. Marriage is holy, while homosexual acts go against the natural moral law. Homosexual acts "close the sexual act to the gift of life. They do not proceed from a genuine affective and sexual complementarity. Under no circumstances can they be approved."[27]

It is not unjust to take note of the differences between homosexual acts and the sexual acts between men and women within marriage. The differences between the two are evident from a merely biological perspective. There are likewise differences in terms of psychological complimentarity, and anthropology. Moreover, there is much evidence to show that the stable union between a husband and wife provides the best environment for the procreation and education of children.[28] Indeed, men and women are designed by nature to procreate together. Two men or two women cannot claim that nature discriminates against them unjustly because their mutual sexual acts are not able to lead to the conception and birth of a child.

In terms of social policy, the question is whether same-sex couples can reasonably claim that their unions are marriages in the traditional and natural understanding of the term. Some well-meaning people claim that we should be able to affirm the good that is to be found in these unions. Thus, we are asked to appreciate the qualities of mutual care and affection present in same-sex relationships. This, though, does not seem to be a strong argument in support of the equivalence of same-sex unions to marriage. An adulterous husband might manifest signs of care and affection toward his mistress. This does not mean his adulterous relationship is the equivalent of marriage. Right reason enables us to distinguish between some relationships that are in harmony with nature and the common

---

27. Congregation for the Doctrine of the Faith, *Considerations Regarding Proposals*, n. 4. The term "homosexual persons" is in the title of the document. To speak of "homosexual persons," however, could give the impression that "homosexual tendencies" are intrinsic to the personhood of some individuals, which is not the case.

28. See, for example, Sullins, "Emotional Problems among Children with Same-Sex Parents: Difference by Definition," 99–120.

good and those that are not. For example, we are able to recognize and condemn sexual unions between adult men and under-aged girls as well as those between adult women and under-aged boys. Incestual sexual relationships between brothers and sisters or between parents and children are rightfully repudiated as are homosexual unions between adult men and minor boys and between adult women and minor girls. Clearly not all forms of sexual unions are equal.

With regard to same-sex "marriages," the question seems to turn on whether it is reasonable to distinguish between such unions and those that exist between men and women united in marriage. The Catholic Church believes it *is* reasonable to distinguish between the two for the reasons given by the Catechism and the Congregation for the Doctrine of the Faith. The push for same-sex "marriage," therefore, is not a movement grounded in right reason. Instead, it is a social movement based on the desire to have laws conform to the unreasonable wishes of certain groups of people.

Conclusion

The Catholic Church opposes all forms of *unjust* discrimination that violate human dignity and equality. Based on Sacred Scripture and the natural law, the church recognizes and defends the equal dignity of all human beings in terms of origin, dignity, and destiny. This is why the church has spoken out strongly against abortion, slavery, racism, the oppression of women, and the abuse of children. The equal dignity of all human beings is based on the common rational nature that is a gift from God who created us in his image and likeness.

Bibliography

Acta Apostolicae Sedis 107. Rome: Typis Polyglottis Vaticanis, 2015. http://www.vatican.va/archive/aas/documents/2015/aas-indice2015.pdf.

Aquinas, Thomas. *Summa Theologica*. Complete English Edition. 5 vols. Translated by Fathers of the English Dominican Province. Allen, TX: Christian Classics, 1981.

Aristotle. "Nicomachean Ethics." In *Introduction to Aristotle*, edited by Richard McKeon, 328–29. New York: The Modern Library, 1947.

Belch, Stanislaus. *Paulus Vladimiri and His Doctrine Concerning International Law and Politics*. 2 vols. The Hague: Mouton and Company, 1965.

Boethius. "Liber de Persona in Duabus Naturis contra Eutychen et Nestorium." In *Theological Tractates and the Consolation of Philosophy*, edited by H. F. Stewart and E. K. Rand, 84–85. London: William Heinemann, 1918.

Catechism of the Catholic Church. 2nd ed. Vatican City: Libreria Editrice Vaticana, 1997.

Congregation for the Doctrine of the Faith. *Considerations Regarding Proposals to Give Legal Recognition to Unions between Homosexual Persons* (2003). http://www.vatican.va/roman_curia/congregations/cfaith/documents/rc_con_cfaith_doc_20030731_homosexual-unions_en.html.

Denzinger, Heinrich, and Peter Hünermann, eds. *Compendium of Creeds, Definitions, and Declarations on Matters of Faith and Morals*, 43rd ed. San Francisco: Ignatius, 2012.

Francis, Pope. *Letter to the President of the International Commission against the Death Penalty* (March 20, 2015). https://w2.vatican.va/content/francesco/en/letters/2015/documents/papa-francesco_20150320_lettera-pena-morte.html.

John XXIII. *Pacem in Terris*. Encyclical Letter, 1963.

Panzer, Joel. *The Popes and Slavery*. New York: Alba House, 1998.

Sullins, Donald Paul. "Emotional Problems among Children with Same-Sex Parents: Difference by Definition." *British Journal of Education, Society and Behavioural Science* 7.2 (2015) 99–120.

Vatican II. *Dignitatis Humanae: Declararation on Religious Freedom*. http://www.vatican.va/archive/hist_councils/ii_vatican_council/documents/vat-ii_decl_19651207_dignitatis-humanae_en.html.

———. *The Documents of Vatican II: Vatican Translation*. Staten Island, NY: St. Paul's, 2009.

———. *Gaudium et Spes: Pastoral Constitution on the Church in the Modern World*. http://www.vatican.va/archive/hist_councils/ii_vatican_council/documents/vat-ii_const_19651207_gaudium-et-spes_en.html.

———. *Lumen Gentium: Dogmatic Constitution on the Church*. http://www.vatican.va/archive/hist_councils/ii_vatican_council/documents/vat-ii_const_19641121_lumen-gentium_en.html.

———. *Nostra Aetate: Declaration on the Relation of the Church to Non-Christian Religions*. http://www.vatican.va/archive/hist_councils/ii_vatican_council/documents/vat-ii_decl_19651028_nostra-aetate_en.html.

Wielgus, Stanislaw. *The Medieval Polish Doctrine of the Law of Nations: Ius Gentium*. Translated by John M. Grondelski. Lublin, Poland: University Press of the Catholic University of Lublin, 1998.

Chapter 2

Sacramental Roots of Canon Law[1]
Fundamental Equality and Functional Differences

ERNEST CAPARROS

Looking for canonical roots means discovering the deep influence of Christian thought and of canon law in the life of interpersonal and societal relationships. There are many manifestations in the juridical sphere, like in consensual agreements or in the role of good faith in the field of contracts or in the establishment of moral persons. Also evident is the impact of Christian principles in western penal law;[2] even law pertaining to refugees could be a modern manifestation of the medieval sanctuary privileges[3] in churches and religious institutions, and many others.

At the roots of all these manifestations is the equality of human beings created in the image and likeness of God, as well as natural differences: "Let us make man to our image and likeness [. . .] and God created man to his own image: to the image of God he created him: male and female he created them."[4] With equality as to the image of God, and difference as to be being female and male, they are eventually called "to be two in one flesh"[5] as they unite themselves in the natural marriage.

If we move from the Old to the New Testament, Christ elevates this equality/difference to a sacramental level. By baptism, human beings are

---

1. Cf. Hervada, "Las raíces sacramentales," 297–319.
2. Cf. Morin, "De l'étude des racines chrétiennes," 213–304.
3. Cf. Lynch, "Medieval Canon Law," 69–89.
4. Gen 1:26 & 27, DRA.
5. Gen 2:24.

raised to be *divinis consortes naturæ*, "partakers of the divine nature"[6]; the baptismal elevation to the adoptive divine filiation establishes by necessity the radical equality among the baptized. But here again, the sacramental equality is developed within the functional differences rooted in the sacrament of Holy Orders—as both the sacrament and the differences are instituted by Jesus Christ. The variety of functions originated by the reception of the sacrament of Holy Orders for service to the people of God does not endanger this fundamental equality. All the baptized are equally children of God, and some of them are chosen by God through the proper authorities, *ex hominibus assumptus*, "taken from among men."[7] "Neither doth any man take the honor to himself, but he that is called by God."[8] They are at the service of all the members of the body of Christ: to help each one answer the universal call to holiness and thus reach the final destination in heaven.

Let us illustrate these fundamental principles of equality and differences with some words of Pope Francis in his homily in Istanbul, on November 29, 2014:

> It is true that the Holy Spirit brings forth *different charisms* in the Church, which, at first glance, may seem to create disorder. Under his guidance, however, they constitute an immense richness, because the Holy Spirit is the Spirit of unity, which is not the same thing as uniformity. Only the Holy Spirit is able to kindle *diversity*, multiplicity and, at the same time, bring about *unity*. When we try to create diversity, but are closed within our own particular and exclusive ways of seeing things, we create division. When we try to create unity through our own human designs, we end up with uniformity and homogenization. [...] the Spirit spurs us to experience variety in the communion of the Church.[9]

The Christianity of the first centuries is the forge in which Western society and law were shaped. Some of the most outstanding traits, like the equality principle, are still the basis of our society, notwithstanding some unfortunate deviations. However, the deep and serious understanding of Christ's answer: "Render, therefore, to Caesar the things that are Caesar's, and to God the things that are God's,"[10] although it took centuries to be put into practice—probably because of the Germanic cultural idea of

---

6. 2 Pet 1:4.
7. Heb 5:1.
8. Heb 5:4.
9. Francis, Apostolic Journey to Turkey, para. 4.
10. Cf. Matt 22:21; Mark 12:17; Luke 20:25.

cuius regio eius religio—cannot be attributed to the Enlightenment. Other important contributions, like the institution of marriage and consensual contracts, are more or less under attack in order to diminish their sociojuridical impact. Let as look at the New Testament for pointers to the equality and variety roots.

Equality, Variety, and Functional Differences in the New Testament

In several instances, the New Testament underlines the equality as well as the functional diversity among people. Saint Paul mentions equality. Writing to the Romans, he says: "For there is no distinction the Jew and Greek: for the same is Lord over all, rich upon all that call upon him."[11] And to the Galatians: "There is [. . .] neither bond nor free: there is neither male nor female. For you are all one in Christ Jesus."[12]

In some cases, lived Christian virtues bring about a true revolution.[13] Baptism transforms each person into a child of God. Hence, each person is entitled to maximum respect. At the same time, every member of the faithful, as a member of the people of God, enjoys a radical and fundamental equality.[14] Despite the fact that its application to every day social life could have been meandering or difficult, this principle was well established in Christianity many centuries before modernity discovered the principle of equality among citizens. Slavery, for instance, is one specific case in which the Christian message introduced a deep transformation to the relationship between master and slave. This is evident in the Epistle of Saint Paul to Philemon, which testifies how much time it took to shape this fundamental principle into legal norms that could influence public social life. Contrariwise, within the life of the church, slaves had the same rights as free men and in some instances a slave could be the presbyter or the bishop of a community, or even the Pope.[15] Equality existed in the

---

11. Rom 10:12.

12. Gal 3:28.

13. Cf. For a point of view, Berman, *Law and Revolution*, 51, 62–66; I don't share his notion of "revolution." For a criticism of some of Berman's theological "perceptions," cf. Soria, "Religion, History and the Growth," 487–519.

14. Cf. Gal 3:26–29; Acts 10:34–35; del Portillo, *Faithful and Laity in the Church*, 18–25 (Original Spanish: *Fieles y laicos en la Iglesia*, 40–47); Brissaud, *Cours d'Histoire générale*, n. 20, p. 148; Biondi, *Il diritto romano cristiano*, nn. 283–88, pp. 328–41.

15. St. Callistus (217–222) was the son of a slave and a slave himself. After his liberation, he was ordained a deacon and elected pope. His adversaries and the first antipope St. Hippolytus (217–235), opposed him because of his past as a slave. Cf. Chapman,

church even though the church had not yet had the proper impact in changing legislation and the society.[16]

Saint Paul mentions unity and variety. Again to the Romans, he writes: "For as in one body we have many members, but all members have not the same office: So we being many, are one body in Christ, and every one members of another."[17] And to the Corinthians he insists: "For we, being many, are one bread, one body, all that partake of one bread."[18] Saint Paul also presents one of the most clarifying expressions of functional variety, explaining to the Corinthians the functioning of the body of Christ.[19] You all remember well the long enumeration he does about the different parts of the body and the diversity of their functions. All are different and all are required.

"Callistus I," 183–87; Coulson, *Dictionnaire historique des saints*, 96, 194–95; Farmer, *Oxford Dictionary of Saints*, 63–64, 194–95; Mathieu-Rosay, *Los Papas de san Pedro*, 36–38; Walsh, *Pocket Dictionary of Popes*, 28–29.

16. Concerning slavery, cf. the repeated exhortations to slaves as well as to masters, mainly in the epistles (Eph 6:5–9; Col 3:22–24, 1; Titus 2:9–10; 1 Pet 2:18–19), and see especially Philemon, the letter in which Saint Paul presents the perspective of early Christianity. For slavery in Roman Law, cf. Watson, *Law of Persons*, 159–200; for the influence of Christianity cf. Biondi, *Il diritto romano Cristiano*, vol. 2, nn. 300–18, pp. 374–444, and vol. 3, n. 351, pp. 88–90; Allard, "Slavery," 36–39; Alvarez, "Esclavitud III," 782–84. For the reappearance of slavery in more recent times, cf. Nicholson, "Legal Borrowing and the Origins," 38–54.

17. Rom 12:4–5.

18. 1 Cor 10:17.

19. "For as the body is one, and hath many members; and all the members of the body, whereas they are many, yet are one body, so also is Christ. For in one Spirit were we all baptized into one body, whether Jews or Gentiles, whether bond or free; and in one Spirit we have all been made to drink. For the body also is not one member but many. If the foot should say because I am not the hand, I am not of the body; is it therefore not of the body? And if the ear should say, because I am not the eye, I am not of the body; is it therefore not of the body? If the whole body were the eye, where would be the hearing? If the whole were hearing, where would be the smelling? But now God hath set the members every one of them in the body as he hath pleased him. And if they all were one member, where would be the body? [. . .] Now you are the body of Christ, and members of member. And God indeed hath set some in the church; first apostles, secondly prophets, thirdly doctors; after that miracles; the graces of healing, helps, kinds of tongues, interpretation of speeches. Are all apostles? Are all prophets? Are all doctors? Are all workers of miracles? Have all the grace of healing? Do all speak with tongues? Do all interpret? But be zealous for the better gifts. And I shew unto you yet a more excellent way." (1 Cor 12:12–19, 27–31). (The [. . .] are not omitting "interior citations," but verses 20–26 of 1 Corinthians).

The Foggy Perception of Fundamental Equality through the History of the Church

If we look at the way these fundamental principles evolved in the history of the church, we realize that the divine constitution of the church and of canon law, to be found in the preaching of Christ and in his development in the New Testament, has not always been clearly perceived.

We mentioned before how the clear distinction established by Christ "Render, therefore, to Caesar the things that are Caesar's, and to God the things that are God's,"[20] took time to be inserted in the social and political fabric.

Similarly, the fundamental equality among the children of God, while perfectly well understood and applied in the first centuries of the church, later on became obscured. Around the fourth century, for historical, societal and political reasons, there developed in the church the conceptualization of a notion of *societas inæqualis* in which society was structured by estates. People in a country were not equal and this influenced the church. The medieval society, with the people enclosed in specific estates, influenced also the perception of canon law and hence we find *Gratianus famous dictum*: *Duo sunt genera christianorum*—often, but not always, interpreted as the governing, teaching clergy and the governed, learning laypeople.[21] We are very far from Saint Peter's proclamation: "You are a chosen generation, a kingly priesthood, a holy nation, a purchased people,"[22] as applied, twenty centuries later, to all baptized by *Lumen Gentium* 10.

Besides, at the time of the Reformation, the need to defend the hierarchy in the Catholic Church facing opposing ideas helped consolidate the medieval concept of an unequal society.[23]

The Rediscovery of the Fundamental Concepts of Equality, Variety, and Functional Differences: Vatican II

One of the great contributions of the Second Vatican Council is the rediscovery and the consolidation of the fundamental equality of human beings as such and of all baptized within the church. Establishing at the same time that such equality does not lead to uniformity but to a variety of ways for

---

20. Cf. Matt 22:21; Mark 12:17; Luke 20:25.
21. Cf. Fornés, "*Duo sunt genera christianorum*," 607–32.
22. 1 Pet 2:9.
23. Cf. Fornés, "Diversidad de los fieles," 431–35.

each one to fulfil one's share in the common mission of the people of God. There is unity in the mission and functional differences.

Fundamental Equality

We find several developments in the documents of Vatican II underlining the fundamental equality of all human beings. Rooted in the biblical previous quotations of *Genesis, Gaudium et Spes* underlines: "Since all men possess a rational soul and are created in God's likeness, since they have the same nature and origin, have been redeemed by Christ and enjoy the same divine calling and destiny, the basic equality of all must receive increasingly greater recognition" (*GS* 29).

We find also abundant explanations of this fundamental equality of all members of the People of God, among other possible quotations, *Lumen Gentium*, referring to Ephesians and Galatians, states: "There is, therefore, one chosen People of God: 'one Lord, one faith, one baptism' (Eph. 4:5); there is a common dignity of members deriving from their rebirth in Christ, [. . .]. In Christ and in the Church there is, then, no inequality" (*LG* 32).

Unity in Variety

The principle of *unity within the variety among human beings* is well put forward by *Gaudium et Spes*: "Therefore, although rightful differences exist between men, the equal dignity of persons demands that a more humane and just condition of life be brought about. [. . .] Nevertheless, with respect to the fundamental rights of the person, every type of discrimination [. . .] is to be overcome and eradicated as contrary to God's intent. For in truth it must still be regretted that fundamental personal rights are still not being universally honored" (*GS* 29).[24]

Unity and variety is as well applied to the people of God. First of all, it is the universal calling "to belong to the new people of God." Then the unity and universality: "while remaining one and only one, is to be spread throughout the whole world." Differences in participation are also underlined: "In virtue of this catholicity each individual part contributes through its special gifts to the good of the other parts and of the whole Church." This is exemplified in the following terms: "This diversity among its members arises either by reason of their duties, as is the case with those who exercise the sacred ministry for the good of their brethren, or by reason of their

---

24. Cf. also *LG* 13, 28, 63; *GS* 5, 24, 33, 42; *DH* 6; *NÆ* 1, 5.

condition and state of life." The same paragraph includes also a mention of the Eastern Churches (*LG* 13).[25]

Unity of Mission and Functional Differences

The mission of all baptized is one and the same; nevertheless it is accomplished through the proper functional differences as well as the specific condition of each member of the people of God. Referring to *LG* 33, the Decree on the Apostolate of Lay People, describes it in a nutshell sentence:

> In the Church there is a diversity of ministry but a oneness of mission. To the apostles and their successors Christ has entrusted the office of teaching, sanctifying, and governing in His name and by His power. But the laity are made to share in the priestly, prophetic, and kingly office of Christ; they have therefore in the Church and in the world their own assignment in the mission of the whole People of God (*AA* 2).[26]

---

25. The full text reads: "All men are called to belong to the new people of God. Wherefore this people, while remaining one and only one, is to be spread throughout the whole world and must exist in all ages, so that the decree of God's will may be fulfilled. [. . .] In virtue of this catholicity each individual part contributes through its special gifts to the good of the other parts and of the whole Church. Through the common sharing of gifts and through the common effort to attain fullness in unity, the whole and each of the parts receive increase. Not only, then, is the people of God made up of different peoples but in its inner structure also it is composed of various ranks. This diversity among its members arises either by reason of their duties, as is the case with those who exercise the sacred ministry for the good of their brethren, or by reason of their condition and state of life, as is the case with those many who enter the religious state and, tending toward holiness by a narrower path, stimulate their brethren by their example. Moreover, within the Church particular Churches hold a rightful place; these Churches retain their own traditions, without in any way opposing the primacy of the Chair of Peter." (Cf. also *LG* 32, *GS* 32).

26. Cf. *LG* 33. Others texts developing similar ideas: "That messianic people has Christ for its head, 'Who was delivered up for our sins, and rose again for our justification,' (Rom 4:25) and now, having won a name which is above all names, reigns in glory in heaven. The state of this people is that of the dignity and freedom of the sons of God, in whose hearts the Holy Spirit dwells as in His temple. Its law is the new commandment to love as Christ loved us (cf. John 13:34). Its end is the kingdom of God, which has been begun by God Himself on earth, and which is to be further extended until it is brought to perfection by Him at the end of time, when Christ, our life, (cf. Col 3:4) shall appear, and 'creation itself will be delivered from its slavery to corruption into the freedom of the glory of the sons of God' (Rom 8:21). So it is that that messianic people, although it does not actually include all men, and at times may look like a small flock, is nonetheless a lasting and sure seed of unity, hope and salvation for the whole human race. Established by Christ as a communion of life, charity and truth, it is also used by Him as an instrument for the redemption of all, and is sent forth into the whole world

Transformation of the Biblical and Magisterial Teachings on Fundamental Equality and Functional Variety into Canonical Language

As it is well known, Saint John XXIII when he announced the Ecumenical Council on January 25, 1959, decided also to revise the 1917 Code of Canon Law. He decided, though, to wait until the end of the forthcoming council in order to incorporate its teachings in the revised code.

Translation of the Conciliar Ecclesiology into Canonical Norms

At the end of the Second Ecumenical Vatican Council, at the beginning of 1966, the Commission for the Revision of the Code began its work. Different groups of experts were constituted to examine the modifications to be introduced. The *cœtus* dealing with the rights and duties of the faithful met for the first time on November 26, 1966. They had received a *votum*, i.e. a very developed study, prepared by Father Alvaro del Portillo (Blessed Alvaro, since September 27, 2014) on the distinction between notions of faithful and laity and proposed a well-structured presentation of the obligations and rights of Christ's faithful, taking into consideration the teachings of the council.[27] In the field we are presenting, this was a first step "to translate the conciliar ecclesiological teaching into canonical terms," to use Saint John Paul II's expression.[28]

The doctrinal contribution of Blessed Alvaro del Portillo facilitates the task of the *cœtus*. First of all, he underlined that the notion of "the faithful" corresponds to all members of the people of God, while the term "laity" is the majority of this people, perhaps best defined in canon 399 of the Codex Canonum Ecclesiarum Orientalium (*Codex Canonum Ecclesiarum Orientalium*—the Eastern Catholic Code promulgated in 1990):

---

as the light of the world and the salt of the earth (cf. Matt 5:13–16)" (*LG* 9). "[. . .] sharing a common dignity as members from their regeneration in Christ, having the same filial grace and the same vocation to perfection; possessing in common one salvation, one hope and one undivided charity. [. . .] If therefore in the Church everyone does not proceed by the same path, nevertheless all are called to sanctity and have received an equal privilege of faith through the justice of God (cf. 2 Pet 1:1). [. . .] Thus in their diversity all bear witness to the wonderful unity in the Body of Christ. This very diversity of graces, ministries and works gathers the children of God into one, because 'all these things are the work of one and the same Spirit' (1 Cor. 12: 11)" (*LG* 32).

27. Cf. Herranz, "Foreword," footnote 14, xiii–xvi.

28. Cf. John Paul II, "*Sacræ disciplinæ leges*, January 25, 1983," 6–7.

"In this Code, the name of lay persons is applied to the Christian faithful whose proper and special state is secular and who, living in the world, participates in the mission of the Church, and are not in holy orders nor enrolled in the religious state."

In his study, published for the first time in Spanish in 1969, del Portillo extracts the duties and the rights of faithful and laity from the teachings of the council. His framework which he used to present those duties and rights is based both on the principle of fundamental equality and the principle of functional differences.

Interestingly enough, the second English edition of his book, links, in footnotes, del Portillo's insights presented to the *coetus* in 1966 with the specific canons of both the Latin and the Eastern codes. It shows that the ways he proposed to translate the teaching of Vatican II into canonical terms were fully accepted by the Legislator.

The Misunderstanding of the Relationship between the Royal and the Ministerial Priesthood

The documents of the Second Vatican Council (Vatican II) quoted above, and many others—as well as the canonical norms presenting the conciliar teachings—clearly establish the unity of the mission of the church and the participation of the whole people of God in the accomplishment of such mission, thereby manifesting the *principle of radical equality* of all the baptised. At the same time, each one participates in the one mission of the church "according to his or her own condition and office," reflecting hence the *principle of variety*. It is noteworthy that both principles are presented in the very same norm in both Codes of Canon Law.[29] Equality does not mean uniformity; nor does variety mean anarchy. Nevertheless, these two principles have not yet been well understood by everyone. Saint Paul VI, a short time after the council, emphasized that some people did not have the required *forma mentis* to properly understand the teachings of Vatican II.

In the domain of the collaboration of laity and clergy in the mission of the church, it seems that, in spite of the half century elapsed since the end of Vatican II, we can find a foggy perception of the relationship between the two ways of participating in Christ's priesthood. This could be the consequence of what some people call *clericalism*.[30] That is, a vision of

29. Cf. *Codex Iuris Canonici* (1983 Code of Canon Law), canon 208; *Codex Canonum Ecclesiarum Orientalium* (1990 Easter Catholic Code of Canon Law), canon 11.

30. The dictionaries I have consulted (English, French, and Spanish) concur in the main elements of the definition. "A policy of supporting the power or influence of the

the church through the lens of the former notion of *societas inequalis*, leading to an attitude of *clericalism*, with a twofold manifestation. On the one hand, clerics sometimes get involved in matters which are not part of their competency (like for instance participation in partisan politics) or they do not allow laypeople to do what pertains to their proper fields. In addition, clerics sometimes deal with laypeople like minors or even try to manipulate them. In a nutshell, clerics do not always mind their own business. On the other hand, there is the contrary application when laypeople, in some cases encouraged by clerics, want to take over roles or responsibilities properly corresponding to clerics, mainly liturgical,[31] but also in governance,[32] over and above what is foreseen in the codes, particularly, when the sacrament of Holy Orders is required to exercise those functions.

Saint John Paul II, in the exhortation *Christifideles laici*, after presenting the positive aspects of the collaboration of laypeople in different functions, he makes the following *caveat*:

> In the same Synod Assembly, however, a critical judgment was voiced along with these positive elements, about a too indiscriminate use of the word "ministry," the confusion and the equating of the common priesthood and the ministerial priesthood, the lack of observance of ecclesiastical laws and norms, the arbitrary interpretation of the concept of "supply," the tendency towards a "clericalization" of the lay faithful and the risk of creating, in reality, an ecclesial structure of parallel service to that founded on the Sacrament of Orders.[33]

This *forma mentis*, often unconsciously rooted in the concept of the church as *societas inequalis*, or even a *forma mentis* somehow pretending that there is no essential difference between the ministerial and the common priesthoods (maybe accepting by osmosis some of the Protestant theories), is promoted by a certain number of people, canonists as well as theologians,

---

clergy in political or secular matters" (*American College Dictionary*, 2nd College edition). I will use the term even when there is not an established policy but a fact of clergy intervening in partisan politics or in secular matter not of their competency. I will use the term as well applying it on a somehow contrary meaning: to laypeople promoting clericalism, having a clerical mind, or trying to occupy clergy functions. The same dictionaries call these kinds of people "clerical," defining them as "A person or party advocating clericalism."

31. For the liturgical dimension, cf. Congregation for the Clergy et al., *Ecclesia de mysterio* (15-08-1997), which set out theological principles and practical considerations.

32. Certainly, laypeople (women and men) can cooperate in the governance of the Church according to law (*Codex Iuris Canonici*, canon 129, *Codex Canonum Ecclesiarum Orientalium*, canon 979).

33. John Paul II, *Christifideles laici*, (30-12-1988) AAS 81 [1989] 431n23.

who insist on the importance of laypeople participating in church governance. They are normally in the same category of the ones pushing for ordaining married men and also for the ordination of women, notwithstanding the Magisterial teachings underlining the impossibility of women ordination.[34] In my opinion this is one of the subtlest manifestations of clericalism.

In general, those people assume that the most important endeavour in the church is to be a priest, because they consider the ministerial priesthood in its different degrees as a manifestation of power, not as it is: a commitment to service, following the example and the teachings of Jesus Christ[35] and they want to "empower" laypeople, women and men.

Two fundamental truths have been completely forgotten. One, the universal call to holiness, hence the most important aim and challenge of every member in the church is to become a saint. If we were to make a list of holy women and men, this exercise would prove that we remember their names, while in most cases the names of their parish priests or of their bishops would be less familiar—even though to reach holiness each one of them would have needed to receive the abundant spiritual riches of the Church, especially the word of God and the sacraments from their pastors.[36] Two, the essential role and great challenge of the laypeople (women and men) is to sanctify the world: the human realities, the family, business, the arts, sports—everything. This truth was crystal clear in the mind and writings of the first Christians, then was forgotten for many centuries, until Saint Josemaría Escrivá resurrected the traditional understanding in 1928,[37] and the Second Vatican Council presented it again with great fervor.[38] The two fundamental principles are presented in several canons of both codes.[39] Yet, they demand constant support from the pastors in the church. It is worth underlining that if priests and laypeople were to embrace their own proper challenges and responsibilities, clericalism could be diminished, if not eliminated.

---

34. Cf. John Paul II, "Apostolic Letter *Ordinatio Sacerdotalis*." Also, Congregation for the Doctrine of the Faith, "Declaration *Inter Insigniores*," 98–116; Congregation for the Doctrine of the Faith, "*Responsum ad Dubium*, 28-10-1995," 1114; Ratzinger, "Letter Concerning the Congregation."

35. Cf. Matt 20:28; Mark 10:45; *LG* n. 28; CCC n. 875–76.

36. Cf. *Codex Iuris Canonici,* canon 213; *Codex Canonum Ecclesiarum Orientalium,* canon 16.

37. Cf. Escrivá, *Conversations with Monsignor Escrivá*, n.10, 114 et passim.

38. Cf. Mainly *Lumen Gentium* and *Gaudium et Spes.*

39. Cf. *Codex Iuris Canonici,* cc. 211, 225, 226, 227; *Codex Canonum Ecclesiarum Orientalium,* cc. 14, 401, 402, 406, 407.

Of course, laypeople, women as well as men, can cooperate in governance according to law,[40] and the codes mention a number of cases in which this cooperation could be accomplished and beneficial (for instance as: chancellors, financial administrators, judges, notaries, etc.).[41] For many years, there have been a good number of women and men occupying these functions and with great capability in diocesan offices. But we cannot forget that these functions are not the most important mission for the laity; besides the number of laypeople exercising them is always a small percentage of the laity. Similarly, also in the case of priests, functions of governance correspond to a small percentage of the *presbyterium*. Of course, the percentage of priests in governance is higher than that the percentage of laypeople, but in both cases we are talking about a minority of lay persons and priests.

The liturgical norms as well the codes foresee a few functions that laypeople can accomplish. Certainly, ministerial priesthood is more often required in the liturgy. Laymen can receive the stable ministry of lectors and acolyte in the Latin Church.[42] Laypeople (women and men) can receive a temporary assignment for exercising other liturgical actions mentioned in the code.[43] The codes also consider the possibility for laypeople, in case of need and absence of priests and deacons, to supply certain functions.[44] As for the participation in governance, laypeople exercising some role in liturgical matters is a very small minority (often, but not always, people with clerical minds).

Due to the fact that women are occupying several functions in Diocesan structures and in view of the study that Pope Francis is carrying out with his advisory group of cardinals, people have raised the question of the importance of having more women participate in the functions of the Roman Curia. Certainly, there are not that many women, and there is room for improvement, but women have occupied and continue to occupy, functions of importance. I like to remind people that for the Beijing Conference on Women, Saint John Paul II appointed Professor Mary Ann Glendon as

---

40. Cf. *Codex Iuris Canonici*, canon 129, *Codex Canonum Ecclesiarum Orientalium*, canon 979.

41. Cf. *Codex Iuris Canonici*, cc. 482, 483, 494, 1421 § 2; *Codex Canonum Ecclesiarum Orientalium*, cc. 252 (the Chancellor has to be a priest or deacon, but not the vice-Chancellor), 253, 262, 1087 § 2.

42. Cf. *Codex Iuris Canonici*, canon 230 § 1. In the Eastern Churches those ministries are minor orders.

43. Role of lector, commentator, cantor, and other such roles (*Codex Iuris Canonici*, canon 230 § 2). Cf. *Codex Canonum Ecclesiarum Orientalium*, canon 403 § 2.

44. Cf. *Codex Iuris Canonici*, canon 230 § 3 (exercise the ministry of the word, preside over liturgical prayers, confer baptism, distribute Holy Communion). Cf. *Codex Canonum Ecclesiarum Orientalium*, cc. 677 § 2, 709 § 2.

head of the Vatican delegation. To my knowledge it was the first time that a woman had the function of a *nuncio*, and had under her leadership, besides other people, an archbishop. Sometime later, she was appointed President of the Pontifical Academy of Social Sciences.

Let us conclude with the question about the participation of non-ordained people in governance from an historical perspective. No doubt there are some who consider that the reception of Holy Orders is required for the exercise of the power of governance or jurisdiction (*potestas regiminis seu jurisdictionis*). Nevertheless, in my opinion the doctrinal debate about the participation of laypeople in such functions has some deep roots and could be linked to the eleventh to twelve centuries old controversy about the exercise of the power of jurisdiction, mainly by the German Emperors (in some cases also kings and lay Lords) who were appointing bishops without the intervention of the pope—the so called "quarrel, controversy or conflict about investitures."[45] The same way that the notion of the *societas inequalis* was partially established in a very specific sociopolitical context, the investitures quarrel developed in a very acrimonious social political context mainly between the popes and the German emperors. At that time, the popes tried to defend their power to freely appoint bishops against interference from the emperors. Such a context was not favorable for clarifying which jurisdictional functions lay people could exercise and which functions theologically demanded the reception of the sacrament of Holy Orders. This is the Gordian knot that needs to be cut: does the Church, theologically always require joining the power of governance or jurisdiction to the power of order? As a matter of fact, as we have seen, the codes present certain cases in which lay people can exercise jurisdictional powers or functions.

Some historical studies underline that laypeople had exercised in specific cases governance functions.[46] At the moment of the codification, a debate took place about the possibility of laypeople exercising governance functions; the result was the inclusion of two canons in the new codifications[47] but they did not solve the fundamental theological doctrinal debate. Commentators of the code indicate that the legislator has established a practical solution in the canons without deciding on the doctrinal

---

45. Cf. Van Hove, "Investiture (Canonical)," 84; Löffler, "Investiture (Conflict of)," 84–89; Rowe, "Investiture (Controversy)," 340; Schieffer, "Investiduras (Querella de las)," 781–84.

46. Cf. Stickler, "*potestatis sacræ natura et origine*," 65–67; Ibid., "La bipartición de la potestad," 45–47.

47. Cf. *Codex Iuris Canonici*, canon 129, *Codex Canonum Ecclesiarum Orientalium*, canon 979.

question.⁴⁸ For the priests they use the expression *habiles sunt* while for laypeople the sentence is *cooperari possunt*. In both cases, in addition, they need the proper appointment by the competent authority to exercise the governance function.

Hervada has some very insightful explanations on the doctrinal understanding of the need to require sacramental ordination. He argues that it is required if the governance function is proper to what he calls the "primary organs"—pope and bishops—as they act *in nomine Christi, in Persona Christi Capitis*, while the "secondary organs" (vicar, delegation, participation) strictly speaking do not need the priestly ordination, as the exercise of such functions is not *in nomini Christi*, but rather in the name and representation of the primary office (although the vicars need to be priests, as they are acting in the name of the bishop).⁴⁹

Obviously, the proper understanding of the sharing of priests and laypeople in Christ's priesthood, each one according to his or her condition, could solve many tensions and allow for a better grasp and fulfillment of the mutual participation in the unique mission of the church.

Conclusion

We should keep in mind that the supernatural aim of Canon Law, the *salus animarum suprema lex*,⁵⁰ is the foundation which gives Canon Law its originality. Here lies the root of the profound transformation brought about by Christianity. The message of the gospel transforms hearts and humanizes people. Once this is done to the point of being rooted in society, often due to a good number of individuals having received it, then following the fundamental conversions, the canonical norms translate the theological and ecclesiological concepts and bring about the juridical framework needed for the transformation of society and the humanization of the law.⁵¹

---

48. Cf. Viana, "Power of Governance" and *sub* c. 129, 815–22; Hill, "Power of Governance," 92–93.

49. Cf. Hervada, *Elementos de derecho Constitucional Canónico*, 237–40. The short résumé doesn't render all the nuances made by the author.

50. Cf. now can. 1752, *Codex Iuris Canonici.*, the expression is not included in canon 1400, *Codex Canonum Ecclesiarum Orientalium*; also Arrieta, "La *salus animarum* quale guida," 343–74, spec. 353–57, 369–74; Agostini, *Droit comparé*, 76n37; Fedele, "*Nihil aliud est æquitas quam*," 82–83; Herranz, "*Salus animarum*, principio dell'ordinamento canonico," 185–206; Hervada, "La *salus animarum*," 55–67; Hervada, *Pensaminetos de un canonista*, 58–60; Moneta, "La *salus animarum* nel debatitto," 307–26.

51. Cf. Agostini, *Droit comparé*, 75–76n36; also Gaudemet, *La formation du droit séculier*, nn. 109–10, pp. 160–62, nn. 120–31, pp. 187–89.

Bibliography

Agostini, Eric. *Droit comparé*. Paris: Presses Universitaires de France, 1988.
Allard, P. "Slavery." In *The Catholic Encyclopaedia*, vol. 14, edited by Charles G. Heberman et al., 36–39. New York: Appleton, 1912.
Alvarez, S. "Esclavitud III." In *Gran Enciclopedia Rialp*, vol. 8, edited by José Maria Casciaro Ramírez et al., 782–84. Madrid: Rialp, 1993.
Arrieta, Juan Ignacio. "La *salus animarum* quale guida applicative del Diritto da parte dei pastoril." *Ius Ecclesiæ* 12 (2000) 343–74.
Berman, H. J. *Law and Revolution*. Cambridge, MA: Harvard University Press, 1983.
Biondi, B. *Il diritto romano Cristiano*. Vol. 2. Milano: Giuffrè, 1952.
Brissaud, J. *Cours d'Histoire générale du droit français*. Vol. 1. Paris: A. Fontemoing, 1904.
Chapman, J. "Callistus I," *The Catholic Encyclopaedia*, vol. 3. New York: R. Appleton, 1912.
Congregation for the Clergy, et al. *Ecclesia de mysterio. On Certain Questions Regarding the Collaboration of the Non-Ordained Faithful with the Sacred Ministry of Priests*. August 15, 1997. http://www.vatican.va/roman_curia/congregations/cclergy/documents/rc_con_interdic_doc_15081997_en.html
Congregation for the Doctrine of the Faith. "Declaration *Inter Insigniores*, (Oct 15, 1976)." *AAS* 69 (1977), 98–116. http://www.vatican.va/roman_curia/congregations/cfaith/documents/rc_con_cfaith_doc_19761015_inter-insigniores_en.html.
———. "*Responsum ad Dubium* (Oct 28, 1995)." *AAS* 87 (1995) 1114. http://www.vatican.va/roman_curia/congregations/cfaith/documents/rc_con_cfaith_doc_19951028_dubium-ordinatio-sac_en.html.
Coulson, J., ed. *Dictionnaire historique des saints*. Paris: SEDE, 1964.
del Portillo. Á. *Faithful and Laity in the Church*, 2nd English ed. Edited by P. Hayward and W. Daniel. Gratianus Series. Montréal, Wilson & Lafleur, 2014.
———. *Fieles y laicos en la Iglesia*, 3rd Spanish ed. Pamplona: Eunsa, 1991.
Escrivá, José Maria. *Conversations with Monsignor Escrivá*. Princeton, NJ: Scepter, 1993.
Farmer, D. H. *The Oxford Dictionary of Saints*. Oxford: Oxford University Press, 1982.
Fedele, Pio. "*Nihil aliud est æquitas quam Deus.*" In Études d'histoire du droit canonique dédiées à Gabriel Le Bras, 73–87. Paris: Sirey, 1965.
Fornés, J. "Diversidad de los fieles (Principio de)." In *Diccionario general de derecho canónico*, vol. 3, edited by Javier Otaduy, et al., 431–35. Pamplona: Editorial Aranzadi, 2013.
———. "*Duo sunt genera christianorum* del Decreto de Graciano." *Ius Canonicum* 60 (1990) 607–32.
Francis, Pope. Apostolic Journey to Turkey (28–30 November 2014). November 29, 2014. http://w2.vatican.va/content/francesco/en/homilies/2014/documents/papa-francesco_20141129_omelia-turchia.html.
Gaudemet, J. *La formation du droit séculier et du droit de l'Église aux IVe et Ve siècles*. Paris: Sirey, 1957.
Herranz, Julian. "Foreword." In *Faithful and Laity in the Church*, 2nd English ed., edited by P. Hayward and W. Daniel, xiii–xvi. Gratianus Series. Montréal: Wilson & Lafleur, 2014.

———. "Salus animarum, principio dell'ordinamento canonico." In *Giustizia e pastoralità nella missione della Chiesa*, edited by Julian Herranz, 185–200. Milano: Giuffrè, 2011.

Hervada, Javier. *Elementos de derecho Constitucional Canónico*. 2nd ed. Pamplona: Navarra Gráfica Ediciones, 2001.

———. "La *salus animarum* y la *merces iniquitatis*." *Vetera et nova I* (1991) 55–67.

———. "Las raíces sacramentales del Derecho Canónico." In *Vetera et Nova: Cuestiones de Derecho Canónico y afine (1958–2004)*, 2nd ed., edited by Javier Hervada, 297–319. Pamplona: Navarra Gráfica Ediciones, 2005.

———. *Pensamientos de un canonista a la hora presente*. Pamplona: Navarra Gráfica Ediciones, 1989.

Hill, R. A. "The Power of Governance." In *The Code of Canon Law-Text and Commentary*, edited by James A. Coriden et al., 92–93. New York: Paulist, 1985.

John Paul II, Pope. "Apostolic Letter *Ordinatio Sacerdotalis*. May 22, 1994." http://w2.vatican.va/content/john-paul-ii/en/apost_letters/1994/documents/hf_jp-ii_apl_22051994_ordinatio-sacerdotalis.html.

———. "*Christifideles laici*, December 30, 1988." *AAS* 81 (1989) 393–521. http://w2.vatican.va/content/john-paul-ii/en/apost_exhortations/documents/hf_jp-ii_exh_30121988_christifideles-laici.html.

———. "*Sacræ disciplinæ leges*, January 25, 1983." In *Code of Canon Law Annotated*, 2nd ed., edited by E. Caparros & H. Aubé, 6–7. Gratianus Series. Montréal: Wilson & Lafleur, 2004.

Löffler, K. "Investiture (Conflict of)." In *The Catholic Encyclopedia*, vol. 7, edited by Charles G. Heberman et al., 84–89. New York: Robert Appleton Company, 1909.

Lynch, J. E. "The Medieval Canon Law on Sanctuary with Particular Reference to England." In *Unico Ecclesiæ servitio*, edited by M. Thériault and J. Thorn, 69–89. Ottawa: Saint Paul University, 1991.

Mathieu-Rosay, J. *Los Papas de san Pedro a Juan Pablo II*. Madrid: Rialp, 1990.

Moneta, Paolo. "La *salus animarum* nel debatitto della scienza canonistica." *Ius Ecclesiæ* 12 (2000) 307–26.

Morin, A. A. "De l'étude des racines chrétiennes des droits pénaux français, britannique et canadien." *Revue générale de droit* 32 (2002) 213–304.

Nicholson, B. J. "Legal Borrowing and the Origins of Slave Law in the British Colonies." *American Journal of Legal History* 38 (2004) 38–54.

Ratzinger, Joseph Cardinal. "Letter Concerning the Congregation for the Doctrine of the Faith's Reply Regarding Ordinatio Sacerdotalis." October 28, 1995. http://www.vatican.va/roman_curia/congregations/cfaith/documents/rc_con_cfaith_doc_19951028_commento-dubium-ordinatio- sac_en.html.

Rowe, J. G. "Investiture (Controversy)." In *The Encyclopedia Americana*, vol. 15, edited by Mark Cummings, 340. Danbury, CT: Grolier, 1993.

Schieffer, R. "Investiduras (Querella de las)." In *Diccionario general de Derecho Canónico*, vol. 4, edited by Javier Otaduy et al., 781–84. Pamplona: Editorial Aranzadi, 2012.

Soria, J. L. "Religion, History and the Growth of Law: An Appraisal of H. J. Berman's *Law and Revolution*." *Studia Canonica* 28 (1994) 487–519.

Stickler, A. M. "La bipartición de la potestad eclesiástica en su perspectiva histórica." *Ius canonicum* 15 (1975) 45–47.

———. "The potestatis sacræ natura et origine." *Periodica* 71 (1982) 65–67.

Van Hove, A. "Investiture (Canonical)." In *The Catholic Encyclopedia*, vol. 7, edited by Charles G. Heberman et al., 84. New York: Robert Appleton Company, 1909.

Viana, Antonio. "Power of Governance." In *Code of Canon Law Annotated*, 2nd ed., edited by Ángel Marzoa et al., 815–22. Gratianus Series. Montreal: Wilson & Lafleur, 2004.

———. "Power of Governance" and *sub* c. 129. In *Exegetical Commentary on the Code of Canon Law*, vol. 1, edited by Angel Marzoa et al., 815–22. Gratianus Series. Montreal: Wilson & Lafleur, 2004.

Walsh, M. *Pocket Dictionary of Popes*. Ottawa: CCCB, 2006.

Watson, A. *The Law of Persons in the Later Roman Republic*. Oxford: Clarendon, 1967.

Chapter 3

The Principles of Equality and Non-discrimination

DANIEL B. GALLAGHER

FOR A LONG TIME, the Catholic Church presumed that the natural law would effectively serve as a common reference point for dialogue between all men and women of good will. It was presumed that since, as St. Thomas Aquinas taught, the precepts of the natural law are "self-evident" (*per se nota*), everyone would be able to perceive them if they just thought hard enough. This engendered an enormous hope, if not an excessive confidence, that the church's doctrine of natural law would make the leading contribution to the building up of a more just society and a greater respect for the dignity and rights of the human person.

This way of speaking of the natural law began to take shape under the pontificate of Leo XIII as a way of delineating the origin and limits of civil authority.[1] St. John XXIII continued in the same vein with *Pacem in Terris* (1963), this time using the natural law as a basis for a common understanding of human rights and duties. Pope Paul VI took this teaching a step further by emphasizing the role of the natural law in establishing a just political order on both the national and international levels. A paradigmatic expression of the use of the natural law as accessible to all people can be found in St. John Paul II's 2003 address to the diplomatic corps accredited to the Holy See, in which he made the following appeal: "we must *rediscover* within States and between States *the paramount value of the natural law*, which was the source of inspiration for the rights of nations and for the first formulations of international law. Even if today some people question its

---

1. See esp. the encyclical *Libertas praestantissimum* (1888).

validity," he continued, "I am convinced that its general and universal principles can still help us to understand more clearly the unity of the human race and to foster the development of the consciences both of those who govern and of those who are governed."[2]

Without denying some validity in looking at the natural law in this way, I would nonetheless contrast it with a comment made in 2004 by the then-Cardinal Ratzinger, now Pope Benedict XVI Emeritus, during a published conversation with Jürgen Habermas about the pre-political foundations of the democratic constitutional state.[3] Cardinal Joseph Ratzinger explicitly *avoided* recourse to the natural law, claiming that, even though it "remained (especially in the Catholic Church) the key issue in dialogues with the secular society and with other communities of faith in order to appeal to the reason we share in common and to seek the basis for a consensus about the ethical principles of law in a secular, pluralistic society," it unfortunately has become a "blunt" instrument (*Instrument ist leider stumpf*).[4] Today, we need to take up the pope-to-be's call and sharpen that instrument. One way of doing so is by "reframing" or "recapitulating" our understanding of the natural law by making a basic distinction between ends and purposes. Doing so will pave the way for a better understanding of what is meant by "nature."

A limited and ineffective understanding of the natural law is to see it as a kind of codex, a set of imperatives that could be formulated in a purely theocratic, systematic exercise, identifiable and arguable apart from any particular moral tradition. Similarly, the use of the term *law* to name what is good by nature reinforces this tendency. If we think of the natural law in this way, we could easily be led into skepticism: If the precepts of the natural law are so lucid and rational, why is there so much disagreement and so much obscurity about them? Indeed, the very fact of moral

---

2. John Paul II, "Address to the Diplomatic Corps," para. 19. The International Theological Commission has, of course, not given up hope on the force of the natural law in circles of dialogue, though the tone is more reserved. See paragraph 52 of *In Search of a Universal Ethics*.

3. Ratzinger, *Dialectics of Secularization*. Reprinted in Ratzinger, *Europe Today and Tomorrow*, 67–81. The original German text, together with responses printed in major European newspapers, appears as *Vorpolitische moralische Grundlagen eines freiheitlichen*, 1–12.

4. Ratzinger, *Dialectics of Secularization*, 69. "Das Naturrecht ist—besonders in der katholischen Kirche—die Argumentationsfigur geblieben, mit der sie in den Gesprächen mit der säkularen Gesellschaft und mit anderen Glaubensgemeinschaften an die gemeinsame Vernunft appelliert und die Grundlagen für eine Verständigung über die ethischen Prinzipien des Rechts in einer säkularen pluralistischen Gesellschaft sucht. Aber dieses Instrument ist leider stumpf geworden, und ich möchte mich daher in diesem Gespräch nicht darauf stützen." Ratzinger, *Vorpolitische moralische Grundlagen eines freiheitlichen*, 6.

controversy—a fact that many of us deal with every day—would, from this vantage point, show that the natural law cannot simply be a codex. If we adopt such a conception, we might conclude at worst that there is no such thing as the natural law, and at best that it would not be helpful—or would even be counterproductive—if representatives of Catholic-inspired non-governmental organizations (NGOs) made reference to the natural law.

If, on the other hand, we recognize that not everyone will have a clear sense of the true ends of things, and if we see that such ends are not grasped beforehand but as differentiating themselves from what I will call purposes, then we will be in a better position to assert that the natural law does play a role in our moral thinking and in the way we evaluate situations and agents. The picture of natural law I would like to suggest is, I hope, more realistic and more persuasive precisely because it accounts for the obscurities associated with moral judgments. Here is an illustration of what I mean. I have a fork, a knife, and a spoon. What is the nature of each of these utensils? You could eat rice with a fork, a spoon, or a knife. Any of them would work. But not all of them were designed for this purpose. You cut a steak with a knife, but only with great difficulty with a fork, and even greater difficulty with a spoon. These utensils, even though they are manmade objects, have natures, and their natures are not determined by us (despite the fact that they came to be as a result of our choice—i.e., a purpose).

Each of these utensils must be understood in its proper cultural context. For example: I love to eat, but I know nothing about cooking. If I walk into the kitchen of a gourmet restaurant, I will see many utensils that I know nothing about. I do not "see" their natures. I need someone to explain their natures to me. When they explain them to me, they cannot avoid talking about what each of these items is *for*. I can tell them what the utensil looks like—it is long, blunt, metallic, etc.—but I need to interact with the person to discover the true nature of the utensil. Based on the features of the object, I can guess what it might be for, but since I do not know the process of cooking, I need someone who does know that process to tell me what it is.

Now return to the fork, and knife, and the spoon. For those who live in cultures that eat with their hands, the purpose of any of those utensils may be contrary to what that culture perceives its nature to be. The spoon, for example, might be taken as an object used to hold incense while making sacrifices to the family gods, but not as something you insert into your mouth to fill it with boiled grain.

The Distinction between Ends and Purposes

What we are getting at here is a distinction between ends and purposes. This is a classic philosophical distinction often overlooked today. The Greek word is *telos*. A *telos* belongs to a thing itself, while a purpose arises only when there are human beings in the picture. Purposes are intentions, something we wish for, deliberate about, or act to achieve. Ends, in contrast, are there apart from any human wishes and deliberations. They are what the thing is when it has reached its best or optimal state, its perfection and completion in itself. In philosophical terms, ends and purposes are both goods, but goods of different ontological orders. Purposes come into existence when human beings set out thoughtfully to achieve something. Purposes are wished-for satisfactions in view of which an agent deliberates and acts. Each of us has probably had various purposes throughout our life: to become a lawyer, to support your family, and even to attend this workshop. We did various things to achieve these purposes: we went to law school, found a job, and registered for some workshop. Once we have a purpose, we articulate the various ways in which the purpose can be achieved. We call this deliberation (or *arbitrium* in classical philosophical language). We then perform the action that, as far as we can see, is the best course of action in the present circumstances to achieve that purpose. This is called choice (*iudicium*).

We can therefore say that purposes exist in the mind and not in things, and they exist only because there are human beings. Purposes are complicated psychological entities because they depend on both thought (reasoning) and feeling (affectivity), but they are different from the ends which are found in things and are there independently of our wishes, actions, thinking, and feeling. Ends, in contrast, do not spring into being through human foresight. In fact, they do not "spring into being" at all; they come about concomitantly with the things they belong to. An end is the finished, perfected state of a thing, the thing when it is acting well as *the type of thing it is*.

The Three Kinds of Ends

There are three kinds of ends. Some ends are entirely unrelated to human beings. The end of an oak tree is to grow, sprout leaves, nourish itself, and reproduce. It is to be active and successful as an oak, as an entity of this kind. The end of a giraffe is to grow to maturity, nourish itself, reproduce, and live with other giraffes. Oak trees and giraffes function well *as* trees and giraffes. It is not an end of a giraffe to grow leaves, because a giraffe is not the *kind of thing* that grows leaves—it is not of its *nature*. A giraffe may break its leg or be eaten by a lion, but possibilities like these do not define what a giraffe is. They are not part of what it is, its essence, which is displayed most fully *not* when the giraffe merely exists but when the giraffe is acting well.

Some ends belong to things that have come into being through human agency. This is category in which the fork, the knife, and the spoon belong. This category includes artifacts and institutions, things brought about by human making and agreements, and these things *have essences and ends*. A museum is designed to hold works of art. A railway station is designed to facilitate the boarding of trains. The *telos* of an art museum is to make works of art available for public viewing, and part of this activity will be the acquisition and preservation of such works. The end of a bicycle is the transportation of individuals, and the end of this pen is writing or drawing. The seemingly obvious but, nonetheless, important thing to note is that in all these cases, *the end defines what the thing is*. Even though artifacts—like knives and forks—and institutions—such as art galleries—are brought about by human beings to serve our purposes and ends, we cannot change what they are. We might suppose that because we have made them, we could turn them into anything we wish, but they resist such manipulation. This spoon and this knife were entirely the result of human artifice. But that does not mean that their use can be entirely determined by human invention. It is more difficult to eat spaghetti with a spoon, and nearly impossible to eat soup with a fork. So even as instrumental beings, they have their own nature or essence and ends. We may have brought them into being, but they do not become our purposes. They retain their own ends and we have to subordinate ourselves to them.

To claim that institutions and artifacts had no definition, and that they could be changed by us at will, would mean that they could not be ruined or destroyed by us. If I were to take a hammer and smash the prongs of this fork and bend them with a pair of pliers, I would ruin it because it would not perform the function for which it was designed. In other words, if it were not part of the definition of a fork to pick up food, it would remain an effective fork even after I had smashed and distorted it.

Human beings themselves have ends. They have an overall end, which we call happiness, which is easy to name but difficult to define; and there are also ends for the various powers that human beings enjoy. There is a *telos* for human sociability, for example, for human thinking, for human sexuality, for bodily nourishment, for dealing with dangerous and painful things. There is also a *telos* for human bodily and psychological health.

Now it is in this third category that it is most difficult for us to discover what the ends truly are, because here human choice comes into play. In the first category, we were dealing simply with ends and not purposes—that is, an oak tree and a giraffe cannot deliberate and choose. In the second category, we were dealing with both ends and purposes, insofar as I can have a purpose to design and fashion a specific object with a specified end, such as a fork or an art museum. In this third category, our purposes and ends become even more entangled with one another, overlapping, complimenting and mutually influencing one another. Our inclinations and desires give rise to purposes, and sooner or later a conflict will arise between what we want and what we truly are. It is quite easy to see what the ends of nonhuman things are; it is more difficult to unravel ends and purposes in regard to institutions and artifacts; but it is extremely difficult to distinguish ends and purposes in regard to our own nature and its powers. But it is not impossible! And this I hope to show.

Differentiating between Ends and Purposes

How ends are differentiated from purposes? We have to begin with a word of caution. It is not the case that ends are presented to us all by themselves, separate from purposes. As all of you know well in your work, it is not the case that we first get a clear idea of the ends of things and then only subsequently attach our purposes to them. If this were the case, everybody would accept what marriage is and how we are to recognize, promote, and defend it. In a world where the *ends* of things are crystal clear to us *apart* from any consideration of what our purposes might be, moral issues would not merely be simpler, there would be no moral problems! This is essentially what Cardinal Ratzinger wanted to point out in his conversation with Habermas. The human problem arises precisely because we must *distinguish* ends and purposes in our activity, and it is difficult to do so.

So let us begin with the example of medicine. The end of medicine is the restoration and preservation of health, but a doctor may have several different purposes for practicing medicine. He may heal people and keep them healthy; he may intend to earn money, he may intend to become famous and well-liked in order to be elected to public office one day. If he is a *vicious* agent, he may want to study medicine in order to become adept at torturing people, just as someone may enroll in aviation school in order to learn how to fly an airplane into a skyscraper and kill people.

So medicine comes to us loaded with many different purposes, and it takes moral intelligence to make the distinction between what belongs to medicine as such (i.e., its end) and what purposes we have in practicing it. There is something else interesting here. Teachers in medical school might talk to their students about the distinction between the end and purposes of medicine, but when the students receive their degree and go on to practice medicine, they must make the distinction for themselves. No one can make it for them, because a distinction is a work of the mind. So the *telos* or essence of a thing comes to light for us precisely in contrast with our purposes, and our purposes come to light in contrast with what belongs to the things themselves. An end acts as a foil to a purpose, and a purpose acts as a foil to an end.

It is misleading to say that ends and purposes come to us entangled with one another, for to say this is to suggest that we have already differentiated between the two. What actually happens is that the very categories are not yet available because we have not yet made the distinction. *What we begin with precedes the distinction, but the distinction must be made nonetheless.* Furthermore, it has to be made not in some static contemplation of stable natures, but in the dynamic tumult of desires, emotions, and interests; in the very thick of the complicated and thorny issues that you deal with every day.

In many cases, our purposes are compatible with the ends of things. Earning income by being a medical doctor is not inherently incongruent with the end of medicine, but it can become so. The same holds for the end of law and the lawyer's practice of it, the end of governance and a politician's actions, etc. The way this usually happens is that the purpose overrides the end and works against it. For example, a lawyer may delay the execution of a will in order to increase his fees, or a doctor may perform unneeded surgeries in order to charge insurance companies more money. To take another example: I can use this fork as a pointer and it does not conflict with its end as an eating utensil, but if I use it to pry open a locked door, it probably will interfere with its end.

When we distinguish the ends of things in contrast to the pressure of our own selfish purposes, we are essentially distinguishing what is truly just against our personal interest. In other words, the objectivity of something like medicine enters our minds but not alone or unaccompanied. It enters our minds *as being differentiated from what we want*. Both are present together out there, but it is we who need to distinguish them.

It is also possible that someone's purpose can coincide with the end of the thing. Let us stick with the example of medicine. As he is operating on my heart, a doctor can have as his purpose here and now the restoration of my health. What he is doing he does in order that I might get better. So in this case, the end of the medical art and the purpose the physician has in mind overlap. Indeed, we would hope that every doctor *always* has the end of medical art *as at least one* of his purposes, and that he would not let other purposes override it.

The important thing to note is that even when purpose and end overlap and indeed are identical, there is still a difference between them. The restoration of health *really is* the end of the art of medicine, and it *really is being chosen* by the doctor the moment he puts the scalpel to my flesh. One and the same good presents itself in two guises: (1) as the end of the art, and (2) as the purpose of the agent. Philosophers call this a formal distinction: in other words, there is one and the same material good—namely the health of the person—which is both the natural end of medicine and the object of my physician's free choice. *Neither does the end turn into a purpose nor the purpose into an end.* Rather, the same good presents itself to us under two forms.

We could imagine, for example, a doctor who thought healing was *only* his purpose (and not an end). Perhaps he was told by his teachers in medical school, "everything you do as a doctor must be ordered to the preservation and restoration of your patient's health." As a result, the doctor has not seen for himself that the art he practices—namely medicine—has that same good as its end *apart from his purpose of achieving it*. He would be deceived into thinking that there is no end of his art apart from that which is chosen by him and his colleagues. He has not perceived the natural ends of things, and he has not been given the opportunity to recognize the natural law. He understands that he *does* have healing as the central and non-negotiable purpose of his art, but he does not see that healing *should* be the central and non-negotiable purpose of his art. In short, *medicine is defined in this way not because society wants to determine it in this way, but because that is what it is.*

The Four Inhibitors to Differentiating between Ends and Purposes

I imagine that in our work, we want to understand what inhibits people from seeing the distinction between ends and purposes. To ask this question is to ask why the "natural law" is not self-evident to everyone. First of all, there are people who are simply impulsive. It takes a certain level of development to be able to have purposes. Children, for example, want things, but they do not distinguish between what they want and what they are doing now. They do not shake out the difference between purposes and the steps to attain them. This is why children are impulsive. If my niece understood that it is necessary for my sister (her mother) to put her daughter's food in the microwave for two minutes before feeding her, she would stop crying. But in fact the delay in receiving food makes her cry all the more because all she knows is that she wants food.

Children have not developed the ability to think clearly about what they wish for, nor can they distinguish between what they wish for and what they can do now, nor can they discover optional ways of getting what they want, nor can they determine which is the best and most feasible way to get what they wish, nor can they take the first step, as well as all the succeeding steps, to get what they want.

The activities described above are what philosophers call practical thinking. Practical thinking is the business of picking out a future objective and the present means to obtain it. In children, the future collapses into their present. What is attainable in the future is trumped by the desire to have it now.

I should mention that the ability to rein in impulsive desires is not simply a matter of having time under your belt. In fact, as we get older, the future begins to collapse into our present again, and we become more childish. Aristotle astutely makes this observation. He writes, "it makes no difference whether the person is young in years or youthful in character; the defect does not depend on time, but on one's living, and pursuing each successive object, as passion directs."

The second inhibitor: perhaps we have become adult enough to establish distinct purposes and to determine the steps that lead to them, but we may still be unable to appreciate the presence of other people with their purposes. We permit entry into our awareness only of what *we* want. We remain unable to see that other people have their viewpoints and needs, and that we are not the only agents involved in our situations. We can call this failure to see objectively moral obtuseness. It is different from sheer viciousness because a vicious person *wants* to harm people, but a morally obtuse person does not.

To take a rather banal example: double parking. One person may simply want to get a coffee and double parks his vehicle; it does not even occur to him that the car will block traffic. All he knows is that he wants a cappuccino. Another person looks into the rearview mirror and sees that a fellow employee he does not particularly like is driving behind him. This second employee happens to be proud that he has never been late for work. So even though the first employee does not particularly want an *espresso* (he already had two at home), he double-parks his car in front of a café precisely to delay the second employee from arriving at the office on time. This first employee is a vicious agent, but not necessarily morally obtuse.

One more thing to note. Let's say that I am driving behind these drivers—neither of whom I know—and I see this whole thing transpiring before my eyes. Can I tell whether the first person is morally obtuse or vicious? No. The appearance of the event is the same. One person parked his car in the middle of the street and at least three other cars—including the one driven by person number two—are unable to pass. I have to *know* the person in order to know his or her character. Let's say I worked in the same office as the other two drivers, and as the first driver got out of his vehicle, I recognized him to be the vicious guy from the office, and I immediately had my suspicions regarding his intentions. I might even think he deliberately double-parked his car to annoy *me*. But then I notice the other fellow employee get out of his car and start yelling at employee number one. Then, knowing that employee number one cannot stand the prim, proper sense of responsibility of employee number two, I realize what the first employee is up to because I know him to be precisely the *kind of person* who would do such a mean thing.

In this example, the first driver is not unable to distinguish means and purposes. To take another example of moral obtuseness, a patient in a hospital room may keep the television playing all night long "so that she can sleep," oblivious to the other patients in the room. *Moral obtuseness is a failure in practical thinking, but it is different from vice and from the childishness we described earlier.*

The third inhibitor is immaturity. This is the state of mind in which we are unable to distinguish what we (and others) want from the demands and obligations of the world itself: that is, we fail to distinguish our purposes from the ends of things. To be able to make this distinction is to be "objective" in a new way that is different from simply recognizing the presence of other agents. If we merely recognize other people and acknowledge that they too have purposes, all we would have is a world of conflicting purposes and ultimate violence which would amount to a war of all against all. This is precisely what happens if we make autonomy and choice the sole norms and values of our deliberations. The only way to avoid this all-out war is to recognize the ends of things and the ends of our own nature. To do so is a mark of what we might call moral maturity. It is simply the ability to see that things themselves have their own essence, nature, ends, or "excellences" that need to be respected if the things are not to be destroyed. It is a virtue that enables us to take up a viewpoint that goes beyond our own desires and the desires of others.

The fourth inhibitor is vice. This is the case where we may acknowledge the ends of things and the viewpoints of other persons, but we deliberately and maliciously let our purposes override them. *We fail in regard to justice not because we are impulsive, obtuse, or immature,* but because we are unjust. We *want* to destroy the thing in question—the educational institution, the work of art, the church—and we want to injure others. A truly vicious person does not simply *do* unjust things, he *is* unjust; he does not, say, simply *commit* a murder, he *is* a murderer. He gets to be this way because of choices he has made in the past. The inclination to destroy the thing is always associated with some malice toward others; a vicious person destroys a thing because it could be a good for others.

In summary, I have proposed four ways in which the truth of ends can be obscured: impulsiveness, moral obtuseness, immaturity, and vice. In any given case, the lack of moral insight into the ends of things might be explained by some combination of these four, just as an agent's deficiency might be caused by something intermediate between weakness and malice. What we are discussing here is the way that the difference between ends and purposes comes to light, which amounts to the way in which the truth of things is disclosed. If we are to show how truth occurs, it is necessary to show what impedes such an occurrence—i.e., what hides the truth. We can appreciate a disclosure or unveiling of the truth only in contrast with the forms of concealment that are proper to the thing in question.

I have proposed these four inhibitors not to enable us to categorize fellow colleagues. Rather, I have used these four inhibitors as a philosophical tool to place the difference between ends and purposes in greater relief. The fact is that much of our work with Catholic-inspired NGOs involves the perception of multiple ends, ordering them hierarchically, and finding constructive and effective ways to pursue those ends. It is in this regard that the natural law, as I have tried to reframe it and recapitulate it, might help.

Conclusion

So what is natural law? How do we understand it? The way I am proposing today can be formulated thus: natural law is the ontological priority of ends over purposes. Natural law is shown to us when we recognize that there are ends in things and that our purposes and choices must respect their priority. This understanding of natural law would imply that our discussion of ends and purposes thus far has been a treatment of natural law and the way it is manifested to us. The precedence of ends over purposes occurs especially in regard to the ends that are proper to human nature and its various powers. For example, the ends built into human nourishment must be seen to govern the way we eat, and the ends built into human sexuality must be seen to govern the way we live with our sexuality. In both of these human powers, we ought not be governed by what we simply want and the *purposes* we set for ourselves; we must differentiate between what we want and the reality and the *telos* of the thing we are dealing with. We must have a sense that our purposes must be measured by the way things are, which means that they must be measured by the way things should be. The way things should be is simply what philosophers call their *end*. The important thing to recognize is that ends are not separate from things, but part of their very natures. Furthermore, the distinction between purpose and end has to dawn on us, and when it does dawn on us, we experience the pressure and the attraction of the way things *have* to be. In short, we have encountered "the natural law."

As a very brief footnote, I want to touch upon what we call "personalism" in natural law. It picks up strands suggested by Rocco Buttiglione, and it has to do with human affectivity. In short, we cannot persuade people to accept that there is a natural law merely by deductive or logical reason. We ultimately must persuade them with reasons of the heart. Saint Thomas Aquinas taught that the natural law is promulgated by being written in the human heart. "The law written in the hearts of men is the natural law: *lex scripta in cordibus hominum est lex naturalis.*" Aquinas also quotes a passage from Saint Augustine's *Confessions,* where Augustine speaks about God's law as written in the hearts of men, and of course both authors hearken back to Saint Paul who, in the Letter to the Romans, writes: "For when the Gentiles who do not have the law observe the prescriptions of the law; they are a law for themselves even though they do not have the law." They show that the demands of the law are written in their hearts. We should understand the full meaning of the words used for the heart in such passages as *cor* or *kardia*. The concepts designated by these words can help to heal the separation of heart and head that we take for granted in a world marked by Cartesian dualism. It is ingrained in us that the head or the brain is the seat of cognitive processes and the heart is the seat of emotion and feeling; but when Aquinas appeals to the heart, he is not saying that the natural law is somewhere given to our feelings or impulses instead of our minds. Rather, he is claiming that we are able to acknowledge, rationally, what the good is, *but precisely with the help of human affectivity, or the integral unity of head and heart that is intrinsic to our nature as ensouled beings created for and destined for love.* Only in this context do we fully understand what Aquinas means when he refers to our capacity for truth; more specifically, our capacity to perceive the natural ends of things—and consequently our supernatural end as human beings destined for God—by initially distinguishing them from purposes.

Bibliography

International Theological Commission. *In Search of a Universal Ethics: A New Look at the Natural Law* (2009). http://www.vatican.va/roman_curia/congregations/cfaith/cti_documents/rc_con_cfaith_doc_20090520_legge-naturale_en.html

John Paul II, "Address to the Diplomatic Corps (Jan. 13, 2013)." http://w2.vatican.va/content/john-paul-ii/en/speeches/2003/january/documents/hf_jp-ii_spe_20030113_diplomatic-corps.html.

Ratzinger, Joseph Cardinal, *Dialectics of Secularization*. San Francisco: Ignatius, 2007.

———. *Europe Today and Tomorrow: Addressing the Fundamental Issues*. San Francisco: Ignatius, 2007.

———. "Vorpolitische moralische Grundlagen eines freiheitlichen Staates." In *Zur Debatte: Themen der Katholischen Akademie in Bayern*. Vol. 34. (2004) 1–12.

Chapter 4

How to Think About Sexual Orientation and Gender Identity (SOGI) Policies and Religious Freedom

Ryan T. Anderson

Openness to win-win policy solutions that address the needs and concerns on all sides of a policy debate are all to the good. This is just as true in current debates about the needs of people who identify as LGBT (lesbian, gay, bisexual, transgender) as it is in current debates about infringements of religious liberty or any other policy area. In the aftermath of the US Supreme Court's decision in *Obergefell v. Hodges*,[1] all Americans—wherever they fall on the political spectrum and whether religious, secular, or agnostic—should join the effort to find ways to coexist peacefully.

But recent public policy proposals portrayed as win-win in this context are actually win-lose, and better policy solutions are possible. Current proposals to create new LGBT protections with varying types of religious exemptions will not result in fairness for all. Instead, they will penalize many Americans who believe that we are created male and female and that male and female are created for each other—convictions that the Court recognized are held "in good faith by reasonable and sincere people here and throughout the world."[2]

---

1. See *Obergefell v. Hodges*, 576 U.S. ___ (2015), http://www.supremecourt.gov/opinions/14pdf/14-556_3204.pdf.

2. Ibid., 576.

There is a better way to think about the concerns animating these new policy proposals and the best solutions. While SOGI antidiscrimination laws are unjustified, that does not exclude the idea of more tailored policies to prevent the mistreatment of people who identify as LGBT and at the same time would leave all Americans—not just the lucky few who are sufficiently well-connected to be exempted from "sexual orientation and gender identity" (SOGI) laws—free to act on their good-faith convictions.

"Fairness for All": Fundamentally Misguided

The most prominent model for creating specific LGBT policies while showing concern for religious freedom is known as "Fairness for All," a phrase used by proponents to describe a law first adopted in Utah and similar proposals in other states and potentially at the national level.[3] This approach creates new protected classes in antidiscrimination law based on sexual orientation and gender identity and then grants limited exemptions and protections, mainly to religious organizations. Proponents argue that nothing short of elevating SOGI as protected classes in law is sufficient to address existing problems for people who identify as LGBT. Although several religious organizations have endorsed such proposals and are actively promoting them, other prominent religious voices oppose the idea.

Proponents of "Fairness for All" assume that adoption of SOGI laws in some form is both a good thing and inevitable, and their arguments focus largely on how to mitigate the religious liberty harms of such laws. They do not argue the need for SOGI laws robustly, with facts and studies, and thus avoid the question of whether that need requires SOGI laws to address it as opposed to some less drastic measure or measures.

Because new SOGI laws change the status quo and impose new penalties on people (in some cases, jail time), the burden is on their proponents to prove the need for such laws, the "fit" between the law and the harms to be addressed, and either the lack of infringement of a preexisting right or the sufficient justification for its infringement. The record indicates clearly that proponents have failed to carry their burden on all counts.

---

3. The "Utah Compromise" was a law enacted in Utah in the spring of 2015 that created sexual orientation and gender identity antidiscrimination policy in employment and housing while also creating certain religious liberty exemptions and protections. Indiana attempted, but failed, to pass similar legislation in January 2016. See Anderson and George, "Liberty and SOGI Laws." Thus far, no "Fairness for All" legislation has been introduced at the federal level, but there is discussion among advocates about doing so.

Unfairness for Many, Exemptions for Few

The "Fairness for All" approach creates bad SOGI public policy[4] and then tries to forestall some of its worst consequences through limited religious exemptions. Exemptions, however, do not convert an otherwise bad policy into a good one, and the result here is not fairness for all, but unfairness for many with exemptions for a fortunate few.[5]

SOGI laws, including "Fairness for All," threaten the civil rights of Americans who believe basic truths about the human condition articulated by ancient Greek and Roman philosophers, members of the Abrahamic faiths, and secular people who believe in freedom of inquiry. Orthodox Jews, Roman Catholics, Eastern Orthodox and Evangelical Christians, Latter-Day Saints, Muslims, and people of other faiths or none at all will be at risk. Where similar SOGI policies have been enacted, bakers, florists, photographers, adoption agencies, schools, and providers of services to the needy have been penalized or threatened not because they "discriminated" against someone because they identify as LGBT, but because they judged in conscience that they could not endorse certain morally relevant *conduct*.

Because of the *Obergefell* decision, which required the government to recognize same-sex relationships as marriages, the people who need legal protections are those who believe that male and female are objective biological categories and that marriage unites a man and a woman. Although *Obergefell* did not compel private citizens and their private associations to change their beliefs about marriage, in case after case, corporate and cultural pressures are mounting against those who seek to live and work consistent with their belief that marriage is the union of a man and a woman and sex is a biological reality.[6] SOGI laws establish in law and culture the principle that acting on these beliefs is bigotry.

The Fundamental Difference between Religious Freedom and Antidiscrimination Policies

Current "Fairness for All" proposals are fundamentally misguided because they fail to recognize the essential difference between antidiscrimination policies and religious freedom policies. Antidiscrimination laws are about government coercing people to live according to the majority's values.

---

4. See, for example, Anderson, "Sexual Orientation and Gender Identity," and Anderson, *Truth Overruled*.

5. Anderson and George, "Liberty and SOGI Laws."

6. For a litany of such incidents, see Anderson, *Truth Overruled*.

Religious liberty laws are about removing government coercion and allowing people to live by their own beliefs. While there can be good justifications for certain antidiscrimination policies, there is not a human right to them. Religious freedom, however, *is* a human right. "Fairness for All" mistakenly conflates these rather different concepts.

When Mozilla Firefox forced CEO Brendan Eich to resign because he donated to California's marriage initiative, many people thought the company was doing the wrong thing, but there were no widespread calls for the government to penalize the company for acting on its socially liberal convictions. And when A&E suspended Phil Robertson from *Duck Dynasty* and Cracker Barrel removed his products from its stores because he expressed support for Biblical views of sexuality, many Americans thought A&E and Cracker Barrel were in the wrong. Nevertheless, they were free to act on their socially liberal beliefs in running their businesses.

Similarly, even those who disagree with the beliefs of a baker, florist, photographer, adoption agency, or religious school that supports the historic understanding of marriage should agree that the government ought not to penalize them for running their organizations according to their moral and religious convictions. Yet this is exactly what SOGI laws do.

It is not "Fairness for All" when one side uses the law to coerce the other side, and all the other side gets is limited exemptions for freedom. Nor is it a "compromise"—or at least not a good one—when one side gets special new legal privileges applicable almost everywhere, and "in exchange" the other side gets limited exemptions (which are not guaranteed to last[7]) from this bad public policy. Compromise suggests that each side gets something that it wants, though less than everything, and that both sides stand roughly equal at the end of negotiations. In practice, "Fairness for All" means that one side advances and the other retreats.

---

7. Once established, SOGI rules have come to swallow religious exceptions. After all, once the law has established a principle that sexual orientation and gender identity are akin to race, why should they not receive the same legal protections? Under such policy, what would prevent morally conservative people from being branded as bigots equivalent to racists (a charge many LGBT activists already make, but one that would be backed by law under SOGI policy)? For example, when Ireland first passed its SOGI law, it included exemptions for certain "religious, educational, or medical institutions." In December 2015, the Parliament voted to repeal this section of the act. Likewise, Congress protected the religious freedom of religious schools in the District of Columbia with respect to sexual orientation, but in December 2014, the D.C. City Council rescinded those protections.

Teaching that the Truth Is Discriminatory, Enforcing Government Sexual Orthodoxy

Beyond the particulars of current "Fairness for All" proposals, there are broader and deeper problems with the general model of adding sexual orientation and gender identity to existing antidiscrimination statutes. "Fairness for All," like other SOGI laws, uses the government and the power of the law to send the message that traditional Judeo-Christian beliefs are not only false, but also discriminatory and rooted in animus.

SOGI policies attempt to impose by force of law a system of orthodoxy with respect to human sexuality: the belief that marriage is merely a union of consenting adults, regardless of biology, and that one can be male, female, none, or some combination—again, regardless of biology.[8] SOGI laws impose this orthodoxy by punishing dissent and treating as irrational, bigoted, and unjust the beliefs that men and women are biologically rooted and made for each other in marriage.

Sexual Orientation and Gender Identity v. Race and Sex

Current SOGI laws, including "Fairness for All," lack the nuance and specificity necessary for cases they seek to address. They take the existing paradigm of public policy responses to racism and sexism and assume that this paradigm is appropriate for the policy needs of people who identify as LGBT. This is misguided for both conceptual and practical reasons.

Conceptually, sexual orientation and gender identity are unlike race and sex in important ways. This is one of the reasons why adding the concepts "sexual orientation" and "gender identity" to laws meant to protect on the basis of race and sex does not produce good legal outcomes. SOGIs, including "Fairness for All," create legal privileges for new protected classes based not on objective, verifiable traits, but on subjective identities. Furthermore, unlike race and sex, sexual orientation and gender identity are partly defined in terms of actions, and actions are subject to moral evaluation, while one's status in terms of race and sex is not. As a result, existing and proposed SOGI laws, including "Fairness for All," define "discrimination" with respect to sexual orientation and gender identity much too broadly, penalizing people for simply seeking not to facilitate, support, or participate in actions—such as same-sex weddings or sex "reassignment" surgeries—that they reasonably deem to be immoral.[9]

---

8. For more on this, see Anderson, *Truth Overruled*.

9. People opposed to interracial marriage or racially integrated lunch counters

SOGI laws are not about the freedom of LGBT people to engage in certain actions, but about coercing and penalizing people who in good conscience cannot endorse those actions. SOGI laws do this by coercing and penalizing people who act on an understanding of human sexuality that is at odds with the prevailing viewpoint that the government seeks to enforce. It is one thing for the government to allow or even endorse conduct that is immoral to many religious faiths, but it is quite another thing for government to force others to condone and facilitate it in violation of their beliefs.

There is also a practical difference between proposals for SOGI antidiscrimination policies and policies prohibiting discrimination on the basis of race or sex. The nature and extent of SOGI discrimination in the United States today is unlike racism and sexism when antidiscrimination laws were enacted (and unlike racism and sexism even today). When the Civil Rights Act of 1964 was enacted, blacks were treated as second-class citizens. Individuals, businesses, and associations across the country excluded blacks in ways that caused grave material and social harms without justification, without market forces acting as a corrective, and with the tacit and often explicit backing of government.

Blacks were denied loans, kept out of decent homes, and denied job opportunities—except as servants, janitors, and manual laborers. These material harms both built on and fortified the social harms of a culture corrupted by views of white supremacy that treated blacks as less intelligent, less skilled, and in some respects less human. Making it harder for blacks and whites to mingle on equal terms was not just incidental: It was the whole point. Discrimination was so pervasive that the risks of lost economic opportunities or sullied reputation were acceptable to the many who engaged in it. Social and market forces, instead of punishing discrimination, rewarded it through the collusion of many whites (with a heavy assist from the state). Given the irrelevance of race to almost any transaction, and given the flagrant racial animus of the time, no claims of benign motives are plausible. Resort to the law was therefore necessary.[10]

---

could claim they were opposed to certain actions when blacks and whites did them together, but that stops the inquiry too soon. Why were they opposed? The reason they were against blacks and whites doing things together was an attitude of white supremacy that viewed and treated blacks as less intelligent, less skilled, and in some respects less human. They thus opposed blacks interacting with whites on an equal plane. One can and should hold that we are created male and female, with male and female created for each other, without holding any hostility toward people who identify as LGBT. For more on this, see the section on discrimination in this paper. See also Corvino et al., *Debating Religious Liberty and Discrimination*.

10. Portions of this paragraph are adapted from Corvino et al., *Debating Religious Liberty and Discrimination*.

However, a similar legal push is not necessary today. There is no widespread heterosexual supremacy akin to white supremacy. There is no widespread treatment of LGBTs as second-class citizens akin to Jim Crow. There are no denials of the right to vote, no lynchings, no signs over water fountains saying "Gay" and "Straight." This is not to deny that there has been historic bigotry against those who identify as LGBT or that it has vanished. It exists and should be addressed appropriately. As with other forms of mistreatment, our communities must fight it. But the remaining instances simply cannot be compared to the systematic material and social harms wrought by racism in the 1960s and earlier.

Put another way, the legal response that was appropriate to remedy the legacy of slavery and Jim Crow is not appropriate for today's challenges. Simply adding SOGI to far-reaching antidiscrimination laws and then tacking on some exemptions is not a prudent strategy. The policy response to the legitimate concerns of people who identify as LGBT must be nuanced and appropriately tailored. Antidiscrimination laws, however, are blunt instruments by design, and many go beyond intentional discrimination and ban actions that have "disparate impacts" on protected classes. Policymakers therefore need to rethink how to formulate and implement policy in this area.

LGBT Policy Needs

In responding to the legitimate needs of people who identify as LGBT while also respecting the religious freedom rights of all, policymakers must first assess the nature and extent of the problem and then determine whether governmental intervention is required and, if it is, what the appropriate remedy should be.

Consideration of the needs of people who identify as LGBT should look to both material and social needs. This is illustrated, for example, in the way that Jim Crow not only prevented blacks from accessing certain basic goods and services, but also treated blacks as second-class citizens. Once a legitimate need has been identified, policymakers must ask two questions:

- Is a governmental response appropriate? Are the needs of such a magnitude and extent to warrant government attention?
- Is a government response required? Are social, economic, and cultural forces sufficient to address these needs on their own?

If a government response is judged necessary, it must be tailored to address the documented need at the appropriate level of government (federal, state, or local) while doing everything possible to avoid burdening such rights as the freedoms of contract, conscience, religion, and speech.[11]

The Needs

Before any law can be justified and crafted, there must be a documented need for it, Advocates of SOGI laws must therefore provide evidence proving the need for a coercive governmental response—a requirement they have failed to meet. This is not to say conclusively that such a need does not exist or that we live in a country that is free from discrimination against people who identify as LGBT. It *is* to say, however, that evidence of discrimination comparable to the evidence used to justify passage of our civil rights laws on race and sex has not been demonstrated. Absent such demonstration, civil rights laws used to combat racism and sexism are not the proper models to use in addressing discrimination against those who identify themselves as LGBT.

As to broader trends, there is no evidence that people who identify as LGBT have been turned away by a single hotel chain, a single major restaurant, or a single major employer.[12] In fact:

- The Human Rights Campaign (HRC)—the nation's premier LGBT advocacy group—reports that 89 percent of *Fortune* 500 companies have policies against considering sexual orientation in employment decisions.[13]

- According to Prudential, "median LGBT household income is $61,500 vs. $50,000 for the average American household."[14]

- An August 2016 report from the U.S. Treasury—based on tax returns, not surveys—shows opposite-sex couples earning on average $113,115, compared to $123,995 for lesbian couples and $175,590 for gay male couples. For couples with children, the gap is even more

---

11. Ibid.

12. The Equal Employment Opportunity Commission suggests that it secured a total of $4.4 million in awards for complainants of LGBT discrimination last year, but these figures appear to be overstated, because "[m]onetary benefits include amounts which have been recovered exclusively or partially on non-LGBT claims included in the charge." U.S. Equal Employment Opportunity Commission, "LGBT-Based Sex Discrimination Charges FY 2013–FY 2016," https://www.eeoc.gov/eeoc/statistics/enforcement/lgbt_sex_based.cfm.

13. Human Rights Campaign, "LGBTQ Equality at the Fortune 500."

14. Prudential Financial, Inc., "LGBT Financial Experience 2016–2017," 10.

dramatic: $104,475 for opposite-sex couples but $130,865 for lesbian couples and $274,855 for gay couples.[15]

When it comes to the denial of services to LGBT people, Professor Andrew Koppelman, an LGBT advocate, acknowledges that:

> Hardly any of these cases have occurred: a handful in a country of 300 million people. In all of them, the people who objected to the law were asked directly to facilitate same-sex relationships, by providing wedding, adoption, or artificial insemination services, counseling, or rental of bedrooms. There have been no claims of a right to simply refuse to deal with gay people.[16]

Those three sentences shatter the strongest case for SOGI laws. Amid several years of fierce debate and intense media attention, all but one of the cases have involved vendors opposed to serving same-sex weddings and professionals and nonprofits convinced that children ought to have a mother and father, that marriage unites husband and wife, or that sex is for marriage. The cases do not involve people or organizations treating people who identify as LGBT differently just because they identify as LGBT. The fact is that the strongest grounds for enacting policy to ensure that people who identify as LGBT have access to basic services are rare to vanishing.

Furthermore, the few cases that have garnered media attention—cases involving bakers, a florist, and a photographer—hardly diminish a single person or couple's range of opportunities for room, board, or entertainment. If businesses started to refuse service specifically to gays and lesbians, it is hard to imagine a sector of commerce or a region of the U.S. where media coverage would not provide a remedy swift and decisive enough to restore access in days.

Think, for example, of the pizzeria in small-town Indiana that, after the local news reported that its owners would not cater a hypothetical gay wedding, became the target of protests, boycotts, and death threats that forced it to shut down for several months.[17] Had this been an actual case, not a mere hypothetical, and had it involved a blanket "No Gays Allowed" policy, not simply a conviction about marriage, the resultant media coverage and social pressure would likely have been even more intense. This example and others like it highlight a related point: The LGBT community's political influence is profound and still growing.

---

15. Fisher et al, "Joint Filing by Same-Sex Couples," 28.
16. Andrew Koppelman, "Zombie in the Supreme Court," 77–95.
17. Buckley, "Threats Tied to RFRA," para. 1.

In reality, there is neither a national nor even a local problem of bakers vilifying people who identify as gay. They have no problems crafting birthday cakes for customers regardless of sexual orientation, but some bakers cannot in good conscience use their talents to help celebrate a same-sex wedding by designing a cake topped by two grooms or two brides. Similarly, religious schools have no problem employing teachers with same-sex attractions who support their religious mission and teachings, but some religious schools have had to dismiss teachers who *fail to model or who outright oppose those teachings*. These decisions do not count as mistreatment based on sexual orientation, and preventing them should not be counted as a legitimate need.

Cultural Forces and Government Responses

As for the mistreatment that remains, it is being driven ever more to the margins by media, markets, and culture. Where we can leave these more efficient forces to do the job, we should do so. Market forces are already curbing wrongful discrimination based on factors that are irrelevant to employment ability or performance without the costs and inevitable side effects of heavy-handed legal coercion. Market competition can provide nuanced solutions that are far superior to coercive, costly, one-size-fits-all government policy.

When corporate giants like the NBA, the NCAA, the NFL, Apple, Salesforce, Delta, and the Coca-Cola Company threaten to boycott a state over laws that merely give conscientious objectors their day in court, it is hard to see the case for legally coercing such dissenters to achieve progressives' social goals. SOGI laws, including "Fairness for All," are legal hammers purportedly justified by extensive, entrenched, and unjust discrimination. SOGIs, including "Fairness for All," are solutions in search of a problem.

Nevertheless, supposing that the evidence showed a need both large enough and entrenched enough to justify a policy response, how should such a policy be structured? Specifically, how can policymakers be precise in tailoring such a law to meet the underlying need while not prohibiting legitimate actions and interactions and not burdening the rights of conscience, religion, or speech?

Scope of Coverage: The Case of "Public Accommodations"

Any policy response to a legitimate need must be appropriately tailored. If a policy is justified by a housing or employment need, the scope of who counts as an employer or what counts as relevant housing must be defined accurately so that it can address the problem without unnecessarily burdening others. One problem with current SOGI laws, however, is that they apply to too many sectors of life and employ unreasonably expansive definitions. The scope of coverage—areas where the law applies, penalizes, and coerces—is far too broad.

For example, the Equality Act,[18] the centerpiece of the Human Rights Campaign's Beyond Marriage Equality Initiative,[19] would add "sexual orientation" and "gender identity" to virtually all federal civil rights laws covering race—"Public Accommodations, Education, Federal Financial Assistance, Employment, Housing, Credit, and Federal Jury Service"[20]—and expand them beyond their current reach. It is also explicitly designed to shrink existing religious liberty protections.[21] It also would stretch the scope of "public accommodations" quite far. The Civil Rights Act of 1964—the purpose of which was to integrate half of the continental United States after centuries of race-based slavery and Jim Crow—covered entities like hotels, restaurants, theaters, and gas stations. The Equality Act would cover almost every business serving the public.

Likewise, a 2014 SOGI law passed by the Houston City Council—but later repealed by a supermajority of the city's voters—would have covered "every business with a physical location in the city, whether wholesale or retail, which is open to the general public and offers for compensation any product, service, or facility."[22] No inch of the public square would have been spared its costs to conscience, pluralism, and speech.

By contrast, at common law, the term "public accommodations" is used to refer to public utilities, common carriers, and other natural monopolies that have a general duty to serve the public.[23] Likewise, the federal Civil

---

18. Equality Act, S. 1858, 114th Cong., 1st sess., https://www.congress.gov/114/bills/s1858/BILLS-114s1858is.pdf. The House version of the bill is H.R. 3185.

19. Human Rights Campaign, "Beyond Marriage Equality."

20. Merkley et al., "The Equality Act," 1.

21. Equality Act, S. 1858, Sec. 9.

22. City of Houston, Texas, Ordinance No. 2014-530, May 28, 2014, Exhibit A, pp. 2–3, http://www.scribd.com/doc/228533432/Equal-Rights-Ordinance.

23. Separately, under common law, individuals who open their private property to the public to conduct business, though they have no general duty to serve, may exclude

Rights Act of 1964 does not apply to bakeries, but racial discrimination is not rampant at Dunkin' Donuts, not least because all incentives are aligned against it. Because "sex" is not a protected class for federal antidiscrimination law for public accommodations, federal law allows restaurants of any size to refuse to admit women. It also allows theaters and stadiums to turn away Democrats just for being Democrats and Republicans just for being Republicans. And yet culture and commerce prevent these and other forms of discrimination without any help from the law.

Thus, the first step to finding an appropriate policy solution is to consider the scope of coverage. A policy response must be tailored to the need that justifies it in the first place. This entails defining key terms such as "public accommodations" appropriately.[24]

Definition of Key Terms: "Discrimination"

The second step is to define "discrimination" accurately. The biggest problem with current SOGI laws, including "Fairness for All," is that they do not appropriately define what counts as discriminatory. To illustrate this, consider several different cases of putative "discrimination." The law must be nuanced enough to capture the important differences in these cases.

Invidious and Rightly Unlawful Discrimination

Racially segregated water fountains were one form of discrimination that took race into consideration—in a context where it was completely irrelevant—and then treated blacks as second-class citizens precisely because they were black. The entire point was to classify on the basis of race in order to treat blacks as socially inferior. As a result, such actions were rightly described as invidious race-based discrimination, and—given the entrenched, widespread, state-facilitated nature of the problem—they were rightly made unlawful.

Likewise, throughout much of American history, girls and women were not afforded educational opportunities equal to those available to

---

members of the public from the premises only for a valid reason. At common law, race is never a valid reason for exclusion, but many other reasons can be valid, depending on the circumstances of the case. Such reasons would include the inability to perform actions that violate the conviction that marriage is the union of a man and woman. See MacLeod, "Tempering Civil Rights Conflicts," 643–711.

24. The same is true for defining housing or employers that are covered should the need be in housing or employment.

boys and men. This form of discrimination took sex into consideration and then treated girls and women poorly precisely because of their sex, barring them from education in certain subjects or at certain levels despite being otherwise qualified. As with invidious racial discrimination, such treatment took a feature (in this case, sex) into consideration precisely to treat women as less than men. The law rightly deemed such actions as invidious sex-based discrimination, and—again, given the entrenched, widespread, and state-facilitated nature of the problem—Title IX of the Education Amendments was enacted to ensure that girls and women received equal educational opportunities.

Appropriate and Rightly Lawful Distinctions that are not Classified as Discrimination

When Title IX was enacted in 1972 and its implementing regulations were promulgated in 1975, the law made clear that sex-specific housing, bathrooms, and locker rooms were not unlawful discrimination. Such policies take sex into consideration, but they do not treat women as inferior to men or men as inferior to women. They treat both sexes equally *because* they take sex into consideration (they "discriminate"—in the nonpejorative sense of "distinguish"—on the basis of sex) precisely in a way that matters: by appreciating the bodily sexual difference of men and women in things such as housing, bathroom, and locker room policy.

Would we really be treating men and women equally in anything but an artificial way if we forced men and women, boys and girls, to undress in front of each other? Justice Ruth Bader Ginsburg, in her majority opinion for the Supreme Court forcing the Virginia Military Institute to become co-ed, wrote that it "would undoubtedly require alterations necessary to afford members of each sex privacy from the other sex in living arrangements."[25] Yet we certainly would be treating people unequally if access to intimate facilities were based on factors wholly unrelated to privacy, such as race.

As a result, policymakers did not consider sex-specific intimate facilities as discriminatory in the first place, and laws explicitly reflected that commonsense understanding while rightly declaring racially segregated facilities to be unlawful. The lesson here is that not all distinctions in fact should be deemed unlawful discrimination.

---

25. *United States v. Virginia*, 518 U.S. 151, 550n19 (1996), https://supreme.justia.com/cases/federal/us/518/515/case.html.

Not Discriminatory at All

If sex-specific intimate facilities are an example of lawful, legitimate policies that take sex into consideration, pro-life medical practices are examples of policies that are legitimate and lawful because they do not take sex into consideration at all. That only women can get pregnant has no bearing whatsoever on the judgment of the conscientious doctor or nurse who refuses to kill the unborn. The insistence of LGBT activists that men actually can become pregnant highlights the point: Pro-life medical personal refuse to do abortions on pregnant women *and* "pregnant men" (i.e. women who identify as men).

Thus, we can identify three different types of cases:

- Cases of invidious discrimination, in which an irrelevant factor is taken into consideration in order to treat people poorly based on that factor, as with racially segregated water fountains;
- Cases of distinctions without unlawful discrimination, in which a factor is taken into consideration precisely because it is relevant to the underlying policy and people are not treated poorly, as with sex-specific intimate facilities; and
- Cases with neither distinctions nor discrimination, in which a particular factor simply does not enter into consideration.

Any proposed policy intended to address the documented needs of people who identify as LGBT must take these categories into account without conflation.[26]

SOGI Discrimination: Real and Imagined

Consider a florist who refused to serve all customers who identify as LGBT simply because they identified as LGBT. That would be a case of invidious discrimination because the mere knowledge that they identify as LGBT should have no impact whatsoever on the act of the florist selling flowers, because there is no rational connection between the two.

---

26. There is a fourth category of "discrimination": nonmalicious oversight or neglect. Consider the type of discrimination the Americans with Disabilities Act is meant to combat. Before enactment of the ADA, many movie theaters, for example, did not have wheelchair ramps. This was the result of an oversight with respect to the needs of people with disabilities, not because of any hostility toward them. Because such oversights were so widespread and contributed to the exclusion of people with disabilities from full participation in society, Congress acted.

Now consider Baronelle Stutzman, the 71-year-old grandmother who served one particular gay customer for nearly a decade but declined to do the wedding flowers for his same-sex wedding ceremony. The customer's sexual orientation did not play any role in Stutzman's decision. Her belief that marriage is a union of sexually complementary spouses does not spring from any convictions about people who identify as LGBT. When she says she can do wedding flowers only for true weddings, she makes no distinctions based on sexual orientation at all.[27]

This is seen most clearly in the case of Catholic Charities adoption agencies. They decline to place the children entrusted to their care with same-sex couples not because of their sexual orientation, but because of the conviction that children deserve both a mother and a father. That belief—that men and women are not interchangeable, mothers and fathers are not replaceable, the two best dads in the world cannot make up for a missing mom, and the two best moms in the world cannot make up for a missing dad—has absolutely nothing to do with sexual orientation. Catholic Charities does not say that people who identify as LGBT cannot love or care for children; it does not take sexual orientation into consideration *at all*. Its preference for placing children with mothers and fathers is not an instance of discrimination based on sexual orientation—and the law should not say otherwise.[28]

Purported gender identity discrimination presents similar problems. *The Washington Post* recently reported on a woman who was suing a Catholic hospital for declining to perform a sex reassignment procedure on her that entailed removing her healthy uterus. In that report, the *Post* captures the conflation of real and imaginary discrimination:

> "What the rule says is if you provide a particular service to anybody, you can't refuse to provide it to anyone," said Sarah Warbelow, the legal director for the Human Rights Campaign. That means a transgender person who shows up at an emergency room with something as basic as a twisted ankle cannot be denied care, as sometimes happens, Warbelow said. That also means if a doctor provides breast reconstruction surgery or hormone therapy, those services cannot be denied to transgender patients seeking them for gender dysphoria, she said.[29]

The two examples given, however, differ in significant ways. A hospital that refuses to treat the twisted ankles of people who identify as

27. See discussion in Anderson, *Truth Overruled*.
28. Ibid.
29. Somashekhar, "Catholic Groups Sue," n.p.

transgender simply because they identify as transgender would be engaging in invidious discrimination, but a hospital that declines to remove the perfectly healthy uterus of a woman who identifies as a man is not engaging in "gender identity" discrimination. The gender identity of the patient plays no role in the decision-making process: Just as prolife physicians do not kill unborn babies, regardless of the sex or gender identity of the pregnant person, doctors do not remove healthy uteruses from *any* patients, regardless of how they identify themselves.

As for the Human Rights Campaign spokesperson's claim that emergency rooms "sometimes" refuse to treat the twisted ankles of transgender patients, there is no evidence— including on the HRC's website—that it or anything similar in fact happens. Furthermore, insofar as this "sometimes happens," it seems reasonable to think that the media would focus so much attention on it that the hospital would reverse course within hours. It therefore seems highly unlikely that this alleged problem merits a governmental response.

In any event, if analysis of the scope and extent of a need and the cultural and social forces at play indicates that people who identify as LGBT have a legitimate need that justifies governmental action, then the government's response must be limited to the proper scope and must accurately define what counts as "discrimination."

Need for Policy Shapes the Nature of Policy Response, Definitions, and Protections

The preceding sections provide a framework for thinking through how to (1) identify the needs of people who identify as LGBT that government must address, (2) tailor the scope of any policy remedy appropriately, and (3) carefully distinguish which circumstances count as discrimination and which do not. If all of those steps are accomplished, another consideration comes to the fore: Any legal remedy must not penalize valid forms of action and interaction or burden the rights of conscience, religion, and speech.

Because there was such widespread, entrenched systemic and institutional racism throughout American society in the 1960s, for example, and because social and market forces were not sufficient to remedy the problem, it was appropriate for government to respond. That response was properly tailored to meet this need. It defined discrimination to include racially segregated accommodations, places of employment, and housing providers while providing thin religious liberty protections. Because the justification for antidiscrimination laws based on race was so strong and the need was so great, the law was appropriately broad with limited exemptions.

By contrast, consider laws that address discrimination based on sex. Because the nature of sex and the history of sexism did not represent an exact parallel to racism, the law did not treat them in entirely the same ways. To this day, for example, sex is not a protected class for federal antidiscrimination law as applied to public accommodations. Discrimination was legally defined so as not to include sex-specific intimate facilities, and much broader—and in some cases total—religious liberty exemptions were included. In other words, because the justification for laws against sex-based discrimination was weaker than the justification for laws against race-based discrimination, the legal response was more modest: It covered less terrain, defined discrimination more narrowly, and provided greater protection for religious liberty.

Any proposed policies intended to meet the needs of people who identify as LGBT would need to be crafted in a similar manner. Without greater evidence of the justification for specific policy responses—greater documentation of what the needs truly are—it is hard to be specific. In general, however, the need clearly seems weaker than the need for policies designed to deal with discrimination on the basis of race and sex. A policy response would therefore need to cover less ground, target discrimination more narrowly, and avoid undermining the rights of conscience, religion, and speech.

Policy Responses Matter Because of the Messages They Send

Getting public policy right matters both because the law is binding and because the law is a teacher. A law that burdens and penalizes nondiscriminatory actions and violates the rights of conscience, religion, and speech is purely and simply unjust, and an unjust law that supposedly applies to all Americans while exempting a select few from its provisions hardly represents "Fairness for All."

"Fairness for All" advocates who believe the truth about marriage, human nature, and embodiment should consider how the law would teach future generations that this truth is a lie and that a lie is the truth. Any good that an exemption from the law preserves for religious communities will pale in comparison to the damage that the law does in its pedagogical function.

Some LGBT activists express concerns about the message that religious exemptions send. They claim that such laws teach that people have a "license to discriminate." But their criticism proves the point made earlier: SOGI laws will teach that legitimate conduct and judgments discriminate, are morally wrong, and should therefore not be given a "license." Much better, then, not to have the law define such actions as discrimination in the first place.

In the aftermath of the judicially imposed legal redefinition of marriage, the law should not be used to punish and hound those who continue to believe that marriage unites husband and wife. The law should respect their full and equal status as citizens. If *Obergefell* was about respecting the freedom of people who identify as LGBT to live as they wish, as LGBT activists claim, then that same freedom should be respected for Americans who believe in the conjugal understanding of marriage as the union of husband and wife. The law should not force these Americans into the closet.

Lessons from *Roe v. Wade* Applied to *Obergefell v. Hodges*

After the Supreme Court's decision in *Roe* v. *Wade*, Americans responded by protecting the rights of pro-life citizens—religious and nonreligious, for-profit and nonprofit—to lead their lives in accordance with their beliefs. Americans did not pass "Fairness for All" legislation that would have made it unlawful sex discrimination to decline to perform an abortion with some limited exceptions. After *Roe*, Americans did not give even greater legal privileges to the forces promoting abortion; they instead sought to enshrine stand-alone conscience protections in law and over time succeeded.

Americans enacted legislation at the local, state, and federal levels to protect the rights of pro-life Americans not to be punished by government for living out their beliefs. The Church and Weldon Amendments have protected the conscience rights of pro-life medical personnel to refuse to perform or assist with abortions, and the Hyde Amendment and Mexico City policy prevent the use of taxpayer money to support abortion.

The same needs to happen in the aftermath of *Obergefell* for Americans who believe that male and female are objective biological categories and that marriage unites a man and a woman. Public policy must ensure that government never penalizes people for expressing or acting on their view that marriage is the union of husband and wife, that sexual relations are properly reserved for such a union, or that maleness and femaleness are objective biological realities. An example of good policy along these lines is the First Amendment Defense Act.[30]

30. H.R. 2802, 114th Cong., 1st Sess., https://www.congress.gov/bill/114th-congress/house-bill/2802. See also Anderson, "First Amendment Defense Act."

Some argue that *Obergefell* was only a first step and that Congress and state legislatures should get ahead of the coercive laws they fear will come by enacting their own coercive law with some exceptions under the mantle of pragmatism. This it is more akin to "burning the village in order to save it" because such a proposal in reality favors one side of a cultural debate—the culturally and politically powerful LGBT lobby—at the expense of citizens of goodwill who believe reasonably that we are created male and female and that marriage unites a man and a woman but who lack the influence and power of the LGBT lobby (and cannot therefore bring the power of Google, Microsoft, the NBA, the NCAA, Starbucks, and similar organizations to bear in helping them to defend their rights or achieve their political goals).

Some proponents of "Fairness for All" go beyond pragmatic arguments and claim that it would be unjust not to adopt SOGI laws, but that those laws must have religious exemptions. These proponents, however, spend relatively little time arguing for the rules under which they propose others should live compared to the large amount of time they spend on the benefits of exceptions to those rules. Suffice it to say that it is unusual for proponents of any laws to focus on what the laws do *not* do as opposed to what they actually *do* and why we need such actions in the first place. As noted previously, SOGI proponents, including those of the "Fairness for All" variety, have failed to demonstrate the requisite need to enact SOGI laws.

While such proposals may have some superficially appealing aspects, they would only increase cultural tensions, further empower an already powerful special-interest lobby, and impose unjustly on Americans of many different faiths and all walks of life. Big Business and Big Law are using Big Government to impose their cultural values on small businesses and ordinary Americans. Corporate elites are using their privilege and positions of power to have government coerce people whose convictions on matters of profound moral import differ from theirs.

Conclusion

If it is determined that the needs faced by people who identify as LGBT are legitimate and significant enough to warrant government attention, then proposed policy solutions must do three things:

- They must be nuanced and narrowly tailored to address the documented need;
- They must employ accurately defined terms to avoid punishing good actions and interactions; and

- They must respect the rights of conscience, religion, and speech.

SOGI antidiscrimination laws are unjustified, but if other laws are passed that prevent the mistreatment of people who identify as LGBT, they must leave people free to engage in legitimate actions based on the conviction that we are created male and female and that male and female are created for each other. This would leave all Americans—not just the lucky few who are sufficiently well-connected to be exempted from SOGI laws—free to act on those convictions.

Bibliography

Anderson, Ryan T. "First Amendment Defense Act Protects Freedom and Pluralism After Marriage Redefinition." Heritage Foundation Issue Brief No. 4490 (November 25, 2015). http://www.heritage.org/research/reports/2015/11/first-amendment-defense-act-protects-freedom-and-pluralism-after-marriage-redefinition.

———. "Sexual Orientation and Gender Identity (SOGI) Laws Threaten Freedom." In Heritage Foundation *Backgrounder* No. 3082 (November 30, 2015). http://www.heritage.org/civil-society/report/sexual-orientation-and-gender-identity-sogi-laws-threaten-freedom.

———. *Truth Overruled: The Future of Marriage and Religious Freedom.* Washington, DC: Regnery, 2015.

Anderson, Ryan T., and Robert P. George. "Liberty and SOGI Laws: An Impossible and Unsustainable 'Compromise.'" http://www.thepublicdiscourse.com/2016/01/16225/.

Buckley, Madeline. "Threats Tied to RFRA Prompt Indiana Pizzeria to Close its Doors." Updated April 3, 2015. http://www.indystar.com/story/news/2015/04/02/threats-tied-rfra-prompt-indiana-pizzeria-close-doors/70847230.

Corvino, John, et al. *Debating Religious Liberty and Discrimination.* New York: Oxford University Press, 2017.

Fisher, Robin, et al. "Joint Filing by Same-Sex Couples After Windsor: Characteristics of Married Tax Filers in 2013 and 2014." In U.S. Department of the Treasury, Office of Tax Analysis, Working Paper No. 108 (August 2016). https://www.treasury.gov/resource-center/tax-policy/tax-analysis/Documents/WP-108.pdf.

Human Rights Campaign. "Beyond Marriage Equality: A Blueprint for Federal Nondiscrimination Protections," http://hrc-assets.s3-website-us-east-1.amazonaws.com//files/documents/HRC-BeyondMarriageEquality-42015.pdf.

———. "LGBTQ Equality at the Fortune 500," http://www.hrc.org/resources/entry/lgbt-equality-at-the-fortune-500.

Koppelman, Andrew. "A Zombie in the Supreme Court: The *Elane Photography* Cert Denial." *Alabama Civil Rights & Civil Liberties Law Review* 7 (2015) 77–95.

MacLeod, Adam J. "Tempering Civil Rights Conflicts: Common Law for the Moral Marketplace." *Michigan State Law Review* 3 (2016) 643–711.

Merkley, Jeff, et al. "The Equality Act." https://www.merkley.senate.gov/imo/media/doc/EqualityAct_OnePager.pdf.

Prudential Financial, Inc. "The LGBT Financial Experience 2016–2017." http://www.prudential.com/lgbt.

Somashekhar, Sandhya. "Catholic Groups Sue Over Obama Administration Transgender Requirement." *The Washington Post*, December 29, 2016. https://www.washingtonpost.com/news/acts-of-faith/wp/2016/12/29/catholic-groups-sue-over-obama-administration-transgender-requirement/?utm_term=.85ff03f50d40.

U.S. Supreme Court. *Obergefell v. Hodges,* 576 U.S. ___ (2015). http://www.supremecourt.gov/opinions/14pdf/14-556_3204.pdf.

Chapter 5

The Necessity for a Contextual Analysis for Equality and Non-Discrimination

Iain T. Benson

"All Animals are Equal but Some are More Equal than Others."[1]

Introduction: Who Can Oppose Equality or Non-Discrimination, Yet Who Understands What They Are?

In his masterful and important 1946 essay, "Politics and the English Language" George Orwell, whose famous line from the closing chapter of *Animal Farm*, written a year earlier, I have placed at the head of this chapter, identifies "equality" along with many words including two other currently popular words—"values" and "progressive"—as "meaningless words," part of a catalogue of "swindles and perversions" that can, due to their vagueness, lead to the avoidance of accountability and, eventually, the corruption of thought.[2] He believed that corrupt thought corrupts politics and that corrupt politics can further corrupt thought. We live in a time of both and close to the center of some of what is going wrong is this term "equality"—everyone thinks it is a good thing but not one in a hundred can give any good account of what it means and how it is to be achieved.

---

1. George Orwell, *Animal Farm* (London: Penguin, 1945) 112.

2. George Orwell, "Politics and the English Language," in *The Collected Essays, Journalism and Letters*, Sonia Orwell and Ian Angus (eds.) Vol. IV, 1945–1950 (London: Penguin), 156–170 at 161–162.

With my students, I begin the class in the Philosophy of Law, in which we discuss different theories of equality, by asking them to do a thought experiment:

Step One: Imagine that we all write on a piece of card the bank balances of ourselves and our parents.

Step Two: we note that there are large discrepancies between the numbers that are on the cards as a result.

Step Three: We address this question: "Would they accept as a valid approach to 'equality' that we simply add all the numbers up and divide equally by the number of students so that now all the families have an 'equal' share of money?" Would they think this represents "equality?"

This usually leads to interesting discussions in which, always, some student asks whether there is a correlation between work and money or merit and money, or even whether inheritance from a long line of wealth or good luck should not be taken into account. Everyone rejects the suggested rebalancing of bank accounts since they recognize that it misses key aspects of justice. When they think about it more deeply, such a proposal involves adjustments by the state and by law that are highly coercive unless everyone agrees with the specific rebalancing. Equality is not, so they soon realize, sameness.

The students also reject the superficial formula made popular by Karl Marx in his 1875 essay in which he sets out the ideal as: "from each according to his abilities, to each according to his needs."[3] The formulation that seems to work is that there can be but one form of equality that is important and valid in a society that runs under the rule of law and this is—"equality before the law." This is a statement that the laws should be applied without fear or favor and that everyone should have equal benefit of the laws as protection and as the protection and sometimes advancement of rights. This, however, does not result in everyone having the same result and may not even mean they have the same opportunities. Our discussions usually end up with us agreeing that "unfair" or "unjust" or "irrational" barriers to participation and opportunity should, as far as possible, be removed (by law protecting against, for example, unjust discrimination) but even here the form of these protections raise other questions—such as, in Australia, whether the proper place for protections are legislatures or the courts operating under more abstract Bills of Rights. In Australia at least there is a live discussion about the problem of "unelected judges" reading things into Bills

3. "Karl Marx, "Critique of the Gotha Program" (1875) in Kory Schaff (2001). *Philosophy and the Problems of Work: a Reader.* (Lanham, Md: Rowman & Littlefield), 224.

of Rights that people did not imagine being there (such as euthanasia in Canada or same-sex marriage in the United States).

Equality, unfortunately, is surrounded by all kinds of claims—some impossible to achieve except through inordinate application of state force and others simply mischievous manipulation to achieve ends that do not respect an idea that is and must remain close to the essence of "law"—respect for difference and context. In the "marriage equality" discussions, for example, a large part of the concerns of some people relate to whether different viewpoints on marriage will be allowed if and when same-sex marriage becomes accepted. They are right to ask questions about this given what has been seen in so many countries about pressures put on religious individuals and their communities in relation to a wide variety of issues from "adoption agencies," marriage photographers, cake-makers, state marriage commissioners, printers, hall and camp rental groups, academic freedom, employees in large corporations, and so on. What "marriage equality" unleashes on a society is a host of issues that really should be addressed ahead of time not litigated piecemeal at huge social and financial cost over many years.

Will "equality" include the right to hold a variety of viewpoints on what constitutes a valid marriage? That should be made clear in legislation and in public discussions. Will "equality" allow parents to still determine the substance matter of courses that touch on sexual morality in public and denominational schools? Will other vague terms such as "hatred" or "safety" be used to usher in what is indoctrination about sexuality by other names or will genuine diversity be protected? I say "genuine diversity" because clearly the use of "diversity" like the use of "equality" is all too often used in a manipulative and cynical way to hide what is actually going on. Catholic schools in the Canadian Province of Ontario a couple of years ago, for example, were told that their "zero tolerance" policy against bullying was not enough and they had to advance a particularly sexualized agenda called "Gay/Straight Alliance Clubs" ("GSA's"). They were instructed by Provincial law that they had to have GSA's in any school where a student requested them. This despite the fact that the Catholic schools had a zero-tolerance policy against bullying and did not wish to have clubs focused on sexual identity which, as they patiently tried to explain to zealous bureaucrats, was not even a leading cause of bullying in their schools. This did not matter and the entire Catholic system was subjected to the views of a few people in the government and the bureaucracy who had bullied others to endorse their version of sexuality—is this "equality"?

In this chapter, I will examine a few concepts of equality before addressing some recent developments that ought to make us very nervous. When equality is being used as it is in Australia now with "Marriage Equality" those who have different moral views in certain areas (and this includes the religious) ought to beware of what Orwell so clearly understood about what happens when vague and meaningless language is used as a rallying cry for action and force.

Various Views of Equality and Non-Discrimination

In an article entitled "The Empty Idea of Equality" and published many years ago now in the *Harvard Law Review*, Peter Westen, then Professor of law at the University of Michigan, explored the fact that "equality is commonly perceived to differ from rights and liberties."[4] He notes that a common error in thinking about equality is induced by equality itself, namely "the tendency to assume that what makes for equality in mathematics also makes for equality in law and morals."[5] This point is one my students notice in relation to the thought experiment set out earlier.

In his conclusion, Westen points out that equality is derivative of other rights and that "people do not realize this" and as a result they "allow equality to distort the substance of their decision making" because "equality erroneously implies that it entails unique remedies and standards all its own" and "because the proposition that likes should be treated alike is unquestionably true it gives an aura of revealed truth to whatever substantive values it happens to incorporate by reference." As a consequence of this, Westen notes that "arguments in the form of equality invariably place all opposing arguments on the "defensive."[6] That is why "equality" has been chosen as the framework for advancing "identity movements" whether of the feminist or sexual identity sort.

Saying that two people should be treated equally or its correlative, without discrimination, does not supply us with the reason why they *should* be treated equally when the context provides alternative and weighty justifications for different treatment. For example, considerations of equality or discrimination in relation to sex (male and female) or physical ability may well be relevant if a certain physical attribute (say "speed" or "weight-lifting capacity" or being able to walk and run) is key to the job. While we may generally not-allow discrimination in relation to disability or age or sex or religion, all of these may have to give way to particular contextual requirements based on these very characteristics. Equality then must be understood, not in abstract, but in context and once we are dealing with context we must

4. Westen, "Empty Idea of Equality," 537.
5. Ibid., 583–84.
6. Ibid., 592–93.

look, not at "equality" but what the arguments are for differential treatment. These may include physical necessity or even "membership" (say for religious leadership choices) or age (say in relation to drivers' licenses or liquor laws). And can a society allow different beliefs to co-exist? Must it do so? We understand that expression and association matter to open societies and part of that is the ability to disagree about morality. Thus, in the discussions about immigration or the nature of marriage or issues like abortion, different viewpoints on morality are prior to the application of abstract principles such as "equality." Where the issue, such as race is involved, however, we do not allow unequal treatment but where membership in religion or moral views in relation to sexual conduct (marriage, sex outside marriage, the number of partners in a marriage etc.) are at issue, then neither discrimination nor "equality" itself cannot give us an answer. In other words, both notions can be a distraction from aspects of context that are essential in a free society that places importance on genuine diversity.

A common way of describing recent challenges involving "equality" is to put the favoured category, in recent years "sexual orientation," as *the* equality right then juxtapose it with something else—usually "religion" so that the conflicts are inaccurately described as "between religion and equality" when they are nothing of the sort. What is at issue *is a conflict within the category of equality itself*. But note this: in all regimes, religion is listed as an "equality" right. This clever sleight of hand puts, for reasons Westen identifies, "religion" in a defensive position when, in fact, it should be on an equal footing *as another "equality" right itself.*[7] When there is an "intra-equality" conflict, the proper manner for analysis and resolution should involve a searching evaluation of context.

Deepening Vagueness: "Deep Equality," Accommodation, and Tolerance?

In recent years an attempt has been made to give de-contextulalized equality greater weight in relation to contexts that have been protected by the twin principles of accommodation and tolerance. One of the latest drivers for this strategy is the neologism of "deep equality." The vagueness of what is meant by "deep equality," which may be observed in the recent collection of Canadian essays, *Reasonable Accommodation: Managing Religious Diversity*, makes it difficult to actually critique what is being proposed. That said,

---

7. The *Equal Opportunity Act* of Victoria in Australia, for example, at Section 6, includes under the "equality rights" both "sexual orientation" and "religion" as well as a long list of other rights. Therefore, both "religion" and "sexual orientation" are "equality rights," though they are seldom described as such.

reading between the lines, it seems to suggest that we need to accept deep equality because "it requires an abandonment of language that establishes hierarchies of difference, such as 'tolerance' and 'accommodation.'"[8]

One might wonder at the meaning of the conception of "hierarchies of difference" since our rejecting them is implied as is our unqualified endorsement of the analysis of "minority/majority" power relations. Also rejected is the idea that anything should be viewed in terms of "us" and "them." In the editor's "Conclusion" we are told:

> "What is really being argued for, then, when we suggest that the content of religions should be opened to fair and public assessment, is an admission that this is already taking place in the courts. It is therefore important that, in order to achieve deep equality both in the legal processes and in public considerations of religious minorities, the existence of mainstream Christianity as a hegemonic or normative force be acknowledged. We can then begin to develop processes that are fully cognizant of the social and cultural context in which the assessment is being conducted. Related to the recognition of social context, is, of course acknowledgment of power differences and sedimentations, as well as a willingness to cede or reorder such sedimentations to achieve equality. This goes to the heart of the shift from accommodation or tolerance to deep equality. We should not, however, completely ignore the "achievements" of accommodation or tolerance but these are "minimum standards" in both public discourse and legal processes which we may celebrate and move on from: . . . but they have done all the work they can do, and indeed are now doing harm in a country that needs to move past holding fast to privileges if it is to recognize the promise of equality that is constitutionally guaranteed."[9]

Note what is assumed but not spelled out in the statement ." . .the existence of mainstream Christianity as a hegemonic or normative force . . . " that should be publically "*re-ordered.*" Which kind of "mainstream Christianity"? The existence of this as "hegemonic" or "normative"—again, *for whom* and recognized *by* whom? And why is being "a normative force" assumed to be negative? Who is to do the "re-ordering" and "assessment" and *by what authority*? The frankly arrogant lack of clarity is baffling,

---

8. Lori G. Beaman ed., *Reasonable Accommodation: Managing Religious Diversity* (Vancouver: UBC Press, 2012) 213.

9. Ibid., 218–19 (emphasis added). We are invited to accept a "re-ordering" of "the *content* of religions!"

frustrating and unacceptable for a work passing itself off as a scholarly analysis of important issues.

Along the same line are statements such as: ". . .multiculturalism is often seen as a thorn in the side of those who aspire to a *cohesive, homogeneous society* united by common values"[10] and "[a]ccommodation does not include equality and is a framework that forces parties to a discussion into hierarchical relationship. It is a framework that continues unfair and unjust power relations that impede rather than promote the equality of minority groups."[11] Who "aspires to a cohesive, homogenous society . . . "? There are compelling reasons to oppose strongly such visions of the "cohesive" or "homogenous" unless the conditions for this union are very clearly spelled out. Alas, that kind of clarity is not offered by the editor or authors quoted from this recent book and the, frankly, totalitarian assumptions undergirding the framework are astounding.

Further, we are told that "abandoning multiculturalism as a mechanism for creating space for religious minorities is a troubling prospect" and that "negotiating through religious diversity requires more difficult and sustained conversation than we have seen to date on most issues of religious diversity that emerge in the public sphere."[12] What is meant by "abandoning multiculturalism" and how exactly could that be done even if it were a good idea? Again, we are left to guess but the suggestions and the directions are worrying.

However carefully and sociologically couched in terms of "hierarchies" and "power-relations" and "minority-majority interest," the quest for a homogeneous "deep equality" is far from convincing as is the conception that religious diversity is something to be "managed." This kind of "stance from on high" perspective seemingly outside of the "hierarchies" that are critiqued, gives no comfort to those who urge for a more humble and respectful positioning of different communities in relation to each other under the aegis of diversity. Abolishing "us/them," a chimera in any case, has historically come at the expense of respecting differences.

---

10. Ibid., 214 (emphasis added).

11. Ibid., 219–20.

12. Ibid., 215–16. The abuse of language to achieve a dominant position by reducing viewpoints that oppose the dogmatic beliefs of the other (as we see in the *Reasonable Accommodation* volume) is not new. John Locke, in *A Letter Concerning Toleration* (1689) (Buffalo: Promethean Books, 1990) states: "Another more secret evil, but more dangerous to the commonwealth, is when men arrogate to themselves, and to those of their own sect, some peculiar prerogative, covered over with a specious show of deceitful words, but in effect opposite to the civil rights of the community." 62.

In sum, without actually giving any real clarity to the concept of "deep equality" but raising a long series of rather worrying concepts, the volume's introduction and conclusion list a litany of concerns so vaguely and confusingly expressed that one begins to lose any sense that there is a coherent idea or set of ideas being expressed in relation to "deep equality" at all. The conclusion states that:

> "In the first three-quarters of the 20th century tolerance was largely an idea that was invoked to regulate relations between normatively dominant mainstream Christianity and minority Christian groups and Jews. A number of intersecting processes, including increased immigration, post-colonial insights, and the rights revolution, have called into question the validity of notions like tolerance and accommodation as valid governance strategies."[13]

By now it scarce needs noting that we are not told how any of these things have actually " . . . called into question the validity of tolerance and accommodation" as opposed to raising important questions that require contextualized analysis to work around and within. Nor is the development of notions of tolerance understood within a history going back for several thousand years as it can and needs to be. That is the lens through which tolerance and the nature of human communities and associations needs to be seen—not the relative keyhole of the "first three-quarters of the 20th century [. . .]."

There is one essay in the book, however, that makes some of this vagueness about "deep equality" clear; though not in a good way. In one essay, the author analyzes "difference" in the context of "sexual diversity and accommodation." Here the language and purpose are clearer and the grounds for concern greater. Heather Shipley, who is a religious studies scholar, is writing on the "legal and social change" that has been occurring "regarding protection against discrimination for homosexuals and the legalization of same-sex marriage [. . . .]."[14] Dr. Shipley is also Project Manager for the "Religion and Diversity Project" a Social Sciences and Humanities Research Council Major Collaborative Research Initiative at the University of Ottawa. The book on which I am commenting has emerged from this project's work. I mention all this because the conclusion and form of analysis, decrying, in the name of "deep equality," both toleration and accommodation, set the stage for what may be seen as the latest in a series of moves that fit rather

---

13. Beaman, 221.

14. Ibid., 181; also, see "One of These Things is Not Like the Other" in Beaman, *Reasonable Accommodation*, 165–86.

neatly into the framework of "civic totalism," "equalitarian absolutism," and "illiberalism" at the core of contemporary elite analysis. Such approaches routinely ignore if they do not deride or attack outright, diversity and genuine pluralism particularly in relation to religious diversity. Here is how Shipley concludes her essay and it is illuminating for one of the concerns of this chapter and the nonsense that is "deep equality."

> "Legal and social change are occurring regarding protection against discrimination for homosexuals and the legalization of same-sex marriage, yet the language surrounding what homosexuality or sexual difference is, or more accurately, what it is not, and the means by which the changes occur *are much more subversively constructed*. The influence of some religious beliefs and religious groups, which become constructed as "the" religious standpoint, have helped maintain mainstream categories of heteronormativity [. . . .] The necessity to make homosexuality the Other (binary opposite/incompatible) to normative heterosexuality must not be disturbed by an acceptance of the religious homosexual. As a result, homosexuality is posited as contradictory to religiosity such that one cannot be both but only one or the other. As referred to earlier, animosity is often purported (sic) as a rational response to danger. When the hegemonic, heteronormative system faces a challenge, it thus responds by drawing very clear lines in the sand between 'us' and 'them.'"[15]

Many things can be said about this form of analysis, such as its suggestion that the opposition viewpoint is "subversively constructed" (thereby attributing dishonesty to those who hold alternative viewpoints to Dr. Shipley) but two are most important. First that it creates a "straw man" argument. Religions do not, as alleged, suggest that one cannot "be both homosexual and religious"—far from it; most make a distinction between desire/orientation and *conduct* not homosexuality- - understood as homosexual desires—*per se*. They say, clearly and frequently, that for the homosexual as for the heterosexual, there are moral and religious restrictions on *conduct*; not all desires can or should be acted upon. *That* is what is objected to by many who disagree with same-sex *conduct* rather than orientation or desire. Shipley's approach unfairly mischaracterizes the diversity and nuance of religious positions and, in common with many commentators, skates around the moral distinction at the core of the differences.

15. Ibid., 181–82 (emphasis added).

Second, Dr. Shipley's analysis stigmatizes the view that sexual relations should be between male and females as "heteronormative" and like "homophobia" should be resisted by "challenges to the system." Nowhere with respect to sexuality[16] or gender does this volume even attempt to argue for co-existence of alternative viewpoints or suggest that living together with different beliefs might be part of a just legal framework; nor does this book recognize that differing viewpoints on sexuality are permissible and even laudatory in the quest for better understanding between people about the mysteries of sexuality and our moral rules in relation to it. Hegemonic dominance by Dr. Shipley and her supporters is an assumed and acceptable strategy when it should be anything but.

This level of analysis, ignoring as it does the freedom of association and difference of moral and religious viewpoints *having a right to co-exist in society*, does nothing to challenge the importance of either reasonable accommodation or tolerance as ongoing realities; it just hints darkly that they are passé and need to be replaced. By this strategy it seems to be setting the stage to try and challenge both accommodation and tolerance as *defences* to challenges or rationales for difference. This sets the stage for the erection of a "cohesive" and "homogenous" viewpoint that is, well—that of Dr. Shipley and her supporters.

The fact that both tolerance and accommodation are under attack in this recent volume is itself noteworthy since both are used in the law to protect associational difference and, most importantly, religious diversity. But then the volume's sub-title suggests that it is about "*managing* religious diversity."[17] And who manages the managers?

16. The volume contains some more nuanced, clearer, and fairer essays on other subjects. These include Bakht, "Veiled Objections," 71–108, an analysis of debates around wearing of the niqab by Muslim women; and discussing the nature of the test used to analyze claims for religious belief respect in Lefebvre, "Religion in Court," 32–50. My criticisms are directed at the authors expressly quoted in this chapter and the nonsense that is "deep equality."

17. Lori Beaman, in her edited volume *Reasonable Accomodation* (2012), suggests some doubts about the notion of "managing diversity" when she states in a footnote that "The use of the words 'managed' or 'governed' are also problematic. Among other things, the implication is that religious diversity requires management or governing in the first place" (Beaman, *Reasonable Accommodation*, 11n1). Having raised the important question the editor says nothing about it. As with many things about this volume, that is unfortunate as it may lead those concerned about "deep equality" to be more suspicious of it than had the concept been explained clearly in relation to the freedom of association and the maintenance of diversity and the meaning of "management" and its limits spelled out. Canada, while priding itself on its openness and respect for pluralism, is showing some recent very worrying examples of illiberalism and antireligious movements in the higher levels of the legal and scholarly communities and, generally, in the Province of Quebec.

While Shipley recognizes that "...sometimes 'freedom' will mean the freedom to be orthodox, or to make choices that some or many of us would not make"[18] the overall suggestion that both tolerance and accommodation pose impediments to some greater homogeneity is worrying to say the least and "deep equality" looks very much like a concept to be wary of rather than embraced.

Conclusion: Respecting Context Is Essential to Understanding Equality, Non-Discrimination, and Liberty

This chapter has so far examined various ways in which "equality" pushed in certain directions can support "convergence" or "civic totalism" rather than respectful co-existence in relationship to understandings of law and religion.

Understanding how "equality" and non-discrimination are being manipulated is relevant to how religious associations will be treated by the law and politics. Identifying the general problems of "vague language," "manipulation through use of vagueness," "convergence," and "civic totalism"[19] as attitudes to law and identity politics, however, gives us some tools to analyze these moves when they arise in politics, law, religious studies and sociology. Political philosopher and Jewish scholar David Novak appropriately sums up what has been discussed:

> A society dedicated to the protection and enhancements of its participatory cultures surely commands more respect and devotion than does a society established merely to protect and enhance property. *When, however, a civil society no longer respects that communal priority, it inevitably attempts to replace that sacred realm by becoming a sacred realm itself.*[20]

---

18. Beaman, 216.

19. William Galston, *The Practice of Liberal Pluralism* (Cambridge: Cambridge University Press, 2005) 24–34. This notion, from William Galston, suggests the "vanguard party" mentality that Charles Taylor identifies as the alternative to an understanding of "civil society" where diversity is respected (see "Invoking Civil Society" in *Philosophical Arguments* (Cambridge: Harvard University Press, 1995) 204–224.). Civic totalists seek to control and force others to do what they believe all should do—there is no respect for genuine diversity.

20. Novak, "Human Dignity" 56–57, emphasis added. The very useful passage continues: "*As such, it attempts to become the highest realm in the lives of its citizens.* In becoming what some have called a 'civil religion,' civil society usurps the role of historic traditions of faith. It becomes what it was never intended to be, *for the hallmark of a democratic social order is the continuing limitation of its governing range. Without such limitation, any society tends to expand its government indefinitely.* But such limitation

Equality or Inclusion without the express safeguards of a commitment, even legal presumptions in favour of, diversity, is a threat to accommodation and difference.[21] I have argued that a commitment to difference is essential to a vision of society that is pluralistic and that respects the forms of civil society within which variety is at home. The new language of "inclusion" or inappropriate de-contextualized applications of "equality" and non-discrimination that suggest the "binding into" without a respect for the "difference from" poses a threat to the variety of differences that undergirds "deep diversity." Such an undifferentiated inclusion is the kind of thing that might favour "deep equality" rather than "deep diversity" and such a form of "equality" while perhaps attractive to a certain form of statist, monist or "civic totalist"[22], is not consistent with respect for the communities that best nurture civic virtues in the various languages communities have developed over millennia.

A commitment to respect for different contexts and the various moral traditions that can co-exist in a respectful accommodational (but not a totalistic or "vanguard") society is essential to the maintenance of freedoms for everyone. This will not give "totalists" what they seek to achieve through undifferentiated de-contextualized languages of "equality" or "inclusion" but a commitment to freedom is what maintains both accountability and the variety that gives colour and spice and difference to life in community. "Inclusion" should be treated with suspicion unless and until it recognizes expressly a prior commitment to difference, pluralism and associational liberty under the rule of law and appropriately limited forms of government. Forms of de-contextualized "equality" or "discrimination" fail to

---

cannot come from within; it can only come from what is both outside it and above it. *Today that external and transcendent limitation can be found in the freedom of citizens in a democracy to find their primal identity by being and remaining a part of their traditional communities. This is what has come to be known in democracies as religious liberty.*" On the tensions between liberalism, pluralism, religions, and "transformative constitutionalism," see the insightful chapter "Liberalism, Pluralism and Religion" in Beiner, *Philosophy in a Time*, 44–50.

21. I have written elsewhere recently about the possibility and utility of a legal presumption in favour of diversity. See: Iain T. Benson, "Should there be a Legal Presumption in Favour of Diversity: Some Preliminary Reflections" in Iain T. Benson and Barry W. Bussey, eds. *Religion, Liberty and the Jurisdictional Limits of Law* (Toronto: LexisNexis, 2017) 3–27.

22. "Civic totalism" in its various forms denotes the position of those who, implicitly or explicitly, assume that their normative position on contested matters (consider, for example, overturning religious community rules relating to gendered leadership, the acceptance of same-sex marriage, or medical referrals in relation to abortion or euthanasia) should be made obligatory for everyone as a required public duty. See Galston, *Practice of Liberal Pluralism*, 23–44.

respect diversity and will, as Orwell predicted, tend towards authoritarian not free and open societies. We are seeing in many lawsuits that support increasingly authoritarian forms of law and politics, that some animals, apparently, become "more equal than others" when equality and discrimination are approached without regard to contexts that diversity and freedom require.

Bibliography

Bakht, Natasha. "Veiled Objections: Facing Public Opposition to the Niqab." In *Reasonable Accommodation: Managing Religious Diversity*, edited by Lori Beaman, 71–108. Vancouver: University of British Columbia Press, 2012.
Beaman, Lori G., ed. *Reasonable Accommodation: Managing Religious Diversity*. Vancouver: University of British Columbia Press, 2012.
Beiner, Ronald. *Philosophy in a Time of Lost Spirit*. Toronto: University of Toronto, 1997.
Benson, Iain T. "Should there be a Legal Presumption in Favour of Diversity? Some Preliminary Reflections." In *Religion, Liberty and the Jurisdictional Limitations of Law*, edited by Iain T. Benson and Brian W. Bussey, 3–27. Toronto: LexisNexis, 2017.
Galston, William. *The Practice of Liberal Pluralism*. Cambridge: Cambridge University Press, 2005.
Lefebvre, Solange. "Religion in Court, Between an Objective and a Subjective Definition." In *Reasonable Accommodation: Managing Religious Diversity*, edited by Lori Beaman, 32–50. Vancouver: University of British Columbia Press, 2012.
Marx, Karl. "Critique of the Gotha Program (1875)." In *Philosophy and the Problems of Work: A Reader*, edited by Kory Schaff, 224. Lanham, MD: Rowman & Littlefield, 2001.
Novak, David. "Human Dignity and the Social Contract." In *Recognizing Religion in a Secular Society: Pluralism, Religion, and Public Policy*, edited by Douglas Farrow, 51–68. Montreal: McGill-Queens University Press, 2004.
Orwell, George. "Politics and the English Language." In *The Collected Essays, Journalism and Letters of George Orwell Volume 4: In Front of Your Nose 1945—1950*. Sonia Orwell and Ian Angus, eds., 156–70. London: Penguin, 1970.
Taylor, Charles. *Philosophical Arguments*. Cambridge: Harvard University Press, 1995.
Westen, Peter. "The Empty Idea of Equality." *Harvard Law Review* 95:3 (1982) 537–96.

Chapter 6

Non-discrimination Policy in the Context of the European Union

Monsignor Piotr Mazurkiewicz

> Instead of favouring fraternal encounter and mutual aid, the city fosters discrimination and also indifference. It lends itself to new forms of exploitation and of domination whereby some people in speculating on the needs of others derive inadmissible profits. Behind the facades much misery is hidden, unsuspected even by the closest neighbours; other forms of misery spread where human dignity founders: delinquency, criminality, abuse of drugs and eroticism.[1]

> (. . .) the worst discrimination which the poor suffer is the lack of spiritual care.[2]

THE NOTION OF "DISCRIMINATION" is derived from the late Latin's *discriminatio* (separation, distinction, detachment; the verb *discriminare*—separate, discern, assign). It is further related to *discrimen* (division, distance, distinction, decision).[3] Discrimination is therefore associated first of all with *making distinctions*, in the cognitive as well as the ethical sense (*discriminating between what is good and what is bad*), and next, with drawing practical consequences resulting there from. We are hence dealing with a certain intellectual act, which alters (enriches) the view of the world by man and, in consequence, leads also

1. Paul VI, *Octogesima adveniens*, 10.
2. Francis, *Evangelii Gaudium*, 200.
3. Cf. Jougan, *Słownik kościelny łacińsko-polski*, 201.

to a change of his functioning in the world. It therefore exerts a tangible impact in the real world.

The world is tremendously varied. The possibility to enjoy the multitude of beings is closely related to the ability to perceive and name the differences between those beings, which are, at times, very subtle. Discovering new species of creatures resembles the original act of naming animals parading before the eyes of biblical Adam (cf. Gen 2:19–20). He could not only distinguish between an elephant and a rhinoceros, a red deer and a roe deer, a ring-tailed lemur and a red ruffed, red-bellied, brown and a blue-eyed black lemur, but also between ten thousand species of birds flying in the air. Making a distinction required perceptiveness as well as an appropriate vocabulary, although we do not know whether Adam had known the words before, or whether he invented them so that each sound matched the image. As we are fully aware, especially in the case of learning foreign languages, the range of vocabulary is closely related to the ability to express opinions in the outside world as well as to spell out the inner experience. The more notions to express various emotional states a person knows, the subtler the differences in the inner experience he can observe and spell out. In that sense, as the ability of the person to discriminate/distinguish between the surrounding beings, as well as to the scope of the inner states increases, the person's experience of being a human grows richer.

We commonly share the view that people are equal. Equality, however—as can be seen at first glance—is not identical with sameness. It seems that, based on empirical experience alone, it would be less risky to assert the opposite: that people are different. Every man is exceptional, unique and incommunicable (*alteri incommunicabilis*). The conviction of equality of men rests not, however, on empirical data, but rather on the belief in equal human dignity. This belief is rooted in the biblical faith that every man was made in "God's likeness and image" (Gen 1:26) and, on account of that, is the bearer of an inherent and inviolable dignity.[4] The equality of persons redeemed by Christ is so basic in nature that all differences between such persons become something merely secondary. "For as many of you as were baptized into Christ have put on Christ. There is neither Jew nor Greek, there is neither slave nor free, there is no male and female, for you are all one in Christ Jesus" (Gal 3:27–28). Differences, both individual and social, do not become blurred, but qualified as secondary. Respect for human dignity must therefore rest on a healthy balance between respecting what is the same in each human being (inherent dignity) and what is unique in each human being (strengths and weaknesses, virtues and

---

4. Cf. Mazurkiewicz, "Europeizacja Europy," 301–33.

flaws, talents and lacks).[5] Justice demands respecting both these aspects in a specific context. In certain situations man has the right to be treated equally (identically to others), and in others differently (distinctly from others). It seems that *the objective of the non-discrimination policy should be the establishment of proper balance between the right of the individual or group to equal (identical) treatment, and the right to different (distinct) treatment.* A properly performed intellectual discrimination should lead to the discernment between features that are objectively meaningful in a particular situation, and those objectively unimportant, or which are only subjectively deemed to be important.

The Non-discrimination Principle in the Social Doctrine of the Church

The problem of non-discrimination as well as the growing moral sensitivity in the face of discrimination may be recognized as the next sign of the so-called "social issue." For the church, it is a "sign of the times," reminding us of "the constant necessity to pave the ways of equitable development for all and to counteract all forms of discrimination and social injustice."[6] In the documents of the Second Vatican Council we find many references to the issue of discrimination in different social contexts. In *Gaudium et Spes*, for instance, we read:

> True, all men are not alike from the point of view of varying physical power and the diversity of intellectual and moral resources. Nevertheless, with respect to the fundamental rights of the person, every type of discrimination, whether social or cultural, whether based on sex, race, colour, social condition, language or religion, is to be overcome and eradicated as contrary to God's intent. For in truth it must still be regretted that fundamental personal rights are still not being universally honoured. Such is the case of a woman who is denied the right to choose a husband freely, to embrace a state of life or to acquire an education or cultural benefits equal to those recognized for men. Therefore, although rightful differences exist between men, the equal dignity of persons demands that a more humane and just condition of life be brought about. For excessive economic and social differences between the members of the one

---

5. Cf. Commission of the Bishop's Conferences of the European Community, *Developing Fair Non-discrimination EU Legislation*, 6.

6. Nitecki, "Dyskryminacja w ujęciu nauczania społecznego," 189.

human family or population groups cause scandal, and militate against social justice, equity, the dignity of the human person, as well as social and international peace.[7]

Paul VI has also commented on discrimination in *Populorum progressio*, and first of all in *Octogesima adveniens*, where he wrote:

> Among the victims of situations of injustice [...] must be placed those who are discriminated against, in law or in fact, on account of their race, origin, colour, culture, sex or religion. Racial discrimination possesses at the moment a character of very great relevance by reason of the tension which it stirs up both within countries and on the international level. Men rightly consider unjustifiable and reject as inadmissible the tendency to maintain or introduce legislation or behaviour systematically inspired by racialist prejudice. The members of mankind share the same basic rights and duties, as well as the same supernatural destiny. Within a country which belongs to each one, all should be equal before the law, find equal admittance to economic, cultural, civic and social life and benefit from a fair sharing of the nation's riches.[8]

John Paul II joins this line of thinking when he writes:

> *The dignity of the person constitutes the foundation of the equality of all people among themselves.* As a result, all forms of discrimination are totally unacceptable, especially those forms which unfortunately continue to divide and degrade the human family, from those based on race or economics to those social and cultural, from political to geographic, etc. Each discrimination constitutes an absolutely intolerable injustice, not so much for the tensions and the conflicts that can be generated in the social sphere, as much as for the dishonour inflicted on the dignity of the person: not only to the dignity of the individual who is the victim of the injustice, but still more to the one who commits the injustice.[9]

John Paul II's particular attention is given to "[...] the various forms of discrimination and marginalisation to which women are subjected simply because they are women." He strongly reaffirmed "the urgency to

---

7. Vatican Council II, *Gaudium et Spes*, 29.
8. Paul VI, *Octogesima adveniens*, 16.
9. John Paul II, *Christifideles laici*, 37.

defend and to promote the personal dignity of woman, and consequently, her equality with man."[10]

The Catholic Church's unequivocal stance against all forms of unjust discrimination has not automatically removed all its signs, even from areas where the Catholic community is dominant. Hence, the rhetorical question posed by John Paul II:

> How can it be that even today there are still people dying of hunger? Condemned to illiteracy? Lacking the most basic medical care? Without a roof over their heads? The scenario of poverty can extend indefinitely, if in addition to its traditional forms we think of its newer patterns. These latter often affect financially affluent sectors and groups which are nevertheless threatened by despair at the lack of meaning in their lives, by drug addiction, by fear of abandonment in old age or sickness, by marginalization or social discrimination. [...] And how can we remain indifferent to [...] *the contempt for the fundamental human rights* of so many people, especially children?[11]

As we see, in parallel to the progress in the area of theoretical reflection and the development of international law, the policy of non-discrimination has also gained recognition in the official teaching of the Catholic Church.[12]

The European Non-discrimination Policy

The principle of equality and non-discrimination appears already in the Treaty establishing the European Economic Community (1957). It relates to two areas: the prohibition of discrimination on grounds of nationality (Treaty on the Functioning of the European Union ("TFEU"), Article 18, Article 45) as well as the principle of equal pay of male and female workers for equal work (TFEU, Article 157). However, the Treaty of Rome did not

---

10. Ibid., 49.

11. John Paul II, *Novo millennio ineunte*, 50–51. (The *Compendium of the Social Doctrine of the Church* [2004] contains in its index the word "discrimination," which facilitates finding a substantial number of texts and contexts where the Church has been using the notion.).

12. One should invoke such documents of international law as the Universal Declaration of Human Rights (1948), the Geneva Convention (1949), the ILO Convention concerning Discrimination in Respect of Employment and Occupation (1958), UNESCO *Convention* against *Discrimination in Education* (1960), or the UN Declaration on the *Elimination of All Forms of Racial Discrimination* (1966). The documents forbid differentiation by putting at a disadvantage, or by giving privilege based on the characteristics described in each of the documents.

include any general prohibition of discrimination on grounds of sex or other special characteristics.[13] After the Maastricht Treaty was adopted (1992), the principle of equal treatment was developed in the context of the category of EU citizenship. As the categories of EU citizenship develop, the prohibition of discrimination refers not only to the economic freedoms related to access to the common market, but also to political freedoms (voting rights) and, due to the expanding case law of the Court of Justice, to the issue of access to social rights. The Treaty provided for the adoption of measures aimed at promoting equality of men and women with respect to their chances in the labor market and treatment in the working place (TFEU, Article 153). In the Treaty of Amsterdam, arriving at the equality of men and women is one of the objectives of the European Community (the Treaty on European Union, Article 2 and clause 3). But the fundamental change introduced by the Treaty of Amsterdam is the introduction of the article authorizing the Union to "take appropriate action to combat discrimination based on sex, racial or ethnic origin, religion or belief, disability, age or sexual orientation" (TFEE, Article 19). The change is twofold; on the one hand, the list of forbidden bases of discrimination has been significantly expanded (the list seems to be closed). On the other hand, the Union has been *authorised* to combat discrimination (*may take appropriate action to combat discrimination*) within its extended scope, with the use of all necessary means, that is, to pursue an active policy to that respect.

Legal regulations adopted based on Article 19 TFEU are referred to as antidiscrimination law of the European Union. It became the basis for three directives: Council Directive 2000/43/EC of 29 June 2000, implementing the principle of equal treatment between persons irrespective of racial or ethnic origin (the so-called racial equality directive), Council Directive 2000/78/EC of 27 November 2000 establishing a general framework for equal treatment in employment and occupation (the so-called framework directive) and the Council Directive 2004/113/EC of 13 December 2004 implementing the principle of equal treatment between men and women in the access to and supply of goods and services. These directives refer to direct and indirect discrimination, allowing Member States to "take positive action," which includes also accommodation (the racial equality directive) that had not formerly been included in the scope of EU competences.[14] Since 2008 work has been underway on the proposal for a Council Directive on implementing the principle of equal treatment between persons irrespective of religion or belief, disability, age or sexual orientation (2008/0140 (CNS)- the so-called horizontal

13. Cf. Śledzińska-Simon, "Zasada równości i zasada niedyskryminacji," 45–46.
14. Cf. Guiraudon, "Antidiscrimination Policy," 295.

directive). Its aim is "to implement the principle of equal treatment between persons irrespective of religion or belief, disability, age or sexual orientation outside the labour market" (Grounds for proposal).

Article 19 of the TFEU led European equality and non-discrimination policy in a completely new direction. A new group of potential victims of discrimination could be created with the movement from economic freedom concerns to individual rights. It is interesting that just a month after the adoption of the Treaty of Amsterdam, the European Commission announced that "respect for the rights of minorities" will be one of the conditions for the accession of new countries to the EU.[15] It should be noted, however, that the implementation of the principle of equality and non-discrimination by means of directives adopted pursuant to Article 19 TFEU is (should be) limited to the area of competence of the Union, and also that the decisions taken under Article 19 require unanimity in the Council and Parliament's consent, unless they relate only to EU incentives, excluding any harmonization of national legislation.[16] Decisions made on the basis of Article 18 and 157 of the TFEU require a qualified majority voting (QMV) in the Council and co-decision of the Council and the European Parliament.[17]

Since the Maastricht Treaty, the fundamental rights guaranteed by the European Convention for the Protection of Human Rights and Fundamental Freedoms—along with the prohibition of discrimination "for any reason" (ECHR, Article 14)—are part of the Union's law as general principles of law (TEU, Article 6). The next step in the evolution of the principle of non-discrimination in the primary law was the adoption of the Charter of Fundamental Rights of the European Union (2000), which due to the Treaty of Lisbon (2009) became binding. The Charter grants the equality of all people before the law (CFR, Article 20, Article 23) and provides a catalogue of prohibited grounds of discrimination, extended in relation to the ECHR on the prohibition of discrimination on grounds of disability, age and sexual orientation. Article 21 CFR prohibits all kinds of discrimination and "in particular with regard to sex, race, colour, ethnic or social origin, genetic features, language, religion or belief, political or

---

15. Cf. ibid., 296.

16. Cf. "Śledzińska-Simon,:Zasada równości i zasada niedyskryminacji," 48; Commission of the Bishop's Conferences of the European Community, *Developing Fair Non-discrimination EU Legislation*, 21–23.

17. In the current Treaty on the Functioning of the European Union, the principles of equality and non-discrimination—as *lex specialis* of the general prohibition of discrimination on grounds of having the nationality of a particular State (TFEU, Article 18)—are included in Article 36, Article 37, Article 40 § 2, Article 45 § 2, Article 49, Article 57, Article 95 § 1, and Article 110 (Cf. Śledzińska-Simon, "Zasada równości i zasada niedyskryminacji," 49).

any other opinion, membership of a national minority, property, birth, disability, age or sexual orientation" (CFP, Article 21, § 1), and "because of the nationality" (CFR, Article 21, § 2). The wording of this article leads to the conclusion that the list of those grounds in EU law is not closed. The Charter of Fundamental Rights (CFR) protects individuals only against discrimination by the institutions, bodies and agencies of the EU and by the Member States to the extent that they are implementing EU law (CFR, Article 51). The development of EU antidiscrimination law—according to Anna Śledzińska-Simon—will probably seek to lift the principle of non-discrimination to the rank of a universal right of individuals.[18]

The Lisbon Treaty, in addition to giving the binding nature of the CFR, also includes the obligation to remove inequalities and to promote equality between women and men in all activities of the Union (*gender mainstreaming*) (TFEU, Article 8), and introduces the *duty to combat discrimination* based on sex, race, ethnic origin, religion or belief, disability, age and sexual orientation (TEU, Article 3; TFEU, Article 10). According to Śledzińska-Simon, "a literal interpretation of those provisions suggests that the TFEU implies that the pursuit of material equality concerns only sex, because the principle of non-discrimination expresses formal equality (equal treatment)."[19] Other authors, however, apply a broad interpretation of this article recognizing that

> it goes beyond the desire to provide formal equality between different groups in the efforts to ensure substantive equality (i.e. the equality of results) and extends the sense of indirect discrimination by including to it seemingly neutral laws and practices which may lead to a particular disadvantage for certain groups of people. It also introduces the concept of harassment, which constitutes an absolute, not only relative, individual right.[20]

The Treaty on European Union also states that "in all its activities, the Union shall respect the equality of its citizens, who shall receive equal attention from its institutions, bodies and organizational units" (TEU, Article 9). This provision had no equivalent in the earlier version of the Treaty on European Union. It points to the ongoing process of the evolution of the EU antidiscrimination law. Sometimes, therefore, three generations of EU antidiscrimination law are identified. They would be in turn:

---

18. Cf. Ibid., 48.
19. Ibid., 49.
20. Guiraudon, "Antidiscrimination Policy," 295–96.

- the principle of equal treatment on grounds of sex and national origin (TFEU Article 18 and Article 157),
- the laws derived from Article 19 TFEU (prohibition of discrimination),
- any possible laws, which would be based of Article 9 TEU (positive obligation to create institutional conditions for *de facto* equality of certain entities).[21]

If this typology of EU antidiscrimination law were to be considered correct, one could speak of a gradual expansion of the list of groups of potential victims of unequal treatment and discrimination. The emphasis of EU policy would appear to be moving from the negative concepts of discrimination in the direction of positive/reverse discrimination and towards granting the principle of non-discrimination the status of a universal right of individuals.

Problems with the EU Non-discrimination Policy

Whilst observing the evolution of the EU antidiscrimination legislation and policy, it is noticeable, that up to a certain point, they aroused no major reservations on the part of the Catholic Church; indeed in most cases people of faith supported it. This concerns mainly the "first generation" of equality rights. It also seems that the *gender mainstreaming* policy does not raise any serious doubts, so long as it is understood in the classical sense, as an effort to ensure the equality of men and women, respecting their complementarity.[22] However, in the European Parliament

---

21. Cf. Schiek, "From European Union Non-discrimination Law," 5, after Śledzińska-Simon, "Zasada równości i zasada niedyskryminacji," 49–50.

22. John Paul II admits, in his "Letter to Women," that the Church (among others) has not always been faultless in this domain: "Unfortunately, we are heirs to a history which has conditioned us to a remarkable extent. In every time and place this conditioning has been an obstacle to the progress of women. Women's dignity has often been unacknowledged and their prerogatives misrepresented; they have often been relegated to the margins of society and even reduced to servitude. This has prevented women from truly being themselves, and it has resulted in a spiritual impoverishment of humanity. Certainly, it is no easy task to assign the blame for this, considering the many kinds of cultural conditioning which down the centuries have shaped ways of thinking and acting. And if objective blame, especially in particular historical contexts, has belonged to not just a few members of the church, for this I am truly sorry. May this regret be transformed, on the part of the whole church, into a renewed commitment of fidelity to the Gospel vision. When it comes to setting women free from every kind of exploitation and domination, the Gospel contains an ever relevant message which goes back to the attitude of Jesus Christ himself. Transcending the established norms of his own culture, Jesus treated women with openness, respect, acceptance and tenderness.

one comes across calls for redefining the meaning of the term *gender* in the above expression, to cover also LGBTQ persons.

The Church's doubts concerning the EU non-discrimination policy have become incremental with the appearance of Article 13 (TFEU, Article 19) in the Amsterdam Treaty, a basis for the creation of the second generation of antidiscrimination laws. Let us consider, for a moment, what changed in the EU equality and non-discrimination policy since the Amsterdam Treaty. I suggest diverging from a chronological order in favour of the substantive weight of arguments.

The Inherent Dignity of a Person as the Basis of Equality and Equal Treatment

As previously mentioned, the equality of all people can be justified through the conviction that every human being holds an equal, inherent and inalienable dignity. Statements asserting this can be found within the United Nations system in both the preamble and Article 1 of the Universal Declaration of Human Rights as well as the preamble of the International Covenant on Civil and Political Rights, the International Covenant on Economic, Social and Cultural Rights or the Convention on the Rights of the Child. Dignity is also referred to in the preamble (and Article 1) of the Charter of Fundamental Rights of the European Union: "Conscious of its spiritual and moral heritage, the Union is founded on the indivisible, universal values of human dignity, freedom, equality and solidarity; it is based on the principles of democracy and the rule of law" (CFREU, Preamble). The Treaty of Lisbon completely changed the axiological and meta-axiological foundations of EU law. The TEU preamble reads as follows: "Drawing inspiration from the cultural, religious and humanist inheritance of Europe, from which have developed the universal values of the inviolable and inalienable rights of the human person, freedom, democracy, equality and the rule of law" (TEU, Preamble). The values brought up in the above catalogue do not correspond to actual objective properties; they lack ontological status, displaying instead only a cultural and historical quality. Rather than dealing with a metaphysical approach to values, a sociological view is adopted here instead. [23]

In this way, he honored the dignity which women have always possessed according to God's plan and in his love. As we look to Christ at the end of this second millennium, it is natural to ask ourselves how much of his message has been heard and acted upon?" (John Paul II, "Letter to Women," 3).

23. Cf. Juros, "Problem wartości w preambule Traktatu," 39–51; Hambura and Muszyński, *Karta Praw Podstawowych z komentarzem*, 33–37.

The values fail to form a coherent system, nor are they absolute in character, they only remain "common to the Member States" (TEU, Article 2). Today they are seen as fundamental EU values, due to the fact that throughout the course of history they were recognized as such by all of the member states, which is illustrated by national constitutions and the widespread views of EU citizens. Hence comments pointing out the presence of cultural relativism or Max Weber's approach to axiological pluralism in the EU start to become legitimate. This can also be applied to the CFREU ("Conscious of its spiritual and moral heritage [. . .]"), although in this particular case the above thesis is not as straightforward.[24]

In his commentary on the TEU preamble, Marek Piechowiak states the following:

> From a meta-axiological point of view, the discussed topic clearly exhibits signs of recognising cultural relativism. In accordance with the given formula, values are based on Europe's cultural, religious and humanist heritage. If this applies to the values themselves, it must also mean that their prevalence is acknowledged and derived from cultural progress. Disregarding dignity (the term is missing in the preamble) is a consistent occurrence with this perspective, since it is understood as an inherent source of law, essentially independent from culture. Basic human rights are therefore negated. This is also the case with their prevalence and the cause of action concerning the universal recognition of human rights in all cultures.[25]

Negating the inherent nature of human rights means abandoning the traditions of natural law. This makes room for discussion about which qualities should be necessary in order to be subject to those laws. The fundamental rule prohibiting discrimination is called into question. Human rights, detached from intellectual studies, are bound to the will of man. They become a subject of negotiations and contracts established in line with the majority rule. The belief that human rights exist as a threshold that should not be crossed by the will of a person is questioned.[26]

If one delves deeper into the text of the Treaty preamble and the preamble of the Charter, it turns out that the authors of the project, accidently reveal their belief in the metaphysical aspect of values, virtually

24. Some commentators believe that the CFR is the last EU document which consciously invokes the concept of human rights based on natural law, and that consequently it is the last ally of the defenders of traditional values. (Cf. Piechowiak, "Karta Praw Podstawowych UE," 27.

25. Ibid., 26.

26. Cf. ibid., 26.

contradicting their own ideologies. In their opinion human rights are universal (TEU and CFREU preamble), indivisible (CFREU preamble), as well as inviolable and inalienable (TEU preamble). Commentaries on the matter tend to point out that in the TEU authors' opinion, the values in question were probably already regarded as such in national constitutions, and the aforementioned metaphysical aspect of values merely echoes the constitutional traditions of member states. The metaphysical aspect of values itself seems to be treated as an accidental by-product of European history, worthy of respect solely on grounds of being the *differentia specifica* of European culture. If this particular interpretation is correct, it would mean that the metaphysical aspect of values understood in this manner could be disputed through democratic procedures. Were it to be removed from member state constitutions altogether, its remnants left in the TEU would have to meet a similar fate.

The historical and cultural status of EU axiology inevitably impacts the understanding of the EU rules of equality, equal treatment and non-discrimination. The values which the EU should protect and promote as part of its policy, lack objectivity and are defined and redefined by the political elite—who see themselves as representatives of the majority—arbitrarily depending on the social context. The views of those who do not agree with the redefined values are often reduced to irrational superstitions, all because the category of objective truth about human nature is dismissed and removed. It is also commonplace for EU antidiscrimination laws based on Article 19 of the TFEU to neglect the category of inherent dignity, which appears in directives only with regard to the definition of harassment.[27] However in this case, doubts can still arise over whether it is actually inherent dignity being referred to here or simply the subjective sense of dignity.[28]

The Definition of Discrimination

Despite the importance attached to equality policy, equal treatment and non-discrimination, no document of the Union's primary law provides a definition of these notions. As a result, the task of filling them with proper

---

27. Commission of the Bishop's Conferences of the European Community, *Developing Fair Non-discrimination EU Legislation*, 7.

28. "Harassment: where an unwanted conduct related to the sex of a person occurs with the purpose or effect of violating the dignity of a person and of creating an intimidating, hostile, degrading, humiliating or offensive environment" (2000/43/EC, 2000/78/EC, 2004/113/EC, Article 2 § 3).

meaning has been transferred to secondary law and the case law of the European Court of Justice. The understanding of the terms is also influenced by numerous declarations, resolutions and other documents that are part of the so-called *soft law*.[29]

In the general understanding, discrimination is a violation of the principle of justice. Justice— according to the Code of Justinian—is *constans et perpetua voluntas ius suum cuique tribuens*.[30] Granting everyone what they are due means—in the context of equality and diversity of entities—that we could be dealing with unjust discrimination both when people are treated differently, and when they are treated identically. It all depends on whether, in a given context, justice requires emphasizing a similarity or a difference. In other words, whether in a given situation the difference is important or not.[31]

Roger Scruton defines discrimination as:

> differential treatment of persons, bodies or groups, usually with the implication, that there is not sufficient ground for doing this in the actual differences between them. Thus 'discrimination' tends to mean irrelevant, and also invidious, distinction. Some argue, that irrelevance implies invidiousness, since if the differences between *a* and *b* are irrelevant to deciding the question of what treatment should be ministered to either, then it is unjust to discriminate between them.[32]

It would seem that the essence of discrimination lies not so much in different treatment of subjects, but in the irrelevance—from a rational point of view—of the premise at the basis of the distinct and wrongful treatment, where not the individual features or the behaviour of a person is in question, but rather the person's belonging to a specific category or social group.[33] Scruton observes that the conviction that different treatment based on insignificant distinctions is unjust is shared both by critics of discrimination and those who practice discrimination:

> A distinction may be thought to correspond to some deep division of nature between people, and so to give grounds for differential treatment. While the search for that deep division may

---

29. Cf. Commission of the Bishop's Conferences of the European Community, *Developing Fair Non-discrimination EU Legislation*, 10.

30. Justinian, *Institutes*, 1.1.

31. Cf. Commission of the Bishop's Conferences of the European Community, *Developing Fair Non-discrimination EU Legislation*, 16–17.

32. Scruton, *Słownik myśli politycznej*, 80.

33. Cf. Winiarska and Klaus, "Dyskryminacja i nierówne traktowanie," 10.

involve the rationalization of an irrational prejudice (e.g. in the Nazi ideology of race), it may also involve serious hypotheses concerning large and unresolved questions (e.g. the normal grounds for treating children differently than adults).[34]

Another example is the issue of differential treatment of persons with disabilities (i.e. the availability of the driving license for the blind persons, different rules for them in the electoral vote), the special rights of women during pregnancy and childbirth, or the question of the relevance of the difference of sex with regard to access to the institution of marriage or child adoption.

Since the principle of equality in itself does not include the criterion of relevance, a feature which would be considered as significant by some in a given situation, will not be deemed as such by others.[35] Some authors, however, define the term "relevant," as "rationally justified." The rational nature of a justification is not tantamount to it being convincing for everyone.[36] So although, on the one hand, one should avoid differentiation based on irrational premises, yet the awareness of the need to treat people differently as a result of certain differences (e.g. of age, sex, disability) is reflected in

34. Scruton, *Słownik myśli politycznej*, 80.
35. Cf. Lucas, "Against Equality," 138–51.
36. In one of its rulings the Constitutional Tribunal (of the Polish Republic) stated that "equality means, that all addressees of legal norms with a given relevant characteristic would be treated in the same manner, without differentiation resulting in either discrimination or giving an advantage. Equality admits differential treatment by law of entities which differ between themselves; nevertheless any possible differentiation in the treatment of specific entities must be justified, e.g., based on accepted criteria, whereas the relevance of the selected criterion of differentiation must undergo evaluation in every case" (CT Decision dated 11 July 2000, K 30/99, OTK ZU 2000/5, item 145). In another decision, the CT pointed out that differential treatment of similar entities need not mean discrimination or giving an advantage because an additional assessment of the criterion applied is necessary. Any departures from the obligation of equal treatment of entities must be objectively justified. Firstly, the justification has to be relevant, thus in direct relation with the objective and the basic content of the provisions, in which the assessed norm is contained, and to serve the implementation of that objective and content. In other words, the differentiations introduced must be rationally justified. They cannot be made based on a discretional criterion. Secondly, the arguments in favor of differentiation must be proportional, hence the weight of the interest that is to be served by the differentiation of the addressees of the norm, must be proportionate to the interests that will be infringed upon as a result of differential treatment of similar entities. Thirdly, the arguments must relate to other values, principles or constitutional norms that justify differential treatment of similar entities. (See CT Decision dated 23 October 1995, K 4/95, OTK ZU 1995, part II, Item 11; CT Decision dated 3 September 1996, K 10/96, OTK No. 4/1996, item 33; also CT Adjudication dated 18 January 2000, K 17/99, OTK ZU 2000/1, item 4). (Witkowska, "Zasada równości w stosunkach pracy," 209–10).

international law in, for instance, the Convention on the Rights of the Child, Convention on the Rights of Persons with Disabilities, or the Universal Declaration of Human Rights, which stipulates on the right of a man and a woman to marry and establish a family after reaching adulthood (Article 16). It would seem that in these and similar cases one should speak of the right to differential treatment. A properly understood non-discrimination policy—as previously pointed out—should aim at striking the balance between the right of a person to be treated equally (identically), and the right of the person to be treated differently (differentially). This should be preceded by the identification of relevant and irrelevant characteristics in a given situation, based on rational criteria.

What is the nature of the harm suffered by the person who has been discriminated against? The goal of discrimination is to remove specific people and groups from certain areas or domains of public life,[37] to limit or deny their access to power or to prerogatives available to others, to limit their capacity to gain goods or benefits valued in a given culture.[38] In the opinion of Piotr Sztompka, discrimination reduces the chances for "access to education, profession, health, political rights, prestige and other valuable assets, only on the grounds of belonging to a group affected by prejudices, and without consideration for individual qualifications and merits."[39] Discrimination is always social and cultural in nature, since the criteria for evaluating the denied assets are social and cultural in nature.[40]

One of the important problems of definition is the question whether we can speak of discrimination in individual and incidental actions, or else only when dealing with deliberate, repetitive and long-term measures? Could discrimination take place during a random encounter in a store, or in the street, or perhaps only when we are dealing with a systematic occurrence, and some type of institutionalisation in the form of legal regulations, institutional practices? Is it possible to discriminate against someone unwittingly, or is discrimination necessarily deliberate?[41] Does the term refer to horizontal relations, or only to vertical relations? The authors of the report

---

37. Cf. Allport, *Nature of Prejudice*; after: Winiarska and Klaus, "Dyskryminacja i nierówne traktowanie," 10.

38. Cf. Winiarska and Klaus, "Dyskryminacja i nierówne traktowanie," 12.

39. Sztompka, *Socjologia*, 301.

40. Cf. Winiarska and Klaus, "Dyskryminacja i nierówne traktowanie," 12.

41. Observatory on Intolerance and Discrimination against Christians in Europe, for instance, assumes in its reports that intolerance concerns the social dimension of actions aimed at the marginalization of Christians, whilst discrimination refers to the legal dimension (Cf. Observatory on Intolerance and Discrimination against Christians in Europe, *Report 2011*, 8).

of the Commission of the Bishops' Conferences of the European Union (COMECE) point out that the notion of discrimination has been developed in order to protect the individual from improper and unjustified treatment on behalf of public authorities. Hence it naturally refers to vertical relations.[42] On the other hand, the authors of a paper prepared for the Biuro Analiz Sejmowych (Bureau of Parliamentary Analyses) distinguish—in line with G.W. Allport—discrimination from other actions derived from prejudice, such as verbal and physical violence, avoidance, as they are occasional in nature. Although they express disdain, they cannot be qualified as discrimination as such. In the analysts' opinion discrimination is "a form of differential treatment, unjustified by circumstance, characterised by durability and deliberation, based on the presence of a specific feature in an individual or group."[43] Discrimination is not an isolated, individual act, but rather an element of complex social relations. Its manifestations are organised and included in the structure of a given society and the way it functions. "The notion of discrimination will therefore be referenced above all to its institutional and legal form."[44] They recognise, nevertheless, that, "discriminating measures may be undertaken both by public authorities (including the legislature, through the formulation of specific regulations that provide for differential treatment of the representatives of certain social groups), and by private persons, e.g. employers, service companies."[45] This means that it is not the goal of the antidiscrimination policy to provide psychological satisfaction to people who feel "different" and hence not good enough, stigmatised.[46]

In the EU directives, the principle of equal treatment means the lack of any form of direct or indirect discrimination based on a given characteristic (compare 2000/43/EC Article 2 § 1, 2000/78/EC Article 2 § 1, 2004/113/EC Article 2). The determination of the general norm is followed by definitions of three notions: direct discrimination, indirect discrimination and harassment. Direct discrimination occurs when one person is treated less

42. Cf. Commission of the Bishop's Conferences of the European Community, *Developing Fair Non-discrimination EU Legislation*, 12.

43. Winiarska and Klaus, "Dyskryminacja i nierówne traktowanie," 11.

44. Ibid., 24.

45. Ibid., 24.

46. Literature points to the phenomenon of *victimization*, which lies in imposing on certain persons or social groups the conviction that they should feel wronged or discriminated against (Cf. Nisbet, *Przesądy*, 330–34). The current EU non-discrimination policy is an attempt to transfer instruments devised in the United States for disabled persons to new categories of "victims." Yet where disability, just as race or sex, may be objectively defined, the groups to which the non-discrimination policy currently attempts to extend to, are defined according to largely subjective criteria. (Cf. Guiraudon, *Antidiscrimination Policy*, 300).

favourably because of a given characteristic than another person is, was, or would be in a comparable situation. Indirect discrimination takes place in a situation, when an apparently neutral provision, criterion or practice would put persons with specific characteristics at a disadvantage compared to other persons without those characteristics, unless that provision, criterion or practice is objectively justified by a legitimate aim and the means of achieving that aim are appropriate and necessary.[47] Harassment occurs in a situation when an unwanted conduct related to a given feature of a person takes place with the purpose or effect of violating the dignity of a person and of creating an intimidating, hostile, degrading, humiliating or offensive environment (por. 2000/43/EC Article 2 § 2, 2000/78/EC Article 2 § 2, 2004/113/EC Article 2). Direct discrimination implies explicit and intentional action. The concept does not admit any general justification of exceptions or differences in treatment, unless they have been included in the Directive in special clauses which clearly justify them. Indirect discrimination does not require intentionality. It suffices that a seemingly neutral provision, criterion or practice genuinely causes unjustified differences in the outcome of its application. Such differences are not, nevertheless, prohibited, provided that they are properly justified. Harassment need not entail putting someone at a disadvantage, and does not even require comparison with the situation of a different person. It is enough to create an intimidating, hostile, humiliating, or offensive environment, though the directive does not specify in any way, how human dignity may be violated and what could intimidate a harassed person.[48]

Subjective components and the ambiguity of EU definitions could open the doors to abuse, especially in the context of the proposed new "horizontal directive" (COM (2008) 426). It broadens the concept of discrimination deeming instruction to discriminate against someone an act of discrimination, as it does the denial of rational improvement (Article 2 § 4 and 5). But most importantly, it moves the notion of discrimination beyond the labour market by including social protection, education and supply of goods and services, including accommodation (Article 3). Yet, although in the case of discrimination on grounds of disability, it is relatively easy to establish what constitutes a physical barrier for a disabled person and when we are dealing with denial of rational accommodation, in the case of discrimination based on religion or conviction the criteria are the feelings, thoughts and the conscience of a person. In the case of harassment in

---

47. This may be exemplified by the lack of separate regulations on the accessibility of polling stations to people with disabilities.

48. Cf. Commission of the Bishop's Conferences of the European Community, *Developing Fair Non-discrimination EU Legislation*, 17–19.

the workplace, we are dealing with a relation of financial and social dependency and subordination and a constant exposure to a hostile environment. In the case of the supply of goods and services, the contacts between the supplier and customer are frequently occasional and by chance. Moreover, the client generally has the option of choosing an alternative supplier. Since the notion of harassment implies a hostile or intimidating environment, the concept might be misused in the case of a "horizontal directive." The situation is further complicated by a general shift of the burden of proof to the respondent (Article 8).[49]

A Question Regarding the Scope of EU Competency

One of the essential issues in the discussed context is the question of the Union's scope of competency in the area of the EU non-discrimination policy. When looking at the titles of antidiscrimination directives, one realizes that their objective is to "implement the principles of equal treatment," which suggests, that such a general principle exists in the EU legislation. When one reads into the spirit of the directives, however—as emphasized by the authors of the COMECE Report—one discovers, that they lead only to the establishment of framework conditions for combating discrimination on grounds of a specific factor, but are not dedicated to ensuring equality as such. In these directives, the principle of equal treatment is defined only for the purpose of those directives. There is no mention of any general principle. Secondary legislation does not introduce a general and all-embracing principle of equal treatment banning any sort of discrimination. Instead, it focuses on selected aspects of discrimination. This means—as stated in the Report—discrimination on grounds of other reasons, or in different contexts, cannot be viewed as belonging to the competences of the Union. Directive 2004/113/EC is the only one that unequivocally stipulates that its goal is to ensure the implementation of the principle of equal treatment based on sex. But this concerns only access to and supply of goods and services (Article 1).[50]

When following the development of the jurisprudence of the European Court of Justice one will notice, however, that it tries to deduce from the text of the directives the existence of a general principle of non-discrimination, which extends autonomously in scope beyond the scope of the directives themselves. The ECJ decided, for instance, that the general principle of equal treatment based on sex included in Directive 76/207/EEC is part of

49. Cf. Ibid., 19–20.
50. Cf. Ibid., 22.

the fundamental rights of Community law. Because the principle was clearly expressed in primary legislation, the decision of the Court did not provoke a cascade of comments.[51] Recently, however, the Court started interpreting EU competences in the domain of non-discrimination by extension. In cases *Mangold* (C-144/04) and *Kücükdeveci* (C-555/07) the Court recognised the prohibition of discrimination based on age as a general principle of the Union, since it constitutes a concrete application of the general principle of equal treatment, and Directive 2000/78/EC merely specifies the principle.[52] The impression, that such a creative interpretation of the scope of EU legislation in the case law of ECJ lacks solid legal basis, seems strongly justified.[53]

The authors of the COMECE Report point out that the recognition of the existence of a general principle of equal treatment in the ECJ jurisprudence does not automatically lead to the appearance of a directly executable and directly effective law, that could be regarded as an independent, free-standing legal basis for entities to undertake legal action. Neither does it justify the claim that the existence of such a principle may lead to the delegation of legislative powers conducive to the prohibition of discrimination beyond the legal basis included in the Treaties. Such measures would instead undermine the division of competences between Member States and the EU.[54] On this point the Commission of the Bishop's Conferences of the European Community notes:

> General principles of EU law only serve as interpretive guidelines and as standards of review of the legislative and administrative acts of EU law. A general principle most certainly does not provide for an EU competence to adopt legislation pertaining to the prohibition of discrimination outside the framework of Article 19 of the Treaty on the functioning of the Union. The effect of these limitations leads to the conclusion that the principle of equal treatment is not a free standing and independent legal basis for undertaking legal action by individuals nor does it confer a right on an individual.[55]

Many supporters of a progressive approach to EU antidiscrimination legislation concur with this conclusion. Whilst demanding the adoption of the "horizontal directive," they often express their opinion on the

---

51. Cf. ibid., 21.

52. Cf. Śledzińska-Simon, "Zasada równości i zasada niedyskryminacji," 81.

53. Cf. Commission of the Bishop's Conferences of the European Community, *Developing Fair Non-discrimination EU Legislation*, 23.

54. Cf. ibid. 41.

55. Cf. ibid., 23.

insufficiency of the hitherto existing antidiscrimination policy precisely for the above described reason. As one scholar observes:

> In the present shape of EU legislation the principles of equality and non-discrimination—as stated in the BAS analysis—are the source of individual rights limited to the areas within the competence of the EU. In the future, it will be important to adopt a new directive banning discrimination in such fields as education, continuous training, social welfare, including social insurance, living accommodation, health care, the image of groups discriminated against in the media and advertising, physical access of disabled persons to information, telecommunication, electronic communication, transport and public space, social benefits, social access to goods and services and their supply. The current secondary laws lack regulations that prohibit discrimination in all the above areas, though it is not impossible, that the ECJ could interpret such a ban based on the principle of equality and non-discrimination as general principles of EU legislation.[56]

Although today the EU competence in the domain of non-discrimination is limited only to areas where it was clearly granted, such competence based on the Treaties, and the principles of equality and non-discrimination are not autonomous human rights, yet one may be justified in expecting that the development of the antidiscrimination law of the EU will attempt to turn the principle of non-discrimination into a universal human right.[57]

Conflicting Rights

The exercise by a person of their lawful human rights may potentially collide with the exercise of human rights by another person. The authors of the COMECE Report analyse in particular the relationship between the right to non-discrimination and the freedom of speech, freedom of thought, freedom of conscience and religious freedom. This list can undoubtedly be extended by family rights, especially the rights to marriage, adoption rights, the rights of parents and children in the area of education.

There is serious concern that the antidiscrimination laws, and especially laws on "hate speech," could contribute to the actual limitation of the freedom of speech, by spreading a general fear of the consequences of its misuse. Instruments of *soft law* such as declarations or resolutions of the European

---

56. Śledzińska-Simon, "Zasada równości i zasada niedyskryminacji," 82–83.
57. Cf. ibid., 83, 48.

Parliament encourage the application of so called "preventive self-censorship." The undefined category of homophobia they refer to—associated with xenophobia, anti-Semitism and racism—is intended to trigger a *chilling effect* and in itself seems to belong to the realm of "hate speech."[58]

Another aspect of liberty is the freedom of conscience. It is universally associated with legally guaranteed exceptions concerning certain duties and interdictions one might disagree with for religious, ethical, humanitarian or similar reasons.[59] It entails both the right to formulate moral judgments and to articulate them in the public domain, as well as the right to conscientious objection. It must be noted that the right to conscientious objection is included in the *Charter of Fundamental Rights*: "The right to conscientious objection is recognised, in accordance with the national laws governing the exercise of this right." (CFR, Article 10 § 2). A change in the wording of the article, as compared to the version from Nice, clearly shows the intention of the legislator not to limit the scope only to the issue of conscientiously objecting to military service.

The next area of potential conflict is the right to education, which—in line with the proposal of the "horizontal directive" —should be covered by the non-discrimination policy (2008/0140 (APP), Article 3 § 1). A discussion on the ratification of the *Council of Europe Convention* on preventing and combating *violence* against women and domestic *violence* is currently taking place in many European countries. Doubts are raised among others by Article 14 of the Convention, which commits member States to undertake ideologically inspired measures in the field of general education, which would constitute a serious interference with the rights of parents to raise and educate their children. The Article commits countries to "include in the educational content materials on non-stereotyped gender roles, and (allegedly) gender-based violence, which is already an ideologically involved claim."[60] Given the lack of unequivocal definition in the EU legislation there exists a genuine concern, that similar trends may be transferred to EU policies, and to the conflict between the right not to be discriminated against—in particular positive measures geared towards fighting any discrimination—and the right of parents to decide about the religious and moral upbringing of children, as guaranteed in the CFR:

---

58. Cf. Mazurkiewicz, "On Stem Cells and Homophobia," 108–13; Coleman, *Censored*.

59. Cf. Commission of the Bishop's Conferences of the European Community, *Developing Fair Non-discrimination EU Legislation*, 29.

60. Cf. Banasiuk, *Raport Instytutu Ordo Iuris*, 39.

The freedom to found educational establishments with due respect for democratic principles and the right of parents to ensure the education and teaching of their children in conformity with their religious, philosophical and pedagogical convictions shall be respected, in accordance with the national laws governing the exercise of such freedom and right." (CFR, Article 14 § 3).

The Specificity of the Catholic Church

The guarantees of religious freedom and the specificity of the Catholic Church are issues which merit a separate discussion. The right to religious freedom both on the individual and community plane, both private and public, is guaranteed in Article 10 §1 CFR. Moreover, in Article 17 TFEU the Union explicitly conceded that it "respects and does not prejudice the status under national law of churches and religious associations or communities in the Member States." (TFEU, Article 17 § 1). Whilst in Article 17 § 3 the Union acknowledges "the identity and the specific contribution," that Churches and religious associations make to the process of European integration (TFEU, Article 17 § 3). Hence the Union lacks any competences related to the pastoral activities of Churches, or regulating the relation between State and Church in member countries.[61] This lack of mandate should be clearly reflected in determining the scope of EU directives. If, however, the Union enacts antidiscrimination legislation remaining within the area of its competences, the specificity of the Catholic Church (along with other Churches and religions) ought to be considered a relevant factor, when it comes to defining the mode of exercising the right to religious freedom. The issue should be embodied in clearly defined healthy legal exceptions.[62] The underlying reason is to guarantee the Church's right to self-determination, a consequence of recognising the principle of State and Church autonomy. The forms of manifesting religious freedom should be exempt from the scope of non-discrimination instruments.

It must be noted that the word "exception" does not refer here to an exception from the principle of non-discrimination, but to the recognition of the exceptional status of Churches and religious institutions. This is not about the right of these institutions to discriminate against their employees, but to concede—in line with the definition of discrimination—that differential treatment in such a case is not tantamount to discrimination, but on

61. Cf. Mazurkiewicz, "Competenze dell'Unione europea," 43–48.
62. Cf. Commission of the Bishop's Conferences of the European Community, *Developing Fair Non-discrimination EU Legislation*, 36–39.

the contrary: identical treatment of those entities, without regard for their specificity, would in itself be discriminatory.

A separate question—especially given the potential entry into force of the "horizontal directive"—is whether entities, which formally are not of religious nature (for instance, they do not possess a legal identity as a Church), but which in fact have been formed with a religious factor in view (for example a hotel only for people living in the sacrament of marriage), should not be treated similarly to Churches.

In Directive 2000/78/EC the above postulates have been included in two ways. Firstly, through a general clause, applicable to all employees and all forms of discrimination, where it is deemed that

> a difference of treatment which is based on a characteristic related to any of the grounds referred to in Article 1 shall not constitute discrimination where, by reason of the nature of the particular occupational activities concerned or of the context in which they are carried out, such a characteristic constitutes a genuine and determining occupational requirement, provided that the objective is legitimate and the requirement is proportionate" (2000/78/EC, Article 4 § 1).

Secondly, through the clause relative to churches, as well as other public or private organizations, the deontology of which is based on religion or convictions. With regard to those entities,

> a difference of treatment based on a person's religion or belief shall not constitute discrimination where, by reason of the nature of these activities or of the context in which they are carried out, a person's religion or belief constitute a genuine, legitimate and justified occupational requirement, having regard to the organisation's ethos" (2000/78/EC, Article 4 § 2).

In addition, the Directive recognises "the right of churches and other public or private organisations, the ethos of which is based on religion or belief [...] to require individuals working for them to act in good faith and with loyalty to the organisation's ethos." (*idem*). In this case the point is to recognise the justified demand on the part of churches for loyalty and a particular lifestyle in conformity with the ethos and moral ethic of the religious institution in question. The above provisions have been introduced as a result of a controversy concerning whether the directive would not commit churches to employ (including ordaining ministers) persons, who according to the internal rules of the churches could not be assigned to certain functions and tasks. Some commentaries emphasize that the above exceptions should be interpreted very narrowly. "Denial of employment based on religious denomination (or lack thereof)—writes Śledzińska-Simon—does not concern work of a lay nature performed for a church or the institutions described. Neither can it justify discrimination on other grounds (such as sex or sexual orientation)."[63] This opinion, however, does not seem to be sufficiently justified.

Sexual Orientation as a Criterion of Discrimination

The greatest doubts in the EU non-discrimination policy appear to stem from the interpretation of the prohibition to discriminate on grounds of sexual orientation. The problem lies not in the rights of individuals, but in the consequences of EU regulations for family law (equality of same-sex unions with marriages between a man and a woman, the right to adopt children, access to so called reproduction services, access to social privileges reserved for marriages, etc.), or the education system (curricula on sexual education, fighting social stereotypes), which extend significantly beyond the EU mandate.

> Access to the institution of marriage is guaranteed to every person of full age (Universal Declaration of Human Rights, Article 16). However, this concerns entering the marital union with a person of the opposite sex. The difference of sex must be regarded as a relevant factor. The principle of non-discrimination which states that the same rules should be applied to similar situations and different rules to different situations (*Discrimination "can arise only through the application of different rules to comparable situations or the application of the same rule to different situations"*—C-157/02, Rieser, par. 39),[64] requires that in the context of the institution of marriage two persons of different sex be treated differently than two persons of the same sex. Diverging from this principle constitutes a serious infringement of the principles of fairness and could endanger the common good of the society. "The Church teaches that respect for homosexual persons cannot lead in any way to approval of homosexual behaviour or to legal recognition of homosexual unions. The common good requires that laws recognize, promote and protect marriage as the basis of the family, the primary unit of society. Legal recognition of homosexual unions or placing

63. Śledzińska-Simon, "Zasada równości i zasada niedyskryminacji," 63.
64. Cf. Commission of the Bishop's Conferences of the European Community, *Developing Fair Non-discrimination EU Legislation*, 16–17.

them on the same level as marriage would mean not only the approval of deviant behaviour, with the consequence of making it a model in present-day society, but would also obscure basic values which belong to the common inheritance of humanity. The Church cannot fail to defend these values, for the good of men and women and for the good of society itself.[65]

This conflict between an unfortunately misconstrued non-discrimination policy in the EU legislation and the institution of the Catholic Church seems inevitable, all the more so considering that the erroneous approach to the institution of marriage has been included in Article 9 of the CFR EU. The conflict is likely to increase in the future, since the EU not only bans discrimination, but also sets itself the goal of actively fighting all instances of discrimination.[66]

Conclusion

The EU non-discrimination policy brought about many positive effects, particularly in the area of equal treatment of men and women and non-discrimination on grounds of nationality. Yet since the Amsterdam Treaty, many controversial elements have emerged. The principal change lies in the departure from the doctrine of natural law—along with its concept of inherent and inalienable human dignity—to basing EU legislation on a *weak* anthropological foundation. The second meaningful element is broadening the scope of the EU non-discrimination policy and the introduction of instances of reverse discrimination. It appears that without a solid anthropological foundation the EU policy is increasingly exposed to a transformation into an instrument of social engineering. Equality and discrimination (devoid of objective significance) constitute an important political goal, but their definition is an outcome of a purely political decision.[67] Such a decision

65. Congregation for the Doctrine of the Faith, *Considerations Regarding Proposals*, 11.

66. One of the expressions of a distinct understanding of the non-discrimination policy is a letter from over one hundred NGOs to the President of the European Commission with a request to withdraw from further work on the draft "horizontal directive" (European Dignity Watch, "Pressure on Junker Grows").

67. In his presentation of reverse discrimination, Ronald Dworkin states, for instance, that admittance to university should not be granted based on the intelligence of, but a criterion serving, the "proper policy." He also wonders whether this thinking is not obvious for everyone: "Why did so many talented lawyers, who supported his (De-Funis's) claims as morally and legally justified make such an evident error? They would all agree that intelligence is an appropriate criterion for admission to a school of law. They would not consider that someone's constitutional right to be treated as an equal

is often made based on some dubious methodological research (conducted, for instance, by the Agency for Fundamental Rights), prepared to match the preceding ideological assumptions. Among the objectives of this policy an increasingly important role is assigned to the effort to give potential victims a sense of contentment.[68]

From the perspective of the current interests of the Catholic Church the expectation of "healthy exceptions" in the EU non-discrimination policy, which will guarantee the possibility of fully enjoying the right to the religious freedom, is a positive one. Nevertheless, in the long term, the "policy of exceptions" might prove to be counter-productive. It could, in fact, lead to the perception of churches as the last institutions where discrimination is temporarily admissible. But with time, such exceptions will likley be withdrawn. In such a case, the single real effect would be the deterioration of the image of the Catholic Church. As a result, the only long-term strategy open to the Church is the active effort to return to the concept of equality and non-discrimination based on proper anthropology.

Bibliography

Allport, Gordon W. *The Nature of Prejudice*. London: AddisonWesley, 1979.
Banasiuk, Joanna, ed. *Raport Instytutu Ordo Iuris: Czy Polska powinna ratyfikować Konwencję Rady Europyo zapobieganiu i przeciwdziałaniu przemocy wobec kobiet i przemocy domowej?* http://www.ordoiuris.pl/public/pliki/dokumenty/Raport_przemoc_OI.pdf.
Coleman, Paul B. *Censored: How European "Hate Speech" Laws are Threatening Freedom of Speech*. Vienna: Kairos, 2012.
Commission of the Bishop's Conferences of the European Community. *Developing Fair Non-discrimination EU Legislation*. http://www.comece.eu/dl/tLslJKJOMnoJqx4KJK/20100601PUBJUS_EN.pdf.
Congregation for the Doctrine of the Faith. *Considerations Regarding Proposals to Give Legal Recognition to Unions between Homosexual Persons* (2003). http://www.vatican.va/roman_curia/congregations/cfaith/documents/rc_con_cfaith_doc_20030731_homosexual-unions_en.html.
Dworkin, Ronald. *Biorąc prawa poważnie (Taking Rights Seriously)*. Warsaw: Wydawnictwo Naukowe PWN, 1998.

---

to others is restricted by this criterion. Why do they deny that, in the circumstances of the present decade, race may also be a relevant criterion" (Dworkin, *Biorąc prawa poważnie*, 410–11)?

68. Cf. European Parliament legislative resolution of 2 April 2009 on the proposal for a Council directive on implementing the principle of equal treatment between persons irrespective of religion or belief, disability, age or sexual orientation (COM(2008)0426—C6-0291/2008—2008/0140(CNS)), (2010/C 137 E/22), amendment 5, http://eur-lex.europa.eu/legal-content/EN/TXT/HTML/?uri=CELEX:52009AP0211&from=PL.

European Dignity Watch, "Pressure on Junker Grows to Drop the Dangerous 'Equality' Directive." Dec. 1, 2014. http://www.europeandignitywatch.org/pressure-on-juncker-grows-to-drop-the-dangerous-equality-directive/.

Francis, Pope. Apostolic Exhortation, *Evangelii Gaudium* (2013). http://w2.vatican.va/content/francesco/en/apost_exhortations/documents/papa-francesco_esortazione-ap_20131124_evangelii-gaudium.html.

Guiraudon, Virginie. "Antidiscrimination Policy." In *Europeanization: New Research Agendas*, edited by Paolo Graziano and Maarten P. Vink. New York: Palgrave-Macmillan, 2008.

Hambura, Stefan, and Mariusz Muszyński. *Karta Praw Podstawowych z komentarzem*. Bielsko-Biała, Poland: Studio STO, 2001.

John Paul II, Pope. Apostolic Letter, *Novo millennio ineunte* (2001). http://w2.vatican.va/content/john-paul-ii/en/apost_letters/2001/documents/hf_jp-ii_apl_20010106_novo-millennio-ineunte.html.

———. Exhortation, *Christifideles laici* (1988). http://w2.vatican.va/content/john-paul-ii/en/apost_exhortations/documents/hf_jp-ii_exh_30121988_christifideles-laici.html.

———. "Letter to Women (June 29, 1995)." https://w2.vatican.va/content/john-paul-ii/en/letters/1995/documents/hf_jp-ii_let_29061995_women.html

Jougan, Alojzy. *Słownik kościelny łacińsko-polski*. Warsaw: Studium Generale Europa, 1992.

Juros, Helmut. "Problem wartości w preambule Traktatu Konstytucyjnego Unii Europejskiej." In *Ustrojowo-polityczny wymiar Traktatu Konstytucyjnego Unii Europejskiej, Wyższa Szkoła Humanistyczna imienia Aleksandra Gieysztora*. Edited by Karina Karbowska and Anna Wnukowska. Pułtusk, Poland: Wydział Nauk Politycznych, 2004.

Justinian. *Institutes*, 1.1. http://www.thelatinlibrary.com/justinian/institutes1.shtml.

Lucas, John R. "Against Equality." In *Justice and Equality*, edited by Hugo Adam Bedau, 138–51. Englewood Cliffs, NJ: Prentice-Hall, 1971.

Mazurkiewicz, Piotr. "Competenze dell'Unione europea in materia religiosa." In *Le confessioni religiose nel diritto dell'Unione europea*, edited by Laura de Gregorio, 43–48. Bologna: Societa Editrice Il Mulion, 2012.

———. "Europeizacja Europy: Tożsamość kulturowa Europy w kontekście procesów integracji." *Studium Generale Europa* (2001).

———. "On Stem Cells and Homophobia." In *Catholic Theological Ethics in the World Church*, edited by James F. Keenan, SJ, 108–13. New York: Continuum 2007.

Nisbet, Robert. *Przesądy: Słownik filozoficzny* (*Prejudices: A Philosophical Dictionary*). Warszawa: Fundacja Alletheia, 1998.

Nitecki, Piotr. "Dyskryminacja w ujęciu nauczania społecznego Kościoła." In *Dyskryminacja jako nowa kwestia społeczna, Księgarnia św*, edited by Joséf Kupny et al., 189. Katowice, Poland: Jacka, 2007.

Observatory on Intolerance and Discrimination against Christians in Europe. *Report 2011*. Vienna: Kairos, 2012.

Paul VI, Pope. Apostolic Letter, *Octogesima adveniens* (1971). http://w2.vatican.va/content/paul-vi/en/apost_letters/documents/hf_p-vi_apl_19710514_octogesima-adveniens.html.

Piechowiak, Marek. "Karta Praw Podstawowych UE—wróg czy sprzymierzeniec tradycyjnych wartości?" *Chrześcijaństwo—Świat—Polityka* 7.3 (2008) 27.

Schiek, Dagmar. "From European Union Non-discrimination Law: Towards Multidimetional Equality Law for Europe." In *European Union Non-discrimination Law: Comparative Perspectives on Multidimensional Equality Law*, edited by Dagmar Schiek and Victoria Chege. London: Routledge, 2009.

Scruton, Roger. *Słownik myśli politycznej (A Dictionary of Political Thought)*. Poznań, Poland: Zyski S-ka Wydawnictwo, 2002.

Śledzińska-Simon, Anna. "Zasada równości i zasada niedyskryminacji w prawie Unii Europejskiej, Studia." *Studia BAS* 26.2 (2011).

Sztompka, Piotr. *Socjologia: Analiza społeczeństwa*. Kraków: Wydawnictwo Znak, 2003.

Vatican Council II. "Gaudium et Spes: Pastoral Constitution on the Church in the Modern World (1965)." http://www.vatican.va/archive/hist_councils/ii_vatican_council/documents/vat-ii_cons_19651207_gaudium-et-spes_en.html.

Winiarska, Aleksandra, and Witold Klaus. "Dyskryminacja i nierówne traktowanie jako zjawisko społeczno kulturowe." *Studia BAS* 26.2 (2011) 10.

Witkowska, Marta. "Zasada równości w stosunkach pracy na tle orzecznictwa Trybunału Konstytucyjnego." *Przegląd Prawa Konstytucyjnego* 1 (2011).

Chapter 7

Human Rights as Ideology
The Meaning of Equality and Non-discrimination in European Litigation within the Context of Religious Freedom

PAUL DIAMOND

THIS ESSAY EXPLORES THE modern application of human rights law in the courts of the United Kingdom with a particular focus on the principles of equality and non-discrimination. I approach this issue as a practitioner who has argued these issues in the courts and who has been involved in many of the important cases on religious liberty that have arisen in the United Kingdom and in the European Courts. The United Kingdom has rapidly become one of the most aggressively secular States in Europe.[1] A number of bishops, including a former Archbishop of Canterbury have made public statements to the effect that Christian adherents are being persecuted.[2] This new form of destructive secularism is not only seeking a strict divide between Church and State (which, in itself, is problematic in a society founded on Judeo-Christian values[3]), but is specifically anti-Christian.[4] The problem is the manifestation of a philosophical confluence of both these beliefs.

---

1. "Pope Benedict XVI warns against an 'aggressive form of secularism' in Britian," *Sunday Telegraph*, 16 September 2010.
2. *Sunday Telegraph*, 27 March 2010.
3. Benson, "Notes Towards a (re)definition," 520.
4. It is rarely directed at faiths others than Christianity (which includes Jewish values by default).

The new hostile secularism has two facets: 1) the prevailing ideology of human rights, non-discrimination, and equality which dominates all legal discourse and acts as an *a priori* set of principles; and 2) a direct animus towards the Christian faith or to Judeo-Christian beliefs, in which the law appears to be manipulated to secure a *political* adjudication. These two facets have reformulated the traditional legal approach: the free exercise of religion (something "neutral") which requires justification according to the principles of non-discrimination (the "good"); consequently, application of the law induces a detriment in circumstances where any individual manifests faith (Christianity or Judeo-Christian morality) in a form that causes offense or some form of unspecified harm (normally described as discrimination) to a protected (*vulnerable*) group.

A correlative legal theme is the malleability of the meaning (and non meaning of) statutory words and of principles in non-discrimination legislation; giving ever greater discretion to judicial lawmaking resulting in the very undermining of the *rule of law* in the name of the law. The current application of equality and non-discrimination rules raises issues as to the limits of the law (or as we say in England, *where the King's Writ Does Not Run*) and the reach of the law. The current expansive application of the law to the private sphere of the citizen (who must endorse the new public values) means that the correlative principles for the recognition of conscience and of the doctrine of *compelled speech/silence* are both required as a legal counter balance.

The road map for this paper is as follows. Part I commences with some brief background information about the legal system within the United Kingdom. Part II discusses the four stages of State limitations on religious freedom. Part III gives a comparative analysis of two cases that demonstrate the destructive effects of equality and non-discrimination laws on freedom of religion. Part IV considers the general threat of equality and non-discrimination laws *per se*, which includes a discussion about the rule of law; the principle of discordance between social reality and the law; juridification of the political choice; and case law when the political choice is animus towards Christians.

Background Considerations

The United Kingdom has no written Constitution; the legitimacy of the lawmaker is founded on the principle of the sovereignty of Parliament, unwritten conventions, and the common law. This unique combination of constitutional settlement originally engaged no democratic principles and was solely predicated on the rule of law often under a powerful sovereign.[5] The enfranchisement of the electorate in the United Kingdom was a protracted process from 1828 to 1928,[6] which was relatively late in global terms.[7] The important paradox was that the common law created a system for the restraint of power of the King and for the protection of personal liberty, property and liberty rights through the establishment of the rule of law. The 1215 "Magna Carta" represents the first attempt to establish the equal procedural application of the law[8] and of the restraint of arbitrary executive power.

In 1953, the United Kingdom ratified the 1950 "European Convention on Fundamental Freedoms and Human Rights" and since the United Kingdom was a dualist State, the Convention was only incorporated into domestic law in 2000 by the 1998 "Human Rights Act." The United Kingdom entered the European Union (EU), in 1973, and the 1957 "Treaty of Rome" was given effect by the 1972 "European Communities Act," which gives primacy to EU law over national law. The legal structure of the United Kingdom is currently premised on a complex overlapping system of national law, EU law, European convention law assisted by the *"soft law"* of international organisations such as the United Nations, the Council of Europe and the Organisation on Security and Co-operation in Europe (OSCE).

Compliance: The Four Stages

Freedom of religion is a concept that is endorsed collectively in society by the lawmaker, academic, and judge. However, in a world of competing ideologies, one ideology must prevail over the other. The current secular human

---

5. Enlightened despotism was a prevalent ideology in Europe: German historian Wilhelm Roscher (1847).

6. *Tess and Corporation Acts 1828* (Catholics granted emancipation), *Great Reform Act 1832, Great Reform Act 1867, Representation of the People Act 1918* (universal male suffrage), and *Representation of the People (Equal Franchise) Act 1928* (universal suffrage for men and women). There have been numerous constitutional reforms. The United Kingdom still has a hereditary upper house, the House of Lords.

7. The United States had a patchwork system of granting universal suffrage on a State by State basis, but forms of universal male suffrage were recognized by 1800 (Vermont, Pennsylvania, Kentucky) (Radcliffe, "Right to Vote," 232); and extensive female suffrage shortly thereafter. The 19th Amendment (1920) ensured full female suffrage.

8. Drafted by the Archbishop of Canterbury and agreed by King John at Runnymede on 15 June 1215, the first of many Charters.

rights agenda seeks to prevail over Judeo-Christian morality through the process of "domesticating religion."[9] This process develops in four stages.[10]

> *Stage 1:* ridicule and open disrespect of the religious practice predominantly in the media and educational establishments. Although the process is articulated by private actors via the press and audio visual communications, the State acquiesces;
>
> *Stage 2:* denial of a governmental favour, for example, an allocation of grants, consultation on legislation, programmes including the facilitation of a religious practice, on education and employment with conditions on the terms of access to such programmes;
>
> *Stage 3:* imposition of a detriment for adhering to a religious belief, for example, the denial of a benefit or a service available to all and/or a penalty for observance, which could be anything from the denial of recognition of a Christian club at a university to a denial of an ability of a married couple to foster children because of their views on homosexuality; and
>
> *Stage 4:* criminal sanction in the form, for example, of a hate crime and use of the criminal law to cause a "chilling effect" such as the threat of arrest for criticism or for allegedly causing offence to a protected group, as determined by the State.

The United States is moving rapidly from the second to the third stage, while the United Kingdom and Europe are moving slowly but surely from the third to the fourth stage. This process is not random, nor a reflection of current societal trends a facet of which is the inevitable march to the new secularism. Rather, it is a calculated and structured "long march." To flesh this point out, let us consider the British Broadcasting Corporation (BBC). It has televised programming that was blasphemous of the Lord Jesus in a comical manner. For example, the "Jerry Springer Show" on 8 January 2005 portrayed the Lord Jesus, God, and Satan all in a derogatory manner which, in turn, generated the largest number of complaints the BBC had ever received (55,000) and led to various protests throughout the country culminating in a legal case before the courts.[11] The State acquiesced to the

9. Carter, "Liberalism's Religion Problem," 23.

10. Developed from the "Nudge" theory of economic science on behavioral science that have been brought to wider audiences in the writings of Professors Sunstein and Thaler, see Thaler and Sunstein, *Nudge*.

11. *R (Green) v City of London Magistrates Court and Jonathan Thoday and Mark Thompson [2007]* EWHC 2785 Admin. The Divisional Court held that the transmission did not breach the common law offence of blasphemy.

transmission under the rubric of freedom of speech. However, there has never been any transmission of similar content critical of the founder of Islam, Mohammed. Rather, similar public criticism of Islam is generally treated by the State under Stage 4.[12]

Attacks on the Freedom of Religion: The Cases of Ladele and McFarlane

It is important to analyse how and why the doctrine of non-discrimination and equality has had such a destructive effect on religion and related concepts of morality, ethics, conscience and stigma, otherwise known as a societal norm of restraint. The decisions of the domestic courts in the two British cases of *Ladele* and *McFarlane*[13] raise key issues in the conflict between sexual orientation rights and religious rights. By way of a comparative analysis let us consider the facts of each case, the main holdings and then move to a discussion of the issues.

Facts and Holdings

The facts are as follows. Ms. Ladele, a Christian, did not want to participate in same sex civil partnership ceremonies as part of her work as a Registrar for a *public authority*, namely "Islington Borough Council." She could have been accommodated by having other staff members allocated to serve the needs of the small number of same-sex couples that wanted to enter into a civil partnership. However, she was forced to resign from her occupation as her employer insisted that she was acting in a discriminatory fashion.

Mr. McFarlane held the position as a Relationships Counsellor for a *private employer*, namely "Relate" in Bristol. He was good at his work and was progressing in the organisation. He had given relationship counselling to two same-sex couples but he was uncertain about giving directive sexual therapy to a same-sex couple because of his Christian faith. His employer regarded such hesitation as contrary to the "Equality Policy of Relate," when some fellow counsellors at Relate accused him of "homophobia" in response

---

12. *R v Overd (2015)* Taunton Magistrates' Court. Street Preacher charged for a public order offense for criticizing Mohammed's sexual life. In 2012, Channel 4 canceled an educational documentary *Islam: the Untold Story* after Oxford historian Tom Holland was threatened.

13. *Ladele & McFarlane v United Kingdom (2013)*. Both cases ultimately came before the European Court of Human Rights, Strasbourg. The author represented Mr. McFarlane before the Court.

to his manifestation of Christian morality. Mr. McFarlane was required by his employer to, in effect, renounce his Christian views as a condition of employment, that is, to ignore his Christian conscience, whenever it conflicted with an instruction from the employer to give directive sexual therapy to a same-sex couple. Although, Mr. McFarlane was unclear as to his view on the issue, he had never disobeyed a lawful instruction, declined a client or "discriminated" against anyone. His uncertainty as to practice was not sufficient and he was required to endorse same-sex unions.

Moreover, since Relate provides couple counselling, people present themselves on arrival as a couple in a relationship. In this situation, same-sex couples could easily have been directed to a more sympathetic counsellor without difficulty, after all, who would want a counsellor, who finds a same-sex relationship problematic? Nonetheless, Mr. McFarlane was dismissed for gross misconduct, the most serious form of employee misbehaviour and usually associated with theft, violence or drunkenness.

In the Court of Appeal, Lord Neuberger held that Ms. Ladele discriminated against homosexuals by acting on her religious beliefs and it was perfectly reasonable that she should lose her employment for so doing. According to him, she could still worship (not practise her religion) as her views on marriage were not a core part of her religion (a secular court ruling on religious truth).[14] The manifestation of Christian views on the morality of homosexuality was deemed discriminatory against homosexuals. The implications of this assessment of the law are obvious. The complexity of a balance of rights was not recognised as the status of the religious practice was downplayed. In particular, he held the following in *Ladele v Islington LBC*:[15]

> "... it appears to me that the fact that Ms. Ladele's refusal to perform civil partnerships was based on her religious view of marriage could not justify the conclusion that Islington should not be allowed to implement its aim to the full, namely that all registrars should perform civil partnerships as part of its Dignity for All policy. Ms. Ladele was employed in a public job and was working for a public authority; she was being required to

---

14. It is not the function of a (secular) Court to determine religious truth, or the correct exercise of religious practice. In the House of Lords case of *R (Williamson) v Secretary of State for Employment and Education* [2005] 2 AC, it was held at paragraph [23] that a secular court should not assess the religious belief of the adherent, unless there is a reasonable concern that the religious belief is an artifice. This test is very similar to the *sincerity test* as applied by *US Courts*. Thus, the decision in *Ladele* would appear to be *per incuriam* (a lack of care in considering precedent cases) to the *ratio decidendi* of this earlier case.

15. *Ladele v Islington LBC* [2010] 1 WLR 955, CA, para. 52.

perform a purely secular task, which was being treated as part of her job; Ms. Ladele's refusal to perform that task involved discriminating against gay people in the course of that job; she was being asked to perform the task because of Islington's Dignity for All policy, whose laudable aim was to avoid, or at least minimise, discrimination both among Islington's employees, and as between Islington (and its employees) and those in the community they served; Ms. Ladele's refusal was causing offence to at least two of her gay colleagues; Ms. Ladele's objection was based on her view of marriage, which was not a core part of her religion; and Islington's requirement in no way prevented her from worshipping as she wished."

And in paragraph 73:

"however much sympathy one may have with someone such as Ms. Ladele, who is faced with choosing between giving up a post she plainly appreciates or officiating at events which she considers to be contrary to her religious beliefs, the legislature has decided that the requirements of a modern liberal democracy, such as the United Kingdom, include outlawing discrimination in the provision of goods, facilities and services on grounds of sexual orientation, subject only to very limited exceptions."

The case of *McFarlane v Relate* was set for hearing shortly after the binding decision[16] of *Ladele*, and clearly, the judicial opinion cited above, in *Ladele*, needed to be addressed. Lord Carey, the former Archbishop of Canterbury filed a witness statement on behalf of Mr. McFarlane stating:

"The comparison of a Christian, in effect, with a 'bigot' (i.e. a person with an irrational dislike to homosexuals) begs further questions. It is further evidence of a disparaging attitude to the Christian faith and its values. In my view, the highest development of human spirituality is acceptance of Christ as saviour and adherence to Christian values. This cannot be seen by the Courts of this land as comparable to the base and ignorant behaviour. My heart is in anguish at the spiritual state of this country.

"It is, of course, but a short step from the dismissal of a sincere Christian from employment to a 'religious bar' to any employment by Christians. If Christian views on sexual ethics can be described as 'discriminatory', such views cannot be 'worthy of respect in a democratic society.' An employer could dismiss a Christian, refuse to employ a Christian and actively

---

16. *McFarlane v Related Avon Ltd.* [2010] EWCA Civ 880. All decisions of the Court of Appeal are binding on other Courts of Appeal and all lower courts.

undermine Christian beliefs. I believe that further Judicial decisions are likely to end up at this point and this is why I believe it is necessary to intervene now.'"

Lord Justice Laws dismissed Mr. McFarlane's case, which proceeded to the European Court of Human Rights. Let us remember, as noted above, that Lord Neuberger had held in the *Ladele* case that Ms. Ladele discriminated against homosexual persons by acting on her religious beliefs and it was perfectly reasonable that she should lose her employment for so doing.

Some Preliminary Points

It is important to make a few preliminary points. One, Ms. Ladele was employed in the public sector performing a statutory obligation,[17] while conversely Mr. McFarlane was employed in the private sector providing non-statutory services. National courts in the United Kingdom tend to not distinguish between the two, so as to avoid privileging those working for the State.

Two, it should be born in mind that private employers have been restricting the individual rights of their employees for a considerable time and in a number of fields, such as: restraints on trade (intellectual property, customers, official secrets); out of work activity tarnishing the image of the employer; restrictions on speaking and writing; and workplace dress codes. In the United Kingdom, a recent practice of employers has been the introduction of Equality Policies in which speech codes have been introduced to prohibit discrimination by speech as well as behaviour with the employer, virtually assuming the role as prosecutor, jury and judge. Such practices of private actors as well as those of public sector employers have impacted religious freedom in the United Kingdom.[18]

Three, the approach of many National courts has been to give the employer discretion in the running of his or her business. Such deference is premised on the fact that the judiciary is ill suited to make commercial decisions for individual businesses.[19]

---

17. The *Marriage (Same-sex couples) Act 2013* is now in force. Section 2 provides exemptions for clergy, but not marriage registrars (which Ms. Ladele was).

18. In *Mbuyi v Newpark Childcare (Shepards Bush) Ltd. Watford Employment Tribunal* 3300656/2014 (a disagreement between a homosexual and a Christian resulted in the dismissal of the Christian. Ms. Mbuyi won her case on the application of speech codes at work to silence the Christian viewpoint solely.).

19. The Employment Tribunal must consider the reasonable range of responses available to an employer, not whether they would have so acted.

Finally, both Ms. Ladele and Mr. McFarlane offended the "Equality Policy" of the employer in that their Christian views and behaviour were deemed discriminatory against same-sex couples. The issue was not whether the service was denied. This was not the case, since other employees could have performed the function.[20] Rather, the problem was their refusal to *serve* a same-sex couple in the abstract and not fact. In other words, in each case there was no detriment or undue burden to the business of the employer.

Application of Discrimination Law

The application of discrimination law in these two cases shows two important components, namely that religious rights were overridden, and unnecessarily overridden and that the detriment incurred was in response to the manifestation of person of his or her Christian faith. The focus on the non-provision of a service to a same-sex couple in abstract means that it was not reasonable for the employee to disobey the employer's instruction as this undermined the non-discrimination policies.[21] Furthermore, downplaying the motive of the Christian religious believer meant that the reason for the non-provision of the service was unsustainable as a defence to discrimination. The reason could be benign and even noble but the effect of the manifestation of the religious belief was held to be "discriminatory" against same-sex couples. The arguments that the Christian believer voluntarily entered the market place of work or is free to resign or find alternative employment does not change the facts.[22]

The second aspect is the Stage 3 treatment, discussed above, for adhering to a religious belief. Such application of the non-discrimination laws, while not their objective, forces the believer to act against his or her conscience by insisting that the employee conform to non-discrimination policies. The loss of employment, livelihood, or trade is one of the most severe sanctions that can be taken against an individual. The hallmark of totalitarian government is the coercion of the citizenry to an ideology promoted by

---

20. *Elane Photography LLC v Vanessa Willcock* (N.M 2013) 309 P.3d 53. There were plenty of other wedding photographers prepared to offer their services to the same-sex couple.

21. National employment law has long recognized that an employee may disobey an unreasonable order from an employer: *UCATT V Brain* [1981] IRLR 224 CA. In *Ladele*, Elias J of the Employment Appeal Tribunal held that all registrars must comply with the non-discrimination policy, at para. 111.

22. *Eweida and Others v The United Kingdom* (App nos 48420/10, 59842/10, 51671/10 and 36516/10) ECHR 15 January 2013, para. 83

the State.[23] In brief, this constitutes Stage 3 and if the resistance continues, or too many individuals refuse to conform, there is a serious risk that the State will move to Stage 4.

Discrimination law requires a comparator for which the person discriminated against can establish his claim by showing that a person without the protected characteristic (*inter alia*, race, sex, religion) would not have been so treated. In the case of *Ladele*, Lord Neuberger held that the comparator was a person who objected to same-sex marriage without any religious belief.[24] A person with no religious belief, who objected to same-sex marriage, would be more likely than not, be a bigot. Ms. Ladele was described as someone who would "pick and choose what duties to perform" and her refusal to carry out duties was due to "hostility" to same-sex couples and that she was, in effect, "discriminating against gay people" and "her view of marriage, which was not a core part of her religion." In the end, the court held that the practice of Christianity discriminated against homosexual persons.

To respond to this line of reasoning, Lord Carey, in the *McFarlane* case, submitted a witness statement which sought to address the implied association of Christians with those who discriminate against homosexuals on grounds of bigotry. McFarlane appeared to have committed a pure thought crime. He was dismissed for holding the view that marriage is between a man and woman; and the putative belief that giving directive sexual counselling to a same-sex couple 'could' violate his religious beliefs. He was required to approve of same-sex couples, regardless of his conscience. His "inner forum"[25] was completely irrelevant. The inviolability of this inner personal zone was voided by the need of the employer not to have an employee who disagreed with the employer's application of the "Equal Opportunities Policy."

The Balancing Question

Antidiscrimination law has created a "right" not to be discriminated against on a protected ground. In this way, discrimination has graduated from being a principle and accelerated beyond a mere "ancillary right" to a substantive right. It is part of the modern dynamic to eradicate discrimination on "suspect grounds." Where there is a difference in treatment based on a

---

23. Coercion to an ideology that is not accepted by the populace as coercion would be unnecessary if this was not the case.

24. *Ladele v Islington LBC*: in the EAT at paras. 111, 124, and the Court of Appeal at para. 52.

25. Traditionally referred to as the "*Forum Internum.*"

"suspect category," the European Court of Human Rights applies the "very weighty reasons" test in relation to sex,[26] illegitimacy,[27] nationality,[28] race,[29] sexual orientation,[30] disability,[31] and now religion.[32]

Religious freedom necessitates two countervailing premises: an exclusion, not an exemption, from discrimination and equality laws and a respect for the freedom of conscience. The use of exclusions avoids the reversed premise that it is religion that requires justification against the right of discrimination. Religious freedom is a substantive right, while discrimination is a complementary right that should fall within the ambit of the substantive right.[33] It is arguably illogical as well, because it is the ancillary right that requires justification against the substantive right. The exemption principle fares poorly in national courts as the primary purpose of the legislation is to be given effect and so exemptions are to be narrowly construed and subject to the test of proportionality.

The recognition of the right of conscience is necessary, not solely because of obvious reasons of civility, but because conscience prevents State coercion. While conscience is difficult to define,[34] it should be recognised when the legal conflict has reached an impasse. The State must have the capacity to determine the "good," that is, those values the State seeks to preserve or promote. The presumption is that the Christian faith remains a "good;" or, at the very least, is not contrary to public policy. There is no free-

26. *Abdaziz, Burgharta v Switzerland* (1994) 18EHRR 101 at 66; *Stec v United Kingdom* (2006) 43 EHRR 47 at 52.

27. *Sahin v Germany* (2003) 36 EHRR at 94, *Mazurek v France* (2006) 42 EHRR 9 at 49.

28. *Gaygusuz v Austria* (1997) 23 EHRR at 42, *Bah v United Kingdom* Appl No. 56328/07 at 37.

29. *DH v The Czech Republic*.

30. *Schalk & Korp v Austria* (2008) 53 EHRR 20 at 97; *Karner v Austria* (2004) 38 EHRR 24 at 37.

31. *Glor v Switzerland* Appl No. 13444/04 at 84.

32. *Vojnity v Hungary* Appl 29617/07 at 36-39.

33. Article 9, Council of Europe, *European Convention for the Protection of Human Rights and Fundamental Freedoms, as amended by Protocols Nos. 11 and 14, 4 November 1950*, ETC 5 protects rights of thought, conscience, and religious freedom; Article 14, Council of Europe, *European Convention for the Protection of Human Rights and Fundamental Freedoms, as amended by Protocols Nos. 11 and 14, 4 November 1950*, ETC on discrimination is not a substantive right and only applies to a violation that falls within the ambit of a substantive right. Protocol 12 creates a substantive right to non-discrimination, and entered into force on 1 April 2005 after the tenth State ratified it, however it has not been ratified by the United Kingdom.

34. For a helpful discussion, see Adhar and Leigh, *Religious Freedom in the Liberal State*, 125-56.

dom if the State seeks Stage 3 or 4 treatment in relation to the exercise of the Christian faith. However, in recognising the need for the State to determine a "good," depending on the circumstances, the State should act by means of Stage 1 and 2 disadvantages, not Stage 3 and 4 penalties.

The Threat of Antidiscrimination and Equality Policies *Per Se*

It is arguable that one of the greatest threats to religious freedom now stems from antidiscrimination and equality policies. Certain questions are raised: why is this the case? Why does discrimination against Christians, which is prohibited on grounds of religion, not have a counterbalance resulting in a stalemate between two conflicting rights? The irony is that the ideological perspective on difference, pluralism, and diversity achieves the converse result when religious freedom is in issue.

Discrimination law adheres to the principle that the protected characteristics[35] are irrelevant to employment or any other context. For example, it is irrelevant that the person who applies for an employment position is a woman or is black. The discrimination paradigm becomes problematic when transmuted to issues of lifestyle: culture, sexual rights and religion as opposed to immutable characteristics.[36]

Discrimination tends to be divided between "direct discrimination" and "indirect discrimination." The latter is often applied to address structural imbalances affecting groups by invoking the principle of "effective" equality.[37] These structural objectives are further compounded by the stringent test associated with any justification (having "weighty reasons") for difference in treatment on a "suspect ground," in particular for sexual orientation. [38]

In this way, the legal process is used to structurally realign societal goals in relation to issues of lifestyle. It is difficult to see how this cannot transform the legal process into a political process with an assault on Judeo-Christian morality, when societal norms (formulated by the dominant

---

35. This varies from jurisdiction but normally includes race, sex, religion, and sexual orientation.

36. Sex, race, and age, with gender re-assignment sex can be problematic.

37. See Alidad in *European Law Review (2012)*.

38. See *Petrovic v Austria Appl No. 156/1996/775/976* (2001) where the European Court of Human Rights held in para. 34: "It is true that the advancement of the equality of the sexes is today a major goal in the member States of the Council of Europe and very weighty reasons would be needed for such a difference in treatment to be regarded as compatible with the Convention."

narrative) discriminate against those choosing a different lifestyle.[39] The conflict is that discrimination laws seek to void differences of treatment, while freedom of religion requires the need for differentiation of treatment. However, the legal process is ill equipped to handle the conflict, from the perspective of process and legitimacy. The legal process is binary, an assessment of evidence as fact finding as well as lateral in that a simple test is conducted as to discrimination that ignores holistic issues, such as values and morality in society.[40] The legitimacy of the law is undermined when the views of members of the judiciary are deemed more profound or valid than those of any other sector of society. In brief, such juridification of social issues lacks legitimacy in a democratic system.[41]

The application of law on discrimination to both "sexual orientation" and "religion" (including all religions such as Islam, Christianity and Buddhism) forces the court to prioritise one right over the other. The "suspect categories" (vulnerable groups)[42] are presumably all related to a "core component" of a person's identity,[43] therefore there is a clash of rights. As one of the parties must be vanquished, the law amounts to nothing other than a utopian statement. Ultimately, a political choice must be made as to which ideology, or which "core component" of identity prevails and the courts make the political choice as to which "right" prevails. Yet, these judicial decisions can equally be classified as political decisions made inappropriately by the courts on issues relating to social norms, political culture, aspirational objectives and the power of pressure groups. We have seen, that in

39. In *Smith & Grady v United Kingdom* (1999) 29 EHRR 493, the European Court considered the dismissal of servicemen on grounds of their homosexuality and held in paragraph [121] that the discrimination was because of a "predisposed bias on the part of a heterosexual majority against a homosexual minority."

40. In the family law case of *Re G (A Child) (2013) EWCA Civ 965*, the Court of Appeal held that a linear approach to deciding the outcome is not appropriate—this means that it is not appropriate to evaluate and eliminate an individual option, to be left with the alternative (for example, Mother cannot care for the child, so a care order is the alternative). This approach leads to a bias towards the most draconian option. The Court held that a global, holistic evaluation of each of the options available must be conducted.

41. In *Cruzan v. Director, Missouri Department of Health*, 497 U.S. 261 (1990), dealing with the removal of a feeding tube from a woman in a vegetative State, Justice Scalia of the United States Supreme Court said that the issues "are [not] better known to the nine Justices of this Court any better than they are known to nine people picked at random from the Kansas City telephone directory."

42. The Equality Act 2010 prohibits discrimination on grounds of age, disability, gender reassignment, marriage and civil partnership, race, religion or belief, sex and sexual orientation.

43. *Preddy v Bull* [2013] 1 WLR 3741 at 52.

the United Kingdom, the Courts (as illuminated in *Ladele* and *McFarlane*[44]) have interpreted the antidiscrimination legislation to prevent any discrimination against homosexual persons, even where both rights (sexual orientation and religion) could be accommodated. The result is that a primary right has been ignored (Article 9 of the European Convention).

In the end, the hallmark of coercive government is, by definition, the coercion of the citizenry to the public ideology. It is clearly wrong to make individuals approve of conduct that they do not approve of by threat of penalty or sanction. It is a violation of the dignity of the human person and right reason.[45] The State will respond to the persistency of some individuals with strong convictions with sanctions that will gradually increase to Stage 4 (criminalisation) in due course. In matters of religious belief, where the balance is between spiritual or temporal sanctions, such a direction is inevitable.

Disrespect for the Rule of Law

The "rule of law" requires that a law is both sufficiently accessible and precise so as to enable the citizen to act in a law-abiding manner. In short, the law is required to have a degree of precision; and not to be expressed in vague open-ended terms. This principle was expressed in *Maestri v Italy*,[46] where the European Court consider the concept of "prescribed by law." According to that decision, the European Court stated:

> "The Court reiterates that the expressions "prescribed by law" and "in accordance with the law" in Articles 8 to 11 of the Convention not only require that the impugned measure should have some basis in domestic law, but also refer to the quality of the law in question. The law should be accessible to the persons concerned and formulated with sufficient precision to enable them—if need be, with appropriate advice—to foresee, to a degree that is reasonable in the circumstances, the consequences which a given action may entail (. . .)
>
> For domestic law to meet these requirements, it must afford a measure of legal protection against arbitrary interferences by public authorities with the rights guaranteed by the

---

44. There are plenty of other cases such as *Preddy v Bull* [2013] 1 WLR 3741 and *R (Johns) v Derby City Council* [2011].
45. Locke, "Letter Concerning Toleration," 8–9.
46. (2004) 39 EHRR 832 at paragraph 30.

Convention. In matters affecting fundamental rights it would be contrary to the rule of law, one of the basic principles of a democratic society enshrined in the Convention, for a legal discretion granted to the executive to be expressed in terms of an unfettered power. Consequently, the law must indicate with sufficient clarity the scope of any such discretion and the manner of its exercise (. . .).

The level of precision required of domestic legislation—which cannot in any case provide for every eventuality—depends to a considerable degree on the content of the instrument in question, the field it is designed to cover and the number and status of those to whom it is addressed (. . .)

The principle of the "rule of law" has two fundamental components: the adjudication of disputes according to settled precedent and procedure without arbitrary personal predilection of judges, which, in turn, enables the second component, namely that the law-abiding citizen is able to assess how to conduct himself or herself so as to avoid unlawful conduct. It is recognised that the precision of the law is limited in certain fields and cannot cover every eventuality and in a common law system, the law develops incrementally,[47] such as the meaning of the word "offensive."

The "rule of law" is premised on the principle of coherency and certainty. Antidiscrimination law is premised on the equalisation of any "difference" and the promotion of "diversity"[48] as a political ideal. These two concepts of difference and diversity in antidiscrimination law are, thus, in conflict,[49] requiring the never-ending process of litigation over grievances, the determination of the grievances and consequent weakening of the coherence of the law, resulting in further litigation and so on. The transfer of a political dispute to the legal forum makes the matter more acute.

If heterosexual couples can adopt or foster children and same-sex couples cannot, there is a difference;[50] if legitimate children can inherit and illegitimate children cannot inherit, there is a difference;[51] if a married

---

47. *Müller v Switzerland* (1988) 13 EHRR 212 at paragraph 29.

48. The result of the juridification of the political process.

49. They are structurally in conflict over and above the incremental development of the law on a case by case basis.

50. *Fretté v. France* (App no. 36515/97) ECHR 26 February 2002—the European Court upheld a national court ruling that a homosexual man was unsuccessful in seeking an adoption of a child.

51. *Pla and Puncernau v Andorra* (App no. 69498/01) ECHR 13 July 2004—The ECHR held that laws on inheritance for children of a marriage discriminated against children born out of wedlock.

couple is entitled to a hotel room, so is an unmarried couple, and so forth.[52] If same-sex couples in a civil partnership have all the rights of married couples, there is discrimination and the reasoning for the difference cannot be rational. None of the results of each of these scenarios are predictable; each incident of different treatment is premised on the incoherence in the law. This necessitates judicial resolution on a case-by-case basis according to a political culture (the balance of political forces in a State at any given period), and where the socio-political environment enables such disputes to be determined, they are often done so in a linear method resulting in the most extreme outcome from a societal perspective.[53]

The psychological effect of this chaos and unsettled law is the ever-reducing field of lawful conduct that a person is prepared to engage in (whether lawful or not). One of the purposes of the "rule of law" is to enable the citizen to act lawfully. The natural inclination is for a citizen to want to avoid legal entanglement and expense, consequently in a situation of uncertain legal boundaries, the citizen will surrender legal rights in order to be safe.

The US Supreme Court in *Baggett v Bullitt*,[54] a case about the taking of oaths by schoolteachers, recognised the effect of uncertainty in legal boundaries and held that persons "[. . .] steer far wider of the unlawful zone, that if the boundaries of the forbidden area were clearly marked. Those [. . .] sensitive to the perils posed by [. . .] indefinite language, avoid the risk [. . .] only by restricting their conduct to that which is unquestionably safe."

Such uncertainty induces the "concentric circle effect of statutory interpretation"[55] where expansive interpretations of the law causes a "penumbra of uncertainty" as to their application resulting in the creation of "folk law," rather than true law,[56] risks minimising behaviour to ensure that one does not go too close to the boundaries of the law, which, in turn, expands the scope of the law. Further, the boundaries to the law are often an electrified fence because, should the citizen challenge the demarcation, such a citizen is likely required to privately fund his case against the publicly funded State agencies, such as the "Human Rights Commission;" or local,

---

52. *Bull and another v Hall and another* [2013] UKSC 73—The Supreme Court of the United Kingdom held that the restriction of double beds in a bed & breakfast to opposite sex couples who are married solely (due to religious belief) was directly discriminatory against same-sex couples who could not marry (at that time).

53. See note 41, *supra*, as regards *Re G (A Child)*.

54. 377 US 360, 372 (1964).

55. Parkinson, "Enforcing Tolerance," 8–9.

56. This is what people think about how the law will be applied according to the political criteria, rather than what the Legislature has actually said.

administrative, and central government; or the public financing of the opponent's case.[57] Then there is the State 1 treatment that will likely follow, that is, the culture of ridicule from the private media with the acquiescence and approval of the State.

This situation of uncertainty is bad enough for any legal order, but in the field of equality and non-discrimination, State agencies are additionally engaged directly in the dispute. Therefore, such a conflict is not simply a private law dispute. The State directly promotes issues, such as the introduction of same-sex marriages, abortion rights and hate speech laws. It also seeks compliance with the law through normal law enforcement agencies or the creation of "Human Rights Commissions" and "Human Rights Boards." In the end, the State will prevail due to their access to unlimited resources, discretionary prosecutor powers and State 2, 3 and 4 sanctions. It is a legal system stacked in support of one side of the debate.[58]

The Principle of Discordance between the Social Reality and the Law

The recent case of *Hamalainen v Finland* is instructive.[59] It involved an attempt to introduce same-sex marriage into the entire Council of Europe area[60] and introduce the need to differentiate between gender identification and sexual orientation.[61] In 1996 H marries, and husband and wife have a child. In 2009 H undergoes gender re-assignment and is defined as a woman in Finnish law. Finland does not recognise same-sex marriage and H was required to constructively divorce his wife and enter into a civil partnership. Thus, a claim was brought by H under Article 8 (right to family life) and Article 12 (right to marry) pursuant to the European Convention on Human Rights. A decision in favour of *Hamalainen* would

---

57. Public Funding is granted in the United Kingdom due to the national cost rules.

58. I can speak personally on this issue. I have conducted some of the most important national and European cases on religious liberty; in all of my cases, I have never secured the benefit of public funding whilst many of my opponents have received Legal Aid and/or intervention by the "Equality and Human Rights Commission," or used public funds of local government, central departments or even of the United Kingdom itself. In my worst case, I counted 13 publicly funded lawyers arrayed against me.

59. Appl. No. 37359/09 of 16th July 2014.

60. There are 47 States in the Council of Europe area; not to be confused with the 25 Member States of the European Union.

61. An argument before the European Court was that H, who had gender re-alignment to become a woman, still had a heterosexual orientation.

have created a Convention right to marry, however, the European Court rejected the proposition that there was a positive obligation to create same-sex marriage in all Member States. This was especially due to the lack of European consensus on the issue and the matter, thus, fell within the "margin of appreciation" (discretion) of the States; for example, the Court needed to respect the decision of the Finnish Legislature to restrict marriage to a man and a woman.[62]

This issue of same-sex marriage is deeply controversial among the Contracting States to the Council of Europe. Of the 47 States, only 11 permit same-sex marriage,[63] most have varying provisions on same-sex relationships and 12 have Constitutional barriers to same-sex marriage.[64] The Republic of Slovakia only recently failed in a referendum to secure a Constitutional amendment to prevent same-sex marriage,[65] but this reality is countered by the introduction of same-sex marriage in Luxembourg and the recent referendum in Ireland (2015).

The juridification of an essentially political decision is apparent and an obvious consequence of having courts decide controversial political issues, rather than legislatures. The European Court held that there was insufficient consensus in Europe on same-sex marriage, and now with Russia recasting itself as the defender of Christian values, this may not change in the near future.

Another important point was the finding by the European Court of the need for coherence in the law, namely that there is a need in the legal order of the States to secure coherence between the reality of the situation in which an individual finds oneself and a "discordance" in the law. In *Hamalainen*, at paragraph 66, the Court held (emphasis added):

> "The notion of "respect" is not clear cut especially as far as positive obligations are concerned: having regard to the diversity of the practices followed and the situations obtaining in the Contracting States, the notion's requirements will vary

---

62. Appl. No. 37359/09 of 16th July 2014, paras. 72–74, 82. (Note: the "margin of appreciation" gives to States a discretionary area to legislate in controversial and sensitive fields in which there is no European consensus.).

63. The (Netherlands (2001), Belgium (2003), Spain (2005), Sweden (2009), Norway (2009), Portugal (2010), Iceland (2010), Denmark (2012), France (2013), United Kingdom (2013), Luxembourg (2015), Ireland Referendum (2015).

64. Latvia, Lithuania, Poland, Hungary, Bulgaria, Croatia, Moldova, Montenegro, Servia, Slovakia, Ukraine.

65. Ninety-five percent of those voting were against the introduction of same-sex marriage into Slovakia; however, a Constitutional amendment requires a 50 percent turnout; the turnout was only 21.4 percent and so the Referendum failed.

considerably from case to case (. . .). Nonetheless, certain factors have been considered relevant for the assessment of the content of those positive obligations on States. Some of them relate to the applicant. They concern the importance of the interest at stake and whether "fundamental values" or "essential aspects" of private life are in issue (. . .) or *the impact on an applicant of a discordance between the social reality and the law, the coherence of the administrative and legal practices within the domestic system* being regarded as an important factor in the assessment carried out under Article 8 (. . .). Other factors relate to the impact of the alleged positive obligation at stake on the State concerned. The question here is whether the alleged obligation is narrow and precise or broad and indeterminate (. . .) or about the extent of any burden the obligation would impose on the State (. . .)."

The cases associated with the issue of discordance are *B v France*[66] and *Goodwin v United Kingdom*.[67] Both individuals were male to female transsexuals. B was living as a female and was found to have a right for the civil status register to be amended to reflect the new status. Goodwin was a gender re-assigned woman living with a man who was found to have a right to marry. The legal system lacked coherence and there was discordance between the daily reality of the individuals and the restriction of the law. The State permitted the person to live their life as a member of the opposite sex, but denied the outworking of this reality. If a State permits a person to live as a woman and have children,[68] it was a breach of the law not to recognise her right as a woman to marry.

In short the law was incoherent because of a compassionate application of the law. Each concession to difference and diversity results in future incoherence and discordance in the law, and further claims of discrimination, and further movement and development in the law. The important issue is that any restraint on the development of the law is political (the "consensus" of European States), but the Court makes the political decision and assessment of consensus, not the democratic processes of the State.

For an extreme example of this "judicial democracy;" in *W v Registrar of Marriages*,[69] the Court of Final Appeal of Hong Kong[70] rejected the

66. B. v. France, 25 March 1992, § 63, Series A no. 232C.

67. Appl. No. 28957/95 at § 72, ECHR 2002VI.

68. X,Y, Z v United Kingdom (1997) 24 EHRR 143 and recognizing right to family life within Article 8 of female to male transsexual.

69. [2013] 3 HKLRD 90 (Hong Kong).

70. Lord Hoffman of the United Kingdom Supreme Court gave the most important speech in the Hong Kong court.

consensus principle in its entirety as inimical to fundamental rights. In that case a transsexual (man to woman) sought to marry. Hong Kong does not recognise gender re-assignment and a challenge was brought under the "Basic Law of the Hong Kong" and "The Hong Kong Bill of Rights Ordinance,"[71] which gives effect to the 1966 "International Covenant on Civil and Political Rights" (ICCPR). The signatories to the ICCPR are very diffuse[72] and European States comprise a small minority. The consensus under the ICCPR does not recognise marriage for transsexual individuals. The Court of Final Appeal disregarded the consensus argument and as the counter-veiling political pressure (in this case from China[73]) was absent, the case of *Goodwin v United Kingdom* was applied. Transsexual marriage was introduced into Hong Kong absent any democratic input.

Juridification of the Political Choice: The Equality and Human Rights Commission

Antidiscrimination laws and equality law in their political dimension amount to socio-political objectives. The engagement of a utopian statement necessitates a utopian goal; the law has a purpose and is not a procedure. A law with political objectives generates unforeseeable litigation with decisions of judicial organs incrementally going in one direction.

The duties of the "Equality and Human Rights Commission" are set out in section 3 of the 2006 "Equality Act" as:

> "The Commission shall exercise its functions under this Part with a view to encouraging and supporting the development of a society in which— (a) people's ability to achieve their potential is not limited by prejudice or discrimination, (b) there is respect for and protection of each individual's human rights, (c) there is respect for the dignity and worth of each individual, (d) each individual has an equal opportunity to participate in society, and (e) there is mutual respect between groups based on understanding and valuing of diversity and on shared respect for equality and human rights."

---

71. Hong Kong Bill of Rights Ordinance, Cap 383.

72. There are 168 State parties to the ICCPR in February 2015; a State Party has ratified the Treaty (including by accession or succession). The State parties include, inter alia, Afghanistan, Algeria, Bangladesh, Mongolia, and Uganda.

73. Hong Kong is part of China (one state, two systems) and currently with an independent (British) legal system until 2047.

The executive arm of the State has the duty to enforce these objectives; namely the creation of a society where everyone is treated fairly. These objectives are non-legal and utopian. Individuals will disagree with the law when the law is used for political objectives, in the same way as an individual has a right to express political choice. However, the juridification of this political process to create a non-discriminatory society means, that where a person disagrees with these political objectives, such a person is no longer expressing his lawful political views, but is acting unlawfully. For example, the individual is discriminating or the individual may be imposing an incoherent harm on a protected group by the mere expression of such unlawful views. This form of juridification has a direct bearing on free speech and the political process since these Utopian principles are extended to the propositional content of speech.[74] Professor Dworkin has argued that such restrictions on "upstream" free speech (political debate) de-legitimise decisions made to implement antidiscrimination laws "downstream" free speech (e.g., housing, employment, education). Where a person acts unlawfully the principle that the law must be obeyed means that the person must be subject to coercive sanctions. The proposition that the Christian manifestation of faith is now unlawful is a regular feature of life in the United Kingdom. In a recent case deciding that Christians discriminated against homosexual persons by giving two beds, in their bed & breakfast, to married couples of different sexes, Baroness Hale held:[75]

> "We do not normally allow people to behave in a way which the law prohibits because they disagree with the law. But to allow discrimination against persons of homosexual orientation (or indeed of heterosexual orientation) because of a belief, however sincerely held, and however based on the biblical text, would be to do just that."

Individuals hold differing views on the merits or demerits of same-sex marriage. Arguments opposing same-sex marriage may be based upon, for example, religious convictions, natural law principles and human rights concerns. The State weighs in favour of same-sex marriage by offering an additional justification for support. Since opposition to same-sex marriage is subjected to severe sanction and support for same-sex marriage is encouraged by State approval, one may very well conclude,

---

74. Dworkin, "Foreword," i–ix.

75. *Preddy v Bull* [2013] 1 WLR 3741 at [37]. Mr. and Mrs. Bull ran a bed & breakfast establishment who only rented out double rooms to married couples (thus excluding unmarried heterosexual couples and same-sex couples).

on the grounds of expediency, that it is more rational to support same-sex marriage than to oppose it.

When the Political Choice Is an Animus toward Christianity

Wearing the Sign of the Cross: Eweida v. British Airways

In 2006, Ms Eweida brought a claim for religious discrimination. She was not permitted to wear a small cross while working for *British Airways*, but members of other religions were permitted to wear the *Hijab, turban* and *Shikha*.[76] The cross was prohibited, classified as jewellery. This would appear to be a simple case of discrimination against a Christian, since other religious practices were accommodated. However, the courts of the United Kingdom did not agree with this straight forward proposition of law.[77] Rather, the tribunal determined that there was no discrimination because if a Muslim, for example, had decided to wear a cross, the adherent of the Islamic faith would have been treated exactly the same (as a Christian) and sent home without pay. In brief, there was no discrimination as everyone was treated the same.

One objection, of course, is that the comparator is wrong. Muslims and Sikhs do not want to wear a cross, and Christians do not want to wear a Hijab or Turban, which, in turn, underscores the malleability of the meaning of antidiscrimination laws and exemplifies the problem with using a nondiscrimination approach, as opposed to a religious liberty approach.[78]

On appeal the decision was upheld. Lord Justice Sedley of the Court of Appeal criticised the litigation by Ms. Eweida as pursuing a "sectarian agenda," part of a strategy that involved a rejection of an "open offer to settle the claim on generous terms" and appeared to advocate a "blanket ban" on all religious rights in the workplace.[79] It is difficult to see this approach as anything other than hostile when one considers the intemperate scolding

76. A form of Hindu "ponytail" that is worn by some men.

77. Para. 37 of Judgment, January 2008 (not reported). At the reading, Employment Judge Lewis dismissed the claim at first instance holding: "We find that the Respondent [British Airways] would have treated identically . . . An adherent of any non-Christian faith, or of no faith displaying a Cross for cosmetic . . . reasons. An adherent of a faith other than Christianity wearing a symbol . . . round the neck. An employee wearing a visible silver necklace . . . ."

78. Consider the issue of the comparator in *Smith v Safeway plc* [1996] ICR 868 and *Denise v Metropolitan Police Department* EAT [2009] UKEAT/0234/09 (where a woman was permitted to have longer hair. The employers in these cases were entitled to implement different rules of apparel [such as hair length] between men and women.).

79. *Eweida v British Airways* [2010] EWCA Civ 880, CA at paras. 25 and 40.

of Ms. Eweida by Lord Justice Sedley and the decision itself, which was unsustainable. Ms. Eweida was fully entitled to pursue her claim to establish a violation of her Convention right.

The Court of Appeal went further. It held that in order to establish indirect discrimination, disparate impact had to be established against a group of people, known in national law as "group disadvantage." The Court held that the purpose of discrimination law is to eliminate structural discrimination in society, for example, a policy that Policemen should be six-foot tall discriminated against women as a group, since, as a group, women tend to be shorter in stature. In *Eweida,* there was insufficient evidence that Christians, as a group, felt strongly about wearing the cross and that Christians as a class would suffer disadvantage if wearing of the Cross were prohibited. Group disadvantage was not established. Consequently, Ms Eweida had no legal claim to bring before the courts, because the requisite legal foundation had not been established.

Contrast this outcome with the decision in *Noah v The Wedge Hairdresser,*[80] where a trendy hairdresser was held culpable for failing to employ a Muslim job applicant who was wearing a *Hijab*, something contrary to the image of the establishment. Even though no job existed since the hairdresser decided not to recruit, due to economic factors, and that wearing of the *Hijab* conflicted with the image of the establishment, the court held that the employer should have waited and accessed any loss of trade as a result of damage to the branding. In brief, discrimination was found even though there was no job at all because the employer decided against employing anyone and the Employment Tribunal simply accepted that Ms. Noah was a Muslim, who wanted to wear the *Hijab*, and did not employ any test of "group disadvantage."

Consider further the case of *In R (Watkins- Singh) v Governing Body of Aberdare Girls High School,*[81] where the Court found both religious and racial discrimination in preventing a schoolgirl from wearing the *Sikh Kara*. While expert evidence was presented as regards to wearing the *Sikh Kara*, the Court adopted a broad-based approach in recognising that the wearing of a *Kara* was not a requirement of the Sikh faith, but should have been permitted as it was an "extremely important indication of her faith."[82] But this broad-based approach does not seem to apply to Christians, since this case can be directly contrasted with *R (Playfoot) v Governing Body of Millais School,*[83] where the

---

80. Case No. 2201867/2007 of 11 June 2008.
81. [2008] EWHC 1865 (Admin).
82. Ibid., paras. 29, 56, 60, and 70.
83. (2007) EWHC 1698 Admin of 16 July 2007, paras. 24 and 29.

wearing by Christian schoolgirls of a purity ring[84] was not held to be a manifestation of Christian practice. Rather, the wearing of a purity ring was held not to be a mandatory requirement of the Christian faith: "Whatever the ring is intended to symbolise, it is a piece of jewellery."

Holding Sunday, the Sabbath, Sacred: Mba v. Merton[85]

In *Mba v Merton LBC*, Ms. Mba was prevented from being excused from work on Sunday. Ms Mba was a Sabbatarian. She had never worked on a Sunday and had asked to be excused from work on that day. Her employer refused her request and began a practice of requiring her to work Sundays until she was forced to resign and bring a case of "constructive dismissal." In regard to the facts in that case, Ms. Mba was an employee of the London Borough of Merton, employed from 2007 to 2010 as a Residential Care Worker. The London Borough of Merton is a London administrative Council serving a population of approximately 200,000,[86] with a budget of approximately £488 million.[87] It employs 5,430 individuals, of which approximately 4,161 are full time.

She brought her case to the Employment Tribunal, the national Court applied discrimination law, as opposed to human rights law according to Article 9 of the Convention. The claim had to be brought as one of indirect discrimination, namely that the employers' neutral rule which required that employees must be available for work on Sunday discriminated against Christians as a group, that is, group discrimination. Accordingly, a witness statement was submitted by an Anglican Bishop[88] indicating that some Christians observed the Sunday Sabbath. Parenthetically, the very fact that such evidence is required by British courts at all is telling and prior to the case there was concern that the Employment Tribunal would not recognise Sunday, in the same way, that the courts did not recognized the Christian cross, as a religious symbol.

The Bishop gave a short and concise witness statement on the issue of Sunday as a Sabbath day for Christians, but stated in the final paragraph:

---

84. A silver ring worn on the hand of the girl, common in some circles, in the United States.

85. *MBA v London Borough of Merton* [2013] EWCA Civ 1562

86. 199,700 on ONS (2011) census estimate.

87. Summary of Accounts for year 2013/14. Approximately £178 million are spent on services.

88. Bishop Michael Nazir-Ali is one of the most senior and respected Churchmen in the United Kingdom. He was Bishop of Rochester from 1994–2009 with an accompanying seat in the House of Lords.

> "Some Christians will not work on the Sabbath (except for mercies); others may work only on an emergency; some Christians will want to wear a cross to manifest their faith, others will manifest their faith in some other way. What is important is reasonable accommodation by employers of religious faith and practice."[89]

The Employment Tribunal contorted this statement to mean its opposite, namely that Christians do work on a Sunday and that Ms Mba had failed to show any structural disadvantage. The Employment Tribunal held:

> "As stated earlier, we need to weigh in the balance the discriminatory impact of the PCP[90] upon the Claimant. We accept that the PCP impacted upon her genuinely and deeply held religious belief and observance, as we have described above. *However in terms of the degree of disadvantage to her, we bear in mind the following in particular: . . . . (iii) Her belief that Sunday should be a day of rest and worship upon which no paid employment was undertaken, whilst deeply held is not a core component of the Christian faith* (in the sense that the phrase is used in Ladele, see our summary of the relevant legal principles above). *As much is as accepted in terms of paragraph 9 of Bishop Nazir Ali's witness statement (served by the Claimant) where he states that some Christians will not work on the Sabbath.* To adjudicate the matter in this way does not involve a secular court impermissibly adjudicating in evaluative terms upon religious beliefs as Mr Diamond submitted, as opposed to simply proceeding on the basis of evidence before it as to the components of Christian faith."

The decision was upheld on appeal by the Employment Appeal Tribunal,[91] but finally reversed in law, but not in fact, by the Court of Appeal.[92] The case was later submitted to the European Court of Human Rights.

It is deeply concerning that the Employment Tribunal twisted the obvious meaning of the Bishop's witness statement to mean the opposite, namely that it was permissible to require Christians to work on a Sunday because only a minority would be affected. The question remains: why a national Court would do such a thing? The interpretation of the witness statement of the Bishop was mendacious and the decision necessitated an appeal to the Court of Appeal by a private individual, with costs to bear, against a public

---

89. Annexed to the Application.
90. Practice, Criteria, or Provision: PCP in cases of indirect discrimination.
91. Employment Appeal Tribunal [2013] ICR 658.
92. [2014] EWCA Civ 1562.

body. There is a serious risk of abuse with group discrimination as a test for proving indirect indiscrimination under article 9 because of the diversity of beliefs within a single faith group. As Lord Justice held in *Eweida*, at the Court of Appeal, the formula for determining discrimination is simple on grounds of sex, but "impossible to do the same for a solitary believer who fellow believers elsewhere in society may accord different degrees of importance to the same manifestation of faith."[93]

The European Court has taken a more reasonable position. In *S.A.S. v France*,[94] at paragraph 56 the Court held it was irrelevant whether the practice in issue was a minority one within the faith group, but nevertheless upheld the French ban on the wearing of veil coverings. In Judge Bratza's partly dissenting opinion in *Eweida v United Kingdom*, he recognized the reasoning behind the use of group discrimination in cases of indirect discrimination, but in relation to Christianity stated this " . . . may be especially difficult . . . in the cases of a religion such as Christianity, which is not prescriptive and which allows for many different ways of manifesting commitment to the religion."[95]

Christians Fostering Children: R (Johns) v. Derby City Council

In *R (Johns) v Derby City Council*,[96] a Christian couple were prevented from fostering a 5 year old child because of their Christian views on sexual ethics. Mr. and Mrs. Johns were a stable, loving couple with a spare room in their house. They wanted to assist another couple in need, so they asked the local council if they could foster a five year old child (or any other young child) for respite care. Respite care is a form of temporary relief for parents who care for a mentally or physically disabled child, who would otherwise be in an institution. Thus, the Johns sought a difficult child for the weekend to enable another couple, perhaps at the end of their tether, to have some time off together.

The social workers discovered in the interview that the Johns were Christians and proceeded to ask questions about their views on homosexuality. Mrs. Johns wondered why this question was relevant for a five year old, but said she would love any child. Mr. Johns said he would "gently turn" the

---

93. Paragraph [19] in *Eweida v British Airways* [2012] Court of Appeal. Contrast with the decision of the US Supreme Court in *Thomas v Review Board of the Indiana Employment Security Division* 450 US 707 (1981).
94. (2014) 36 B.H.R.C. 617.
95. (2013) Application No. 48420/10.
96. [2011] EWHC 375 Admin.

child away from homosexuality, and the scene was set for court action. The Social Services recognised that Mr. and Mrs. Johns would have provided a good home for any child but for their Christian views.

Paragraph 11 of the judgment records the assessment of the Social Worker as to their suitability:

> "Eunice and Owen are kind and hospitable people, who would always do their best to make a child welcome and comfortable. They would endeavour, I am sure, to respond sensitively to a child and would take their responsibilities as carers seriously. The possible shortfalls described in this report in relation to their potential as foster carers do not detract from the fact that they are well-meaning and caring people, who are clearly well-regarded by their family and friends.
>
> (...)
>
> In addition, Mr and Mrs Johns' views on same sex relationships, which are not in line with the current requirements of the National Standards, and which are not susceptible to change, will need to be considered when panel reaches its conclusion."

In the words of the State-funded "Equality and Human Rights Commission":

> "In addition to the harm that it may cause children in their care, approving foster carers who express antipathy to, or disapproval of, homosexuality and same sex relationships militates against the promotion of sexual orientation equality more generally, providing state sanction as it would to views that are inimical to such equality. This is in conflict with the aspirations of anti-discrimination and human rights law, and *carries the real risk that the child in the care of such a foster carer will become infected with*, or affected by, such views." (emphasis added)

According to the position of the State agency responsible for enforcing human rights norms in the United Kingdom, Judeo-Christian views on sexual ethics were in conflict with human rights law and a child could be "infected" with such views. Due to the media outcry concerning this argument, the "Equality and Human Rights Commission" admitted that it had made a mistake.[97] The argument that equated Judeo-Christian beliefs with an infection was permitted by the Court, though, since objections to this

---

97. Submission to the High Court: This submission was challenged in Court and was not withdrawn. However, there was a public outcry and the Equality and Human Rights Commission issued an apology on 11 March 2011.

argument were dismissed and it was not referred to in the judgment and did not form part of the reasoning of the court. If it had been for the media attention and the subsequent public outcry, the "Equality and Human Rights Commission" would have never made the public retraction and the argument would have been deemed acceptable before the courts.

Contrast this with the positions of other religious or secular groups. It is difficult to believe that the same court would have permitted a submission that a child could be "infected" with Islamic beliefs, on the one hand, or homosexual values, on the other hand. Such a submission would have resulted in significant consequences for any party submitting such a proposition. However, in regard to Christianity, the problem is that the laws on equality and non-discrimination are, in effect, arguing that because discrimination against homosexuality is prohibited, Mr. and Mrs. Johns's Christians ethics would engender discrimination and public authority must prohibit such opinions.

Conclusion

The anti-democratic nature of the human rights paradigm coupled with the fear of unlimited and unknown litigation do not create a legal system under the rule of law. At best, the legal system has been placed under the rule of lawyers and judges. At its worst, the legal system has been placed under the court of public opinion. The principle of coherence and discordance in the modern liberal state (modern in the sense that laws develop and are passed in an incremental fashion and are often incoherent, and liberal in the sense that the liberal state permits lifestyle choices) means that a *carte blanche* is given to the judicial processes to resolve these inconsistencies by litigation. The lateral application of the law can have only one outcome, even if the judges delay this outcome because of political realities. The response to politics in the courtroom is simple. We must return to the rule of law. While societal value shifts will occur, the legitimate means of resolving conflicts is through the passage of laws by the legislative branch, subject to democratic judgment. Certainly, each decision will not please every member of society, but legitimacy would be maintained by the preservation of upstream free speech.

Bibliography

Adhar, Rex, and Ian Leigh. *Religious Freedom in the Liberal State,* 2nd ed. Oxford: Oxford University Press, 2013.

Benson, Iain. "Notes Towards a (re)definition of the Secular." *University of British Columbia Law Review* 33.1 (2000) 520–22.

Carter, Stephen. *The Culture of Disbelief: How American Law and Politics Trivialize Religious Devotion*. New York: Anchor, 1993.

———. "Liberalism's Religion Problem." *First Things* 121 (March 2002) 21–32.

Dworkin, Ronald. "Foreword." In *Extreme Speech and Democracy*, edited by Ivan Hare and James Weinstein, i–ix. Oxford: Oxford University Press, 2010.

Locke, John. "A Letter Concerning Toleration." https://socialsciences.mcmaster.ca/econ/ugcm/3ll3/locke/toleration.pdf.

———. *The Second Treatise of Civil Government and a Letter Concerning Toleration*. Edited and with an introduction by John. W. Gough. Mineola, NY: Dover, 2002.

Parkinson, Patrick. "Enforcing Tolerance: Religious Vilification Laws in Australia." Paper presented at Eleventh Annual International Law and Religion Symposium: "Religion in the Public Sphere: Challenges and Opportunities," Provo, UT, October 2004. http://www.saltshakers.org.au/images/stories/attachments/252_300342_ARTICLES_ON_VILIFICATION.pdf.

Radcliffe, Donald. "The Right to Vote and the Rise of Democracy, 1787–1828." *Journal of the Early Republic* 33.2 (2013) 219–54.

Thaler, Richard H., and Cass R. Sunstein. *Nudge: Improving Decisions About Health, Wealth and Happiness*. London: Penguin, 2009.

Chapter 8

The Inter-American System
Sexual Orientation as a Category and/or Ground of Non-discrimination

CARMEN DOMÍNGUEZ HIDALGO

ONE OF THE MAIN aspects of the liberal agenda is to include sexual orientation as a suspect category in juridical systems around the world. Five years prior to the writing of this essay, the notion of sexual orientation was virtually ignored in the Inter-American system. It was not expressly recognized in the 1969 American Convention, nor in the Constitutions and legislative enactments of the countries that are part of the Inter-American System. This juridical reality has changed very quickly in the last five years as will be developed in this paper. Today, one might say that the Inter-American region "is full of contrasts in LGBTQ (Lesbian, Gay, Bisexual, Transgender, and Queer) issues."[1]

As noted, most of the Constitutions within these regions do not recognize sexual orientation as a suspect category and—as it will be shown—there is still no legislation to this effect. Many countries that are not under the jurisdiction of the Inter-American Court of Human Rights (IACtHR),[2] such as Antigua, Barbuda, Barbados, Belize, Dominica, Grenada, Guyana, Jamaica, Saint Kitts and Nevis, Saint Lucia, Saint Vincent and the Grenadines, still criminalize sodomy, as does Trinidad and Tobago, even though it is a country under the IACtHR jurisdiction.

On the contrary, other countries, such as Nicaragua and Panama, have recently repealed sodomy laws as of 2008. Only six countries (Argentina,

---

1. Alvaro, "Examining Atala-Riffo and Daughters," 72.
2. Hereinafter "IACtHR."

Canada, Mexico, Colombia, the United States, and Uruguay) have approved same-sex marriage. Overall, it is clear that American countries have a very different approach in terms of regulating same-sex marriage, but in terms of those that have legalized it, we can see a similar line of thought. In specific regard to Mexico, on 19 June 2015, the First Chamber of the Mexican Supreme Court ruled that

> denying gay couples the tangible and intangible benefits that are accessible to heterosexuals through marriage, involves treating homosexuals as if they were 'second-class citizens,' and therefore 'the exclusion of same-sex couples from the institution of marriage perpetuates the notion that same-sex couples are less worthy of recognition than heterosexual couples, thereby offending their human dignity and integrity.[3]

A few weeks later the United States Supreme Court ruled "no union is more profound than marriage, for it embodies the highest ideals of love, fidelity, devotion, sacrifice, and family" and that it would be a mistake to argue that people with a homosexual orientation "disrespect the idea of marriage. Their plea is that they do respect it, respect it so deeply that they seek to find its fulfillment for themselves. [. . .] They ask for equal dignity in the eyes of the law. The Constitution grants them that right."[4]

The Judicial Approach

In the past five years, the efforts that have been made in order to introduce sexual orientation as a suspect category in the Inter-American System have been done by the judiciary and/or the legislative branch. Let us first consider the judicial approach before we turn to the legislative method.

Atala vs. the State of Chile

The most relevant decision was made by the IACtHR, on 24 February 2012, when it read sexual orientation into the Convention, which does not expressly recognize the term. In order to understand the decision of *Atala vs. the State of Chile*, it is necessary to present the facts, underline the relevant aspects and address the relevance of such a decision for the future. Let us review the facts briefly. In this case, a married woman separated from her

---

3. Jurisprudential thesis published on the *Semanario Judicial de la Federación*, from the tenth era under registration No.2 009 406.
4. Supreme Court of the United States, 26 June 2015, No.14-556 p. 28.

husband and then, just eight months later, began a lesbian cohabitation. She and her husband had three daughters who had been living with her with the consent of their father. Two months after this situation became known to the father, namely the lesbian cohabitation, he began legal proceedings in order to obtain custody of the girls concerned about the effects that such a cohabitation would have on the children.

The evidence led by the mother consisted essentially in foreign reports or sources which argued that lesbian cohabitation had no effect on children living in such situations. Meanwhile, the father presented ample evidence, namely psychological and social reports and testimonies of the people who had worked with them, especially the housemaids. The evidence proved that the lesbian cohabitation of their mother was producing negative consequences for the girls such as: behavioral changes, sexual identity problems, and social isolation. The psychological assessment of the mother demonstrated emotional instability and self-centered behavior. Various people testified that she was never present in the lives her daughters being mainly occupied with her profession, while the father, with help of the housemaids, took care of the children.

The tribunal of first instance gave provisional custody to the father, but ultimately granted the mother custody of the girls. The Court of Appeal confirmed that decision. The father appealed the decision before the Chilean Supreme Court of Justice and was finally granted custody of the girls. The Supreme Court[5] based its decision upon the following considerations: a) that the custody should be carried out under the basic principle of the best interests of the child as recognized under both national and international law; b) that the evidence presented in the case showed that the decision of the Court of Appeal was based on the general proof led by the mother, who had attempted to prove that the lesbian condition did not violate the rights of the children, rather than upon consideration of the specific evidence presented by the father, namely that which showed the negative effects the life option chosen by the mother had been having on the girls (e.g., sexual identity problems and social isolation); and c) that from a juridical perspective sexual orientation of the mother could not be objected to, even though, in that case, the way that she had been living had been causing particular harm to her daughters. In sum, the Supreme Court stated that:

> It is impossible to ignore that the mother of the children by making the decision to live explicitly in terms of her sexual orientation, as every person can do so freely within [the] sphere of [one's] personal rights in sexual gender, does not deserve

5. Supreme Court of Chile, 31 May 2004, Rol No.1193-2003.

disapproval or reproach; [however] she has placed her own interest before her daughters, especially by commencing to cohabit with her homosexual partner in the same household where she raises and takes care of her daughters.[6]

For this reason, the Court decided that in light of the best interests of the child, giving the custody to the father was the best option. In 2005, the mother filed a complaint before the Inter-American Commission, which was sent to the Court, in 2010. The Commission recommended the condemnation of Chile for: a) a violation of the right to equality and non-discrimination for denying custody to the mother based solely on her sexual orientation, b) a violation of the right to privacy of the mother when the Supreme Court analyzed her sexual orientation; c) a violation of the right to family privacy by considering as a family the lesbian couple and the girls, d) a violation of the duties of special protection of the girls and ensuring equal rights of spouses upon dissolution of marriage by focusing only on the analysis of the mother and her behavior without making the same examination to the father (although in the case file, there is a lot of evidence tending to judge his ability to take care of his daughters); and e) a violation of the right to judicial guarantees and judicial protection since the final judgment of the Supreme Court was obtained by an extraordinary action.

The Commission recommended and ordered the State of Chile: a) to compensate for the loss of profits, pain and suffering caused as a result of the violations alleged by the mother and the girls (although they had never been heard at trial, nor had the father been notified about the process) as well as the pain and suffering caused to the lesbian ex-partner whom had been denied the right to build a family and finally, the pain and suffering of the grandmother, uncle, and half-brother; b) to investigate and impose the corresponding legal consequences on the judges who arbitrarily discriminated and interfered with the private life of Karen Atala's family and violated the international obligations to ensure the best interests of the girls (when what the Supreme Court did was precisely what was needed to protect that interest by analyzing the concrete evidence presented); c) to publicly recognize its responsibility; d) to provide rehabilitation measures; e) to adopt measures that include both legislation and public policies to forbid and eliminate discrimination based on sexual orientation in all aspects of the State, including the administration of justice; and f) to pay for the litigation costs and legal expenses.

Clearly, there are a lot of aspects that can be analyzed in this case, including the Court's jurisdiction to decide on family issues and the

6. Ibid.

important question of whether sexual orientation may or may not constitute a suspect category under the American Convention. Also, there is the substantive issue raised as regards parental care and as to whether or not sexual orientation is an aspect of the life of a parent that should be scrutinized when deciding the custody of a child. In regard to this last point, in the end, a more profound reading of the case shows that law and judicial bodies are not to take sexual orientation into consideration when deciding upon the custody of a child.

The Decision of the IACtHR

The IACtHR condemned Chile on the grounds that it violated: a) sexual orientation as a category protected by the Convention; b) equality and non-discrimination in the custody proceedings; c) the right to privacy and family life; d) judicial guarantees and judicial protection; and e) due process during the disciplinary investigation. Accordingly, the IACtHR ordered reparations to be made by the State of Chile. For the purpose of this essay, let us discuss a few of these aspects.

Sexual Orientation as a Category Protected by the Convention

The American Convention on Human Rights provides, in article 1, as regards equality and non-discrimination, that States must respect the rights and freedoms recognized in the said Convention "without any discrimination for reasons of race, color, sex, language, religion, political or other opinion, national or social origin, economic status, birth, or any *other social condition*."[7]

Accordingly, the IACtHR made a number of findings: a) that "whatever the origin or form it assumes, any treatment that may be considered discriminatory regarding the exercise of any of the rights guaranteed in the Convention is *per se* incompatible with it;"[8] b) that "the fundamental principle of equality and non-discrimination has entered the realm of *jus cogens*;"[9] and c) that sexual orientation has to be considered within the context of any "other social condition" in accordance with article 1 of the American Convention, because as regards interpretation "it is always neces-

---

7. American Convention on Human Rights, 1969 (emphasis added).
8. IACtHR (Judgment) 24 of January 2012, *Atala-Riffo and Daughters v. Chile*, para. 78.
9. Ibid., para. 79.

sary to choose the alternative that is most favorable to the protection of the rights enshrined in the said treaty, based on the principle of the rule most favorable to the human being."[10]

The interpretation of the IACtHR was buttressed with references to other international instruments and decisions that had ruled or decided that sexual orientation was protected by the Convention and so "no regulation, decision or practice of domestic legislation, whether by state authorities or individuals, may diminish or restrict in any way whatsoever, the rights of a person based on their sexual orientation."[11]

The Violation of Equality and Non-discrimination in the Custody Proceedings

The IACtHR found a violation of equality and non-discrimination in the custody proceedings because in such cases the decision had to be made on the best interest of the child which meant that it had to be based "on assessment of specific parental behaviors and their negative impact on the wellbeing and development of the child, or of any real and proven damage or risks to the child's wellbeing and not those that are speculative or imaginary."[12] The IACtHR found that the Supreme Court failed to make a real analysis of the connection between the mother's lesbian cohabitation and the deterioration of the social, family and educational aspects of the girls lives. Also, the Court failed to describe why the father's situation was better and did not give "sufficiently weighty reasons that would support the claim that sexual orientation does not have a negative effect on the child's psychological and emotional wellbeing, development, sexual orientation and social relationships."[13] The IACtHR held that the analysis made by the Supreme Court was one *in abstracto* that discriminated against not only Atala, but also her girls when using "the mother's sexual orientation as a ground for its decision [taking into account some considerations that] "it would not have used if the custody proceedings had been between two heterosexual parents."[14]

---

10. Ibid., para. 84.
11. Ibid., para. 91.
12. Ibid., paras. 108–9.
13. Ibid., para. 130.
14. Ibid., para. 154.

The Violation of the Right to Privacy and Family Life

The IACtHR found a violation of the right to privacy and family life because privacy was a broad concept that included "sex life and the right to establish and develop relationships with other human beings."[15] In this case, although the best interest of the child allowed some interferences in that private sphere of the parents, such interference was not justified and therefore, rendered in an arbitrary manner because an "analysis of parental behavior should not have scrutinized sexual orientation, because such factor is irrelevant when examining an individual's suitability as a parent."[16]

Then, the IACtHR related the right to privacy to the rights of the family, ruled on articles 11 and 17 of the Convention, and affirmed that the protection of the family required States "[to] develop and strengthen"[17] the family unit "in the broadest possible terms."[18] In addition, the IACtHR underlined that "various human right organs created by treaties have argued that there is no single model for a family"[19] and that the relationship between the lesbian couple and the girls was so close that it was "clear that they had created a family unit."[20] According to this rationale, the IACtHR concluded that the separation of the girls from their mother affected both the mother's and the girls' right to have a family life as well as the rights of the child.

The Order for Reparations

The IACtHR ordered the State of Chile to pay a sum of money as compensation for the damages suffered, not only, by the mother but also by the girls, by the lesbian partner of Atala (who, by the end of the trial, was no longer her partner) and by Atala's large family. It also demanded some additional reparations to reform society for such treatment of lesbian persons, ruling that the State of Chile had to "promote structural changes, dismantling certain stereotypes and practices that perpetuate discrimination against [LGBTQ] groups."[21] In addition, it had to implement "educational programs in relation

---

15. Ibid., para. 162.
16. Alvaro, *supra* note 1 p. 62.
17. Ibid., 62.
18. IACtHR (Judgment) 24 of January 2012, *Atala-Riffo and Daughters v. Chile*, para. 169.
19. Ibid., para. 172.
20. Alvaro, *supra* note 1, p. 62.
21. IACtHR (Judgment) 24 of January 2012, *Atala-Riffo and Daughters v. Chile*, para. 267.

to, among others, the protection of LGBTQ people and overcome gender stereotypes and homophobia."[22] It ordered a compensation for the three girls even though one of them sent a letter to the Court asking to not be considered as victim and without any reference in the decision about that letter.

The Scope and Relevance of the Decision for the Future

A number of points are important to underline as regards the relevance of this case for the future. One, this decision clearly extended the expression "other social conditions" in an evolutive interpretation that does not correspond with the recognition of that category by States Parties to the Convention. Moreover, as will be shown *infra*, there are relevant differences between the recognition and comprehension of sexual orientation in the laws of these States Parties. Despite the aforementioned, the IACtHR gave its own interpretation without any consideration of the differences in evolution of the law and chose to push ahead with the recognition of sexual orientation. Clearly, this attitude demonstrates one of the main differences between the IACtHR and the ECHR. The former does not recognize the "margin of appreciation" (margin of State discretion), while the latter has relied on this standard in its decisions on LGBTQ issues.

Two, this is the first decision of the IACtHR on sexual orientation, but there are other cases in the system about to be ruled upon. Three of them are cases presented by non-governmental organizations representing LGBTQ interests against the State of Chile. One case concerns same-sex marriage, the right of a lesbian couple to be both registered as mothers of a child. Another case concerns freedom of religion and the right of a Catholic religion teacher to have a public lesbian relationship. If we consider the decision already noted and the fact that only less than two percent of the cases brought to the IACtHR are dismissed, we can rest assured that the remaining cases will be concluded by an agreement between the parties and the States, one way of concluding a trial, or by a judicial condemnation of the State.

Three, with this decision, the IACtHR has redefined the juridical notion of family under the Convention by considering the family in broad terms and including unstable relationships. In the *Atala* case, the relationship between the lesbian couple did not endure, yet, the couple was considered a family without taking into consideration the fact that Atala was married to her husband at the time she began her lesbian relationship. The IACtHR found that the American Convention "does not define a limited

---

22. Ibid. para. 271.

concept of family, nor does it only protect a 'traditional' model of family."[23] Moreover, the notion of family "is not limited only to marriage and must encompass other *de facto* family ties in which the parties live outside the marriage," because there is not one specific model of family.[24]

Four, the ruling does not constitute precedent for the IACtHR, since the system does not operate on this basis. However, the IACtHR considers such decisions binding on domestic courts which, in turn, oblige States Parties to apply this new interpretation of the Convention. As regards the receptivity of domestic courts to this new interpretation, one will need to wait and see whether it will be adopted or not. This will depend on the internal incorporation of the *Atala* decision within the different legal systems. In Argentina, for example, decisions are repeatedly cited to guide how new cases should be decided. In Chile, however, internal implementation of such cases is scarce.

The effects mentioned above on the various domestic legal systems are relevant to the issue of child custody. Although the IACtHR did not order the State of Chile to reform its family legislation in order to expressly forbid the consideration of sexual orientation by judges, a certain immunity for sexual orientation from judicial consideration was an integral component of the decision. Moreover, it is noteworthy that this is an isolated case brought by the homosexual lobby; in Chile one cannot find a similar case, nor is there any legal provision that allows such immunity.

It is true that both the European Court and domestic courts in several other European countries, and even American Courts, have rejected the consideration of sexual orientation in matters of custody of children. However, on the one hand, this is the first decision of the Court in this regard, and on the other hand, the situation in this case was particularly complex because the decision of the Supreme Court expressly stated that the sexual orientation of the mother was not in issue, but rather how she exercised her sexual orientation in a way that affected her daughters' development. Hence, the decision of the Supreme Court to grant custody to the father was properly focused on the best interests of the children.

Thus, if the ultimate goal is the protection of children and it is within the purview of the States to measure the impact produced by the private behavior of parents on children involved in a decision about custody, the best interests of the child must always be a major issue that should not be neglected by any right claimed by the parents. In addition, the same principle

---

23. Ibid., para. 142.

24. IACtHR (Judgment) 24 of January 2012, *Atala-Riffo and Daughters v. Chile*, para. 142.

applies even in the cases involving adults who have engaged in conduct which, although permissible and legal, could have a detrimental effect on the home environment and the development of children. Indeed, sexual orientation cannot be considered as a "super-category" that outweighs the best interests of the child, which remains the paramount principle in all matters relating to international or domestic protection of children.

Consequently, if the IACtHR desires the bests interests of the child to prevail, in matters relating to their custody, judicial scrutiny of parents should be total as regards care of their children, including all relevant aspects of their lives and conduct that have a bearing on the future life of the child. Sexual orientation ought to be considered on an equal footing with other categories, in accordance with the principle of equality. Furthermore, if it is determined that there is a right to not being discriminated against based on the sexual orientation of an individual under the Convention, and this right has been violated, sexual orientation should be analyzed from an interdependent perspective, as an element that interacts with other categories and as such, should not be considered as a greater or lesser right. If a heterosexual parent cannot avoid judicial scrutiny of his or her private life, then the same principle ought to apply to a homosexual person. In support of this proposition, Commissioner Carozza stated in a separate vote that, such scrutiny in the context of determining the custody of the child's welfare should be allowed and, in fact, requires that courts take into account all the nuances of the lifestyle of parents, even private circumstances and emotional life of parents and how their practices and sexual activity can affect the development and education of children.[25] In other words, an analysis of the sexual life of a father or a mother and the consequences and repercussions for their child's life are always relevant. This is why the claim of the IACtHR that the privacy rights of the complainant were violated was unsubstantiated, since in the context of litigation over the custody of a child, there is no right to privacy regarding the life of a father or a mother. As a final matter, it is evident that this decision could lead to unequal treatment of heterosexual parents, who may be scrutinized in their sexual lives. Also, advocates could use such reasoning of the IAmCHR to advise their clients who are claiming custody of a child, to declare that he or she is homosexual, as an efficient way to prevent judicial scrutiny. For all these reasons creating such an immunity should never be acceptable to judges or legislators.

---

25. Separate Opinion of Commissioner Paolo G. Carozza, 2009, *Karen Atala and Daughters*, Case No. 12.502, Report No. 139/09, OEA/Ser/L/V/II, Doc. 50.

LGBTI Cases before the Commission

Other cases dealing with sexual orientation are moving through the Inter-American System. These cases may be organized as follows.

Other Cases Decided by the Inter-American Court

Some of the cases have already been decided by the Court. These cases concern the work environment as in the case received by the Commission, in 2002, where the responsibility of the Republic of Ecuador is in question. The facts are the following. From a disciplinary process Mr. Flor Freire, an officer from the equatorial Ground Forces, was dismissed in virtue of article 117 of the Regulation of Military Discipline, which provided that if an officer of the Armed Forces engaged in "homosexual acts" the officer would be discharged from service for "misconduct or for incompetence."[26] The Commission determined that the criteria used would have "ascribed a negative moral value to the sexual relationship between same sex people, and such would promote stigmatization against lesbian, gay and bisexual people."[27] Therefore, "regulatory sanctions for a certain group of people, for engaging in a consensual sexual act or practice with someone of the same sex," are not admissible "as this directly contravenes the prohibition of discrimination based on sexual orientation."[28] The Court once again considered whether sexual orientation must be respected and protected in a recent decision of 3 August 2016.[29]

Another case under consideration affects the family, personal and private spaces. In 2005, the Commission received a petition alleging that Mr. Duque was subjected to undue discrimination when he was denied the right to receive his deceased partner's pension based on their sexual orientation.[30] In this regard, the Commission determined that "the effects of the exclusion from the right to the survivor's pension of his deceased life partner, under a discriminatory provision based on sexual orientation" by the State constituted a violation of the "right to personal integrity embodied in Article 5.1 [of] the American Convention, in relation to the

---

26. Regulation of Military Discipline of the Armed Forces, Ecuador, 1998, article. no. 67.

27. Commission's Report No. 81/13, p. 31.

28. Ibid., 32.

29. Available at http://www.corteidh.or.cr/docs/casos/articulos/seriec_315_esp.pdf.

30. Acuerdo de Solución Amistosa, Caso P-946-12, 1–2, "Estado de Chile con Movilh."

obligation to respect rights under article 1.1 thereof, to the detriment of Ángel Alberto Duque."[31] This case was decided on 26 February 2016 by the Court reaffirming the protection of sexual orientation as a category protected by the Convention.[32]

Cases Completed by an Amicable Settlement

Similarly, an amicable settlement was arranged between the petitioner and the State of Chile in a case where a policewoman filed a complaint against the alleged victim, accusing her of having a lesbian relationship. In that case, the petitioner complained about "the excess in the performance of duties by the police authorities in charge of the investigation," causing an "interference with private and family life."[33] The petitioners argued that the State was responsible for the detrimental effect caused to the "honor and dignity of the alleged victim."[34] A similar amicable settlement has been arranged with Chile in a case where two couples wanted to celebrate a marriage although they were same sex. The State of Chile arrived at a settlement which included promises to present a year-long law project to introduce same-sex marriage in Chilean civil legislation.[35]

Cases before the Commission

In addition to the aforementioned cases, the Commission has ruled on the admission of two different cases regarding LGBTI issues, without prejudice to the merits of each case. In 1996, the Commission received a petition against the Republic of Colombia alleging that the petitioner's "personal integrity, honor and equality" were being violated by the refusal of prison authorities to authorize intimate visits with her lesbian partner on the basis of "their sexual orientation."[36] In another case, the Republic of Peru was alleged to have been responsible for the illegal and arbitrary detention of a

---

31. Commission's Report No.5/14, 29.

32. Available at http://www.corteidh.or.cr/cf/Jurisprudencia2/busqueda_casos_contenciosos.cfm?lang=eshttp://www.corteidh.or.cr/cf/Jurisprudencia2/busqueda_casos_contenciosos.cfm?lang=es.

33. Commission's Report No. 81/09, para. 2.

34. Ibid., para. 2.

35. Acuerdo de Solución Amistosa, Caso P-946-12, 1–2, "Estado de Chile con Movilh."

36. Commission's Report No.71/99, 1.

man, who was "subject to sexual violence while being under police custody and torture, motivated by his sexual orientation."[37]

The Legislative Approach

Let us now move from a consideration of the judicial approach to the legislative method for promotion of sexual orientation.

Sexual Orientation and Non-discrimination in the Law

In countries with a Roman-Germanic legal tradition, another way that has been used to include the category of sexual orientation has been through reforms to Constitutions or laws. In the past few years, three countries have passed constitutional reforms in order to include the concept of sexual orientation or "sexual preference" into law (e.g. Mexico) or have approved new Constitutions that recognize such a concept (e.g., Equator and Bolivia). For example, in Bolivia, the Constitution provides: "the State forbids and sanctions all forms of discrimination based on sex, color, age, sexual orientation, gender identity."[38] Similarly, the "Law Against Racism and all Types of Discrimination" include the terms "sexual orientation" and "gender identity" in the definition of discrimination.[39]

Sixteen countries have passed "non-discrimination laws" that extends the suspect categories in order to include "sexual orientation" or "sexual preferences." In the case of Mexico, the category of "sexual preferences"[40] has been the motive for "non-discrimination laws" and in Chile, the terms "sexual orientation" and "gender identity."[41] In Argentina, the sexual orientation issue has been regulated in two normative bodies. In 2010, the Senate and Chamber of Deputies of Argentina united in Congress and modified by the National Law N° 26.618, article 172 of the Argentinian Civil Code

---

37. Commission's Report No.99/14, Petition N°.406-09, 1.

38. Article 14 of the Political Constitution of the Plurinational State of Bolivia, 2009, available at http://www.boliviasites.com/ncpe2/index.php/78-primera-parte.

39. Law against Racism and all kinds of Discrimination No.045, 2010, article No.5, available at http://www.noracismo.gob.bo/index.php/leyes-y-normativas/122-ley-n-045-contra-el-racismo-y-toda-forma-de-discriminacion.

40. Social and Political Constitution of México, 1917, article No.1. available at http://www.diputados.gob.mx/LeyesBiblio/htm/1.htm. See also: Federal Law to Prevent and Eliminate Discrimination, 2003, article 1, available at http://www.diputados.gob.mx/LeyesBiblio/pdf/262.pdf.

41. Law No.20.609, 2012, article No.2.

stating that "marriage will have the same requirements and effects, regardless of whether the spouses are of the same or different sex."[42] In addition, the Gender Identity Law N° 26.743[43] allows persons with a different sexual orientation to request a rectification of sex, and the change of name and image in personal documents among other things. In Honduras, a recent modification to the criminal code has been approved which includes "sexual orientation" and "gender identity"[44] as aggravating factors in crimes and in the Dominican Republic its General Law of Youth recognizes "sexual orientation" as one of the categories to be developed in order to promote the integral development of young men and women.[45] In this regard, Uruguay has included in the definition of discrimination contained in Law N° 17.817, the concepts of "sexual orientation" and "sexual identity."[46]

In contrast, some countries may not rely upon a specific category of sexual orientation, for example, the Brazilian Federal Constitution uses the formulation "any other form of discrimination."[47] In the 1982 Canadian Charter of Rights and Freedoms there are provisions regarding equality and equal protection before and under the law.[48] The Colombian Constitution follows a similar line by stating "all persons are born free and equal before the law [. . .]."[49] The United States[50] and Cuba[51] also use an equality before the law provision. In most of these laws, while there is no definition of the category of sexual orientation, one may nonetheless enjoy broad protection

42. National Law, No.26.618, 2010, available at http://servicios.infoleg.gob.ar/infolegInternet/anexos/165000-169999/169608/norma.htm.

43. Gender Identity Law No.26.747, 2012, available at http://servicios.infoleg.gob.ar/infolegInternet/anexos/195000-199999/197860/norma.htm.

44. "Honduras approves a reform of the Criminal Code to end the violation of human rights based on sexual orientation and gender identity" ONUSIDA, April 5, 2013, available at http://www.unaids.org/es/resources/presscentre/featurestories/2013/april/20130405honduras/.

45. Law No.49-2000, 2000, article No.2.

46. Law No. 17.817, 2004, article No.2.

47. Federative Constitution of Brazil, 1988, article No.3, available at http://seotest.ciberius.info/seo—pdba.georgetown.edu/Constitutions/Brazil/esp88.html.

48. Canadian Charter of Rights and Freedoms, 1982, article No. 15, available at http://laws-lois.justice.gc.ca/eng/Const/page-15.html.

49. Political Constitution of Colombia, 1991, article No. 13, available at http://www.procuraduria.gov.co/guiamp/media/file/Macroproceso%20Disciplinario/Constitucion_Politica_de_Colombia.htm.

50. United States Constitution, 14th Amendment, available at https://www.law.cornell.edu/constitution/amendmentxiv.

51. Constitution of the Cuban Republic, 1940, articles Nos. 41, 42, available at http://www.cuba.cu/gobierno/cuba.htm.

to the same extent, for example, as religious freedom, freedom of conscience, and freedom of expression. Although, such reforms are relevant to the legal system of the particular country, there has been little legal analysis of this category and the problems associated with its recognition, for example, in specific regard to religious freedom. Unfortunately, there are few serious articles written by scholars; most of the literature is generated by NGOs as a form of advocacy for specific lobbying interests.

Conclusion

At the time this essay was written, only recently had the Inter-American system recognized sexual orientation as a suspect category and only recently, had it been promoted in the countries forming part of this system. The highest level of promotion came with the *Atala* decision of the Inter-American Court, when starting, in 2012, all cases concerning "sexual orientation" will now bypass the normal procedure as a *per saltum* proceeding,[52] which means that a lot more cases will be decided in the upcoming years along the same lines, and without any originality from the ones that have been presented and decided at the European Court or any of the Courts of the Countries. Indeed, what we can see in the recent decisions of the Court is reaffirmation of this category of protection. One can expect that similar cases will be filed by NGOs, with arguments that follow the same line of thought and we can expect them to have not only the same, but even a larger acceptance before Inter-American Court. Therefore, in such circumstances an enormous effort will be needed to preserve the common sense understanding of the family and respect for the dignity and beliefs of all persons.

Bibliography

Alvaro, Paul. "Examining Atala-Riffo and Daughters v. Chile, the First Inter-American Case of Sexual Orientation, and Some of its Implications." *Inter-American and European Human Rights Journal* 7:1–2 (2014) 54–74.
Canadian Charter of Rights and Freedoms, 1982, article No. 15. http://laws-lois.justice.gc.ca/eng/Const/page-15.html.
Constitution of the Cuban Republic, 1940, articles Nos. 41, 42. http://www.cuba.cu/gobierno/cuba.htm.
Federative Constitution of Brazil, 1988, article No.3. http://seotest.ciberius.info/seo—pdba.georgetown.edu/Constitutions/Brazil/esp88.html.

52. *Per saltum* proceedings allows the Commission to do the initial review of a case immediately after its presentation and reception, skipping the chronological order of intervention of the courts of first or second instance that is due in the normal procedure.

Political Constitution of the Plurinational State of Bolivia, 2009. http://www.boliviasites.com/ncpe2/index.php/78-primera-parte.

Political Constitution of Colombia, 1991, article No. 13. http://www.procuraduria.gov.co/guiamp/media/file/Macroproceso%20Disciplinario/Constitucion_Politica_de_Colombia.htm.

Social and Political Constitution of México, 1917, article No.1. http://www.diputados.gob.mx/LeyesBiblio/htm/1.htm.

United States Constitution, 14th Amendment. https://www.law.cornell.edu/constitution/amendmentxiv.

Chapter 9

Equality and Non-discrimination
The Peculiar Approach of the American Convention on Human Rights

URSULA C. BASSET

THE 1969 AMERICAN CONVENTION on Human Rights (ACHR) has a number of provisions concerning non-discrimination.[1] Many of them are similar to other regional systems or to provisions in other treaties within the universal system of human rights. At the time the ACHR was drafted, the European Convention and the Universal Declaration of Human Rights were already in force and the 1966 International Covenant on Civil and Political Rights and the 1966 International Covenant on Economic, Social and Cultural Rights had been completed. Notwithstanding these instruments, the ACHR has its own identity within the Inter-American system of human rights, which has a unique approach to humanity, quite distinctive from any other regional human rights system, and for a number of reasons.

One, the ACHR is the only human rights instrument in the world to protect life from the moment of conception, in such a radical manner.[2] As a matter of fact, this happens to be a non-discrimination clause, if it is understood within the context of Art. 1 of the ACHR (see the discussion *infra*), for which the universal recognition of personhood of every

---

1. For a general description of the Inter-American legal system see: De Martini, "El sistema interamericano," 1166. With the same treaty see: Zayat, "El principio de igualdad," 903. For a more general presentation see: Alston and Goodman, *International Human Rights*. For a Commentary see: Burgorgue-Larsen and Ubeda de Torres, *Inter-American Court of Human Rights*.

2. De Jesús et al., "El Caso Artavia Murillo," 75.

human being is an ontological clause, a clause that precedes any positive legal recognition by State parties, a mandate that stems from the "essential oneness and dignity of humankind."[3] Article 4 (1) of the ACHR states that "Every person has the right to have his life respected. This right shall be protected by law and, in general, from the moment of conception. No one shall be arbitrarily deprived of his life."

Two, it is original in the great value ascribed to the family, the protection of the family, and the right to family life. Nothing similar can be found in international human rights treaties, nor regional ones. Therefore, discrimination within family life or discrimination of the family itself is quite different from other regional human rights systems. According to the ACHR, the family is an institution deserving protection with duties to society and its vulnerable members, but it is also an institution for which society and family members are responsible. Compared to the European human rights system, where family life is mostly linked to the rights of the individuals, the ACHR has a completely different framework to deal with discrimination issues related to family life and children have a privileged status as right holders.

Three, Latin America is a cradle of innumerable and various forms of vulnerabilities. Classical discriminatory categories are insufficient. The Latin American experience has real issues relating to poverty, indigenous communities, immigration (an issue now shared dramatically with Europe), dictatorships, or abusive conduct of the State. The Inter-American Court of Human Rights (IACtHR) has developed a rich sensitivity to the various faces of vulnerability, providing fresh views on disadvantages that might bear subtle forms of discrimination if not corrected. This is why the case law and advisory opinions of the IACtHR have established the concept of "protective distinctions," a mandate to discriminate in order to protect the vulnerable. It constitutes a sort of positive discrimination, but of a kind that transmits a deep sense of humanity and empathy towards those who need support.

Finally, the Inter-American system is not without contradictions. Such a rich and deeply humane perspective on discrimination collides with different cultural views on human rights and clashes between the many rights stemming from litigation. Even so, the Inter-American identity and approach to human rights deserves to be credited for its commitment to humanity in every stage of human development with respect for the relational

---

3. Advisory Opinion 17/02, August 28, 2002, on the "Legal Status and Human Rights of the Child," para. 47; and Advisory Opinion 4/84. January 19, 1984 on the "Proposed Amendments to the Naturalization Provisions of the Constitution of Costa Rica," para. 57.

and social nature of the human person and his or her weaknesses. Let us now turn to a discussion of non-discrimination within the Inter-American system of human rights.

The Two General Clauses on Non-discrimination

The American Convention on Human Rights addresses non-discrimination in two different articles. Article 1 on the "Obligation to Respect Rights" provides:

> "1. The States Parties to this Convention undertake to respect the rights and freedoms recognized herein and to ensure to all persons subject to their jurisdiction the free and full exercise of those rights and freedoms, without any discrimination for reasons of race, color, sex, language, religion, political or other opinion, national or social origin, economic status, birth, or any other social condition. 2. For the purposes of this Convention, "person" means every human being."

Article 24 on the "Right to Equal Protection" states: "All persons are equal before the law. Consequently, they are entitled, without discrimination, to equal protection of the law." The questions raised are the following: whether the two clauses are complementary? Whether these provisions are redundant, or rather target different forms of discrimination?

Multiple non-discrimination clauses exist in international treaties such as the 1948 Universal Declaration of Human Rights (UDHR). Both articles 1 and 2 deal with equality and non-discrimination and are correlated, the former article is a positive affirmation of equality,[4] while the latter prohibits all kinds of discrimination derived from the equality clause.[5] Then, article 7 applies the general equality and non-discrimination clauses, when it deals with equality before the law.[6] It could be said that articles 1

---

4. Universal Declaration of Human Rights (UDHR), article 1 ("All human beings are born free and equal in dignity and rights. They are endowed with reason and conscience and should act towards one another in a spirit of brotherhood").

5. Ibid. ("Everyone is entitled to all the rights and freedoms set forth in this Declaration, without distinction of any kind, such as race, colour, sex, language, religion, political or other opinion, national or social origin, property, birth or other status. Furthermore, no distinction shall be made on the basis of the political, jurisdictional or international status of the country or territory to which a person belongs, whether it be independent, trust, non-self-governing or under any other limitation of sovereignty").

6. Ibid., ("All are equal before the law and are entitled without any discrimination to equal protection of the law. All are entitled to equal protection against any discrimination in violation of this Declaration and against any incitement to such discrimination").

and 2 are general enunciations of equality and non-discrimination, while article 7 applies the principles to concrete situation, namely every human being before the law.

In contrast, the ACHR does not have a general equality clause similar to that of article 1 in the UDHR.[7] Rather, article 1 of the ACHR deals directly with non-discrimination, while article 24 treats equality before the law as a species of equality, which, in this author's view, should be addressed separately. Both rules, articles 1 and 24, are of a general nature.[8] Article 1 specifies the grounds of prohibited discrimination and article 24 treats equality in a positive manner. It is noteworthy that article 1 of ACHR is the gateway to the treaty densely worded with obligations of State parties to respect rights, to prohibit all forms of discrimination, and to acknowledge the personhood of every human being. Thus, the point of departure in article 1 of ACHR is a peculiar mix of the duty to respect rights, to respect non-discrimination, and to recognize personhood - as a fundamental and unifying criterion of equality. Placed at the beginning of the ACHR, the reader cannot enter into the human rights system without crossing the portico of equal personhood.

This last point is significant, when one considers other international human rights treaties. In the UDHR, one must wait until article 6 to find the following provision: "[e]veryone has the right to recognition everywhere as a person before the law." But, in the ACHR the very key to equality is the right to personhood. Even the wording differs when it comes to personhood. While Art. 6 of UDHR refers to equality before the law and the right to universal recognition of personhood, article 1 of ACHR is more radical. Every human being is a person, without limitation, before any positive or human laws and before any other right. And this approach to human rights, to humanity, to personhood, is a distinctive feature of the ACHR.

In 1982, the IACtHR, the main interpreting body of the American System of Human Rights, gave an Advisory Opinion which provided:

> "The notion of equality springs directly from the oneness of the human family and is linked to the essential dignity of the individual. That principle cannot be reconciled with the notion that a given group has the right to privileged treatment because of its perceived superiority. It is equally irreconcilable with that notion to characterize a group as inferior and treat it with hostility or otherwise subject it to discrimination in the enjoyment of rights which are accorded to others not so classified. It is impermissible

---

7. See note 4, *supra*.
8. Moeckli et al., *International Human Rights Law*, 163.

to subject human beings to differences in treatment that are inconsistent with their unique and cogenerous character."[9]

There is some uncertainty on how to interpret Art. 1 and Art. 24 ACHR. The Court provides the following interpretation:

"Article 1(1) of the Convention, a rule general in scope which applies to all the provisions of the treaty, imposes on the States Parties the obligation to respect and guarantee the free and full exercise of the rights and freedoms recognized therein "without any discrimination. In other words, regardless of its origin or the form it may assume, any treatment that can be considered to be discriminatory with regard to the exercise of any of the rights guaranteed under the Convention is per se incompatible with that instrument [. . .] Although Articles 24 and 1 (1) are conceptually not identical [. . .] Article 24 restates to a certain degree the principle established in Article 1(1). In recognizing equality before the law, it prohibits all discriminatory treatment originating in a legal prescription. The prohibition against discrimination so broadly proclaimed in Article 1(1) with regard to the rights and guarantees enumerated in the Convention thus extends to the domestic law of the States Parties, permitting the conclusion that in these provisions the States Parties, by acceding to the Convention, have undertaken to maintain their laws free of discriminatory regulations."[10]

The scope of Article 1 (1) is general and applicable to any provision of the Treaty. This means that the same provision can be read in conjunction with any other article, because any other clause could eventually be applied in a discriminatory way. Article 24 restates article 1 recognizing equality, but is limited to equality before any legal provision in the positive law of each State party.

---

9. Advisory Opinion OC-4/84 of January 19, 1984, para. 55.

10. Ibid., paras. 53–54. *See also: Corte IDH. Caso Comunidad Indígena Xákmok Kásek Vs. Paraguay.* Fondo, Reparaciones y Costas. Sentencia de 24 de agosto de 2010. Serie C No. 214, Párrafo 272: "Ahora bien, refiriéndose a los artículos 1.1 y 24 de la Convención la Corte ha indicado que "la diferencia entre los dos artículos radica en que la obligación general del artículo 1.1 se refiere al deber del Estado de respetar y garantizar 'sin discriminación' los derechos contenidos en la Convención Americana[. E]n otras palabras, si un Estado discrimina en el respeto o garantía de un derecho convencional, violaría el artículo 1.1 y el derecho sustantivo en cuestión. Si por el contrario la discriminación se refiere a una protección desigual de la ley interna, violaría el artículo 24" and *Caso Apitz Barbera y otros ("Corte Primera de lo Contencioso Administrativo") Vs. Venezuela.* Excepción Preliminar, Fondo, Reparaciones y Costas. Sentencia de 5 de agosto de 2008. Serie C No. 182, párr. 209.

Compare this to other regional systems. The 1950 "European Convention of Human Rights" (ECHR) does not commence with a general clause concerning non-discrimination, rather such a provisions is found later in article 14.[11] The 2000 "Charter of Fundamental Rights of the European Union" (CFR), on the other hand, provides a whole chapter on discrimination, namely "Title III," containing five articles, thus showing how the issue of discrimination has increased in significance over fifty years. The 1981 "African Charter of Human Rights" (AChHR) addresses non-discrimination and equality in Art. 2 and 3. None of the two regional instruments contain a provision concerning the universal recognition of personhood of every human being.

Returning to the Advisory Opinion of IACtHR, complementary with what has been cited above, the same advisory opinion set out certain rules for the purposes of discerning between justified difference of treatment and unjust discrimination:

> "Accordingly, no discrimination exists if the difference in treatment has a legitimate purpose and if it does not lead to situations which are contrary to justice, to reason or to the nature of things. It follows that there would be no discrimination in differences in treatment of individuals by a state when the classifications selected are based on substantial factual differences and there exists a reasonable relationship of proportionality between these differences and the aims of the legal rule under review. These aims may not be unjust or unreasonable, that is, they may not be arbitrary, capricious, despotic or in conflict with the essential oneness and dignity of humankind."[12]

In sum, a number of criteria are expected to be met, in order to apply the standard of justified difference of treatment: a) when the treatment has a legitimate purpose; b) when it does not lead to situations contrary to justice, reason or nature of things; b) when the classifications are based on substantial factual differences; c) when there is a reasonable relationship of proportionality between differences and aims of the legal rule. Based on this rationale, in the Advisory Opinion, under consideration, the Court found that discrimination based on age in the case of a minor who is not able to exert his or her legal capacity are protective measures because of the special vulnerabilities of minors.[13]

---

11. Espiell, *La Convención Americana*, 70.
12. Advisory Opinion, *supra* note 9, para. 57.
13. Ibid., para. 56 ("There may well exist certain factual inequalities that might legitimately give rise to inequalities in legal treatment that do not violate principles of justice. They may in fact be instrumental in achieving justice or in protecting those who

Equality and the "Rights of the Family"

As a corollary to the unique approach of the American human rights system to personhood, the ACHR contains several articles addressing family life and most notably "the rights of the Family" (the very title of the article). The family is treated as an institution with sufficient stability and consistency so as to be ascribed with a number of rights, at least in the title of the very specific provisions found in article 17 (1): "The family is the natural and fundamental group unit of society and is entitled to protection by society and the state."[14] The contents of article 17 does not flesh out what it means for the family to be a rights-holder.[15] However, it is evident that the family is a reality individuals have a right to and one that needs protection by the State. It is noteworthy that ACHR article 17 (1) is identical to UDHR art. 16 (3).

However, the ACHR conveys a strong sense of family evident in the articulation of other human rights. For example, the family appears in several provisions of the ACHR, namely article 11 on private family life; article 17 on rights of the family; article 19 on rights of the child and duties of the family, society and the State; article 27 which cannot suspend such rights in times of emergency; article 32 on the relationship between rights and duties and that everyone has a duty to his or her family; articles 19, 27 and 32 all deal with the family as rights holder before the State subject to special treatment. This treatment of the family as a fundamental unit of society requiring special treatment is unique.

In addition, the IACtHR has frequently referred to breaches of the right of family life in cases involving State intervention causing an

---

find themselves in a weak legal position. For example, it cannot be deemed discrimination on the grounds of age or social status for the law to impose limits on the legal capacity of minors or mentally incompetent persons who lack the capacity to protect their interests").

14. United Nations, *Family in International*, 5.

15. American Convention on Human Rights art. 17, entitled "Rights of the Family" (1. The family is the natural and fundamental group unit of society and is entitled to protection by society and the state. 2. The right of men and women of marriageable age to marry and to raise a family shall be recognized, if they meet the conditions required by domestic laws, insofar as such conditions do not affect the principle of non-discrimination established in this Convention. 3. No marriage shall be entered into without the free and full consent of the intending spouses. 4. The States Parties shall take appropriate steps to ensure the equality of rights and the adequate balancing of responsibilities of the spouses as to marriage, during marriage, and in the event of its dissolution. In case of dissolution, provision shall be made for the necessary protection of any children solely on the basis of their own best interests. 5. The law shall recognize equal rights for children born out of wedlock and those born in wedlock").

individual to lose his or her family life, such as cases involving enforced disappearances for political reasons. The IACtHR has equally condemned breaches of the right of privacy, right to life, right to human integrity and violations of family life.[16] In this way, the Court has promoted a ubiquitous conception of family life.

Similar to other international human rights treaties, non-discrimination issues in relation to family life arise in a twofold manner. Before the beginning of family life, there is a right to marry. Once there is an existing family life, there is a right to equality within family relations. As to the former, the right to marry should not be subject to any kind of discrimination. Every international treaty has a clause granting contracting parties equal access. However, the right to marry is the only right dealt with from the perspective of the sexes, male and female. The phraseology in the UDHR is noteworthy: article 16 (1) provides: "Men and women of full age, without any limitation due to race, nationality or religion, have the right to marry and to found a family. They are entitled to equal rights as to marriage, during marriage and at its dissolution." Article 17 (2) of ACHR has a slightly different wording, but largely similar: "The right of men and women of marriageable age to marry and to raise a family shall be recognized, if they meet the conditions required by domestic laws, insofar as such conditions do not affect the principle of non-discrimination established in this Convention." In terms of the ACHR, one might argue that family life might be created through marriage, but also through other means.

It worth emphasizing that the right to marry within the ACHR is the only right in which the sex of the contracting parties is relevant.[17] Aside from marriage and the right to raise a family, there is no other provision in which the difference of the sexes is relevant.[18] All provisions are written in

---

16. See for instance: *Corte IDH. Caso Chitay Nech y otros vs. Guatemala*. Excepciones Preliminares, Fondo, Reparaciones y Costas. Sentencia de 25 de mayo de 2010. Serie C No. 212, Párr. 161. *Corte IDH. Caso Gudiel Álvarez (Diario Militar) vs. Guatemala*. Fondo Reparaciones y Costas. Sentencia de 20 noviembre de 2012 Serie C No. 253, Párr. 312. *Corte IDH. Caso Norín Catrimán y otros (Dirigentes, miembros y activista del Pueblo Indígena Mapuche) vs. Chile*. Fondo, Reparaciones y Costas. Sentencia de 29 de mayo de 2014. Serie C No. 279, Párr. 404.

17. With the reasonable exception concerning the prohibition of trafficking in women (Art. 6) and the application of capital punishment to pregnant women (Art. 3). Both of these provisions underline the peculiar vulnerability of women when it comes to certain forms of slavery, on the one hand, and pregnancy, on the other hand, which is related to family life.

18. See e. g. UDHR, art. 16 (1); See also the International Covenant on Civil and Political Rights (1966), Art. 23 (2). ACHR, 17 (2).

a neutral manner, often commencing with the terms "every person" or "no one." This fact underlines the very nature of the family.

Once the family is founded, international treaties seek to protect equality within family relations. Since the legal positions and vulnerabilities of family members are divergent, there is a need for equalizing rules in order to protect vulnerable family members. In the case of *María Eugenia Morale de Sierra vs. Guatemala,* the Inter-American Commission held that imbalances between family members have to be corrected.

> "The Commission finds that, far from ensuring the "equality of rights and adequate balancing of responsibilities" within marriage, the cited provisions institutionalize imbalances in the rights and duties of the spouses. (. . .) Moreover, the dispositions of the Civil Code apply stereotyped notions of the roles of women and men which perpetuate de facto discrimination against women in the family sphere, and which have the further effect of impeding the ability of men to fully develop their roles within the marriage and family. The articles at issue create imbalances in family life, inhibiting the role of men with respect to the home and children, and in that sense depriving children of the full and equal attention of both parents."[19]

Such adjustments in family imbalances must be corrected by legal means through the internal laws of State parties.

Yet, ACHR is unique in another respect. As with other international treaties, the ACHR in article 17 (4) provides for the equality of rights and responsibilities of the spouses "as to marriage, during marriage." But then it adds, " . . . and in the event of its dissolution. In case of dissolution, provision shall be made for the necessary protection of any children solely on the basis of their own best interests." Thereafter, the provision in article 17 (5) states: "The law shall recognize equal rights for children born out of wedlock and those born in wedlock." Art. 19 follows in providing that "every minor child has the right to the measures of protection required by his condition as a minor on the part of his family, society, and the state." In sum, the legal position of children and their protection within the constellation of family relations is recognized and protected.

Contrast the ACHR treatment of the rights of the child with the 1989 International Convention on the Rights of the Child (CRC) and the missing language with respect to the equal protection and consideration of the child within family relations. The ACHR clearly places the interest of the

---

19. *María Eugenia Morales de Sierra vs. Guatemala* Case 11.625, 19/01/2001, para. 44.

child as the "sole basis" in order to determine the measures to be taken in case of marriage dissolution. To say that the interest of the child is the sole basis excludes any other criteria and expresses a prevalence for the rights of the child when compared to any other vulnerable person within the family. Protective measures are a form of correction of inequalities in the case of vulnerabilities within the family.

> "There are certain factual inequalities that may be legitimately translated into inequalities of juridical treatment, without this being contrary to justice. Furthermore, said distinctions may be an instrument for the protection of those who must be protected, taking into consideration the situation of greater or lesser weakness or helplessness in which they find themselves."[20]

The equalization of children born in and out of wedlock and protection of motherhood are provided for in several other international human rights treaties.[21] It ensures the avoidance of any form of formal discrimination against children regardless of the context in which they are born. The irrelevance of marriage when it comes to the rights of children is merely formal, because there is a difference between in the status of children born in and out of wedlock. Legislation has rules to establish parenthood, custody and care and other issues of family life, which are usually more precarious when children are born out of wedlock. Therefore, the equality clause in this case is more of an aspiration, than a reality. In any case, the concern for children evokes a third concept in non-discrimination laws: "the protective distinction," another exceptional view on equality propitiated by the case law of the IACtHR.

The "Protective Distinctions"

Equality means not only the prohibition of unjust discrimination but also the correction of inequalities, when, in cases of vulnerable persons, the law

20. Advisory Opinion OC-17/2002 of August 28, 2002, requested by the Inter-American Commission on Human Rights Juridical Condition and Human Rights of the Child.

21. In the case *Forneron v. Argentina* 27 April 2012, para. 50, the IACtHR held: "(. . .) in cases concerning the care and custody of minors, the determination of the best interests of the child must be made based on an evaluation of the specific conduct of the parents and its negative impact on the well-being and development of the child, if applicable, or on the real and proved, not speculative or imaginary, harm or risk to the well-being of the child. Thus, speculations, presumptions, stereotypes, generalized considerations on the personal characteristics of the parents, or cultural preferences regarding traditional concepts of the family are inadmissible."

seeks to correct the application of human rights for protective purposes. The protective discrimination standard does not stem from the wording of the ACHR, but from the case law of the IACtHR. It has been applied to undocumented migrants, children, adolescents, adolescents self-defining as homosexual, persons with disabilities, indigenous people, people impaired by their socio-economic conditions, racial conditions and women. In specific regard to the standard, the Advisory Opinion 18/03 of the IACtHR states:

> "Distinctions based on de facto inequalities may be established; such distinctions constitute an instrument for the protection of those who should be protected, considering their situation of greater or lesser weakness or helplessness. For example, the fact that minors who are detained in a prison may not be imprisoned together with adults who are also detained is an inequality permitted by law." [22]

As regards women, the Inter-American Commission of Human Rights (IACHR) in the case of *Maria Eugenia de Sierra Morales de Sierra* underlined how the vulnerability of women should be corrected by internal laws of the States:

> "A half of the population was subordinated to the other half (. . .) The gender-based distinctions under study have been upheld as a matter of domestic law essentially on the basis of the need for certainty and juridical security, the need to protect the marital home and children, respect for traditional Guatemalan values, and in certain cases, the need to protect women in their capacity as wives and mothers. (. . .) By requiring married women to depend on their husbands to represent the union–in this case María Eugenia Morales de Sierra–the terms of the Civil Code mandate a system in which the ability of approximately half the married population to act on a range of essential matters is subordinated to the will of the other half."[23]

Protective distinctions are a response to the IACtHR cases in which an indirect discrimination[24] has occurred. Consider, for example, protective distinctions in order to protect: handicapped persons;[25] indigenous

---

22. Advisory Opinion 18/03, para. 89

23. *María Eugenia Morales de Sierra v. Guatemala*, Case 11.625, 19-01-2001, paras. 37–38.

24. For the concept of indirect discrimination see Fredman, *Discrimination Law*, 261.

25. *Ximenes Lopes vs. Brazil*, 4 July 2005, paras. 103–4.

communities that risk losing their cultural traditions;[26] women in their relationships with men.[27] In the case of the *Massacre of Mapiripán v. Colombia* the IACtHR held that there was a disproportionate impact on the human rights of women, in charge of households as well as girls, boys and elderly people.[28] Some additional facts in need of correction in order to attain equality, included remedying the impossibility of persons to use their mother tongue in legal processes.[29] The Court held that discrimination could occur for *jure or de facto* reasons,[30] and that Court was obliged to choose the norm "that protects human persons better."[31]

The Contradictions

Even if the ACHR has remarkable and harmonious standards on the issue of equality and non-discrimination, the application of these standards, in case law, has been controversial and contradictory. Perhaps, the two most salient contradictions in the latest case law of the IACtHR. are the cases of *Artavia Murillo v. Costa Rica* and *Atala Riffo v. Chile*. While this paper has provided citations to very "Latin-American" problems such as enforced disappearances, massacres, tragedies, baby trafficking, immigration and so forth, these two cases could be described as more European or North-American. *Artavia* deals with artificial reproductive techniques, while *Atala* treats the issue of sexual orientation. Undoubtedly, we are dealing with human suffering. However, these two cases are not representative of the Latin American humanistic case law characterized by a sense of urgency to end societal tragedies mentioned above.

---

26. *Pueblo Saramaka vs. Suriname*, 28 November 2007, para. 166.

27. *Penal Miguel Castro v. Peru*, 25 November 2005, 223–24. In this case, among many others, certain characteristics of women are addressed, such as their special notion of modesty.

28. *Mapiripán Massacre v. Colombia*, reparations and costs, Inter-Am. Ct. H.R., Series C No. 134 (Sept. 15, 2005); IHRL 1518 (IACHR 2005), para. 175. ("The reasons for and expressions of the acute vulnerability of displaced persons have been characterized from various perspectives. Said vulnerability is reinforced by their rural origin and, in general, it especially affects women—who are heads of households and constitute more than half the displaced population—girls and boys, youths, and elderly persons.").

29. *López Álvarez v. Honduras*, 1 February 2006, para. 171.

30. Advisory Opinion 18/03, para. 103.

31. Ibid., para. 105. (The author has consulted the Spanish text: " . . . y de conformidad con la norma que mejor proteja a la persona humana"). The English translation lacks the richness in that it refers to the individual.

In *Artavia,* the Court did not hesitate to call the right to life a relative right,[32] in which the parental decision to conceive is put before the child's right to life. The Court went so far as to redefine "conception" (only in the case of children conceived by artificial reproductive techniques), creating thus a double standard: children possessing the right to life from the beginning of their biological existence versus children possessing the right to life depending upon the will of specialists or parents—only when children have been implanted are their lives protected. Similarly, in *Atala,* the Court held that the best interests of the child could not curtail the right to the privacy of adults, especially when it comes to living out one's sexual orientation.[33]

Conclusion

The purpose of this paper is to show how the Court has broken with longstanding traditions and the very identity of Latin American people grounded in coherent provisions related to family life, right to life, personhood, and non-discrimination. The two cases of *Artavia* and *Atala* introduced contradictory statements and claims infusing dissonance into an idyllic world of harmonies. The best example of this is when the Court, in its decisions, pitted children against parents and parents against children, thus creating new forms of discrimination in the spectrum of rights, especially for children.

Bibliography

Alston, Philip, and Ryan Goodman. *International Human Rights.* Oxford: Oxford University Press, 2012.
Burgorgue-Larsen, Laurence, and Amaya Ubeda de Torres. *The Inter-American Court of Human Rights: Case Law and Commentary.* Translated by Rosalind Greenstein. Oxford: Oxford University Press, 2011.
César, Julio, et al. *Tratado de los Derechos Constitucionales.* Vol. 3. Buenos Aires: Abeledo Perrot, 2014.
De Jesús, Ligia M., et al. "El caso Artavia Murillo y otros vs. Costa Rica (fecundación in vitro): la redefinición del derecho a la vida desde la concepción, reconocido en la Convención Americana." *Prudentia Iuris* 75 (2013) 135–64.

---

32. *Artavia Murillo v. Costa Rica,* November 28, 2012, para. 264 ("Moreover, it can be concluded from the words 'in general' that the protection of the right to life under this provision is not absolute, but rather gradual and incremental according to its development, since it is not an absolute and unconditional obligation, but entails understanding that exceptions to the general rule are admissible"). For further analysis see the authors in note 2, *supra.*

33. *Atala Riffo v. Chile,* February 24, 2012 paras. 132–40.

De Martini, Siro. "El sistema interamericano de derechos humanos." In *Tratado de los Derechos Constitucionales, Vol. III*, edited by Julio Césa Rivera et al., 1166–1228. Buenos Aires: Abeledo Perrot, 2014.

Fredman, Sandra. *Discrimination Law*. Oxford: Oxford University Press, 2012.

Gross Espiell, Héctor. *La Convención Americana y la Convención Europea de Derechos. Análisis Comparativo."* Santiago: Editorial Jurídica de Chile, 1991.

Moeckli, Daniel, et al. *International Human Rights Law*. Oxford: Oxford University Press, 2013.

United Nations. *The Family in International and Regional Human Rights Instruments 5*. New York: United Nations, 1999. https://searchworks.stanford.edu/view/4274577.

Zayat, Demián, "El principio de igualdad. Razonabilidad, categorías sospechosas, trato desigual e impacto desproporcionado." In *Tratado de los Derechos Constitucionales, Vol. I*, edited by Julio Césa Rivera et al., 903–27. Buenos Aires: Abeledo Perrot, 2014.

Chapter 10

ASEAN's Declaration of Human Rights (ADHR)
Clashing Cultural and Regional Values

D. BRIAN SCARNECCHIA

> "One fool throws a stone into a river and a thousand wise men can't get it out."
>
> (An old Hungarian proverb)

THE ASSOCIATION OF SOUTHEAST Asian Nations (ASEAN) has thrown cultural and regional relativism into the stream of universal human rights under the rubric of "Asian Values,"[1] formalized in the General Principles of its Declaration of Human Rights (ADHR).[2] What were they aiming at? What threats to national security and public order, health, safety, and morality were the drafters of the ADHR looking to meet by these provisos?

---

1. Desierto, "Universalizing Core Human Rights," 93–94, 114.

2. General Principle 6 requires that "human rights and fundamental freedoms must be balanced with the performance of corresponding duties . . . to all other individuals, the community and the society where one lives." General Principle 7 stipulates that "the realization of human rights must be considered in the regional and national context bearing in mind different political, economic, legal, social, cultural, historical and religious backgrounds." Moreover, General Principle 8 mandates that "the enjoyment of human rights and fundamental freedoms" shall be subject to the "the just requirements of national security, public order, public health, public safety, public morality as well as [to] the general welfare of the peoples in a democratic society." ASEAN Declaration of Human Rights, General Principles 6–8 (Nov. 9, 2012), http://www.mfa.go.th/asean/contents/files/other-20121217-165728-100439.pdf. (See infra Annex 2 for the full text of the ADHR).

Most commentators saw the ADHR references to religion, national security, and public morality as threatening the core principles of universal human rights. The UN High Commissioner for Human Rights called for the revision of the ADHR, lest it "undermine international standards."[3] The Coordination Committee of the Special Procedures of the Human Rights Council complained it failed to meet minimum human rights standards: "For the ASEAN human rights system to complement the work of the United Nations human rights system (. . .) it is imperative that, as a minimum, ASEAN's landmark human rights instrument maintains international human rights standards."[4] The European Union's High Representative warned it fell short of the principles articulated in the Universal Declaration of Human Rights: "I emphasize the need to ensure that implementation addresses adequately any problems of compatibility with international standards, notably the Universal Declaration of Human Rights and the relevant United Nations human rights treaties."[5] The United States Department of State concurred, and stated it was "deeply concerned that many of the ASEAN Declaration's principles and articles could weaken and erode universal human rights and fundamental freedoms as contained in the UDHR."[6]

Western/Northern Cultural and Regional Values

On the other hand, the explicit affirmation of regional values in the ADHR may be seen as a reaction to the imposition of Northern/Western cultural and regional values. Postmodern ideologues have corrupted the core principles of universal human rights articulated in the Universal Declaration of Human Rights (UDHR). Contraception, abortion, and sodomy have been introduced in many international soft and hard law documents under the guise of sexual and reproductive health/services/rights and gender mainstreaming. Now they hope to further embed these First World cultural and regional disvalues and misbehaviors into the stream of human rights as penumbras of the UDHR's principles of "equality" and "non-discrimination."[7]

---

3. Asian Forum for Human Rights and Development, *Still Window-Dressing* [hereinafter Forum-Asia, *Still Window Dressing*].

4. *Open Letter from the Coord. Comm. of the Special Procs. of the Hum. Rts.Council on the Draft ASEAN Hum. Rts. Decl.*, 16 Nov. 2012, in id. annex 47, at 160.

5. *Stmnt. by EU's High Rep. Catherine Ashton on the adoption of the ASEA Hum. Rts. Dec.*, in id. annex 44, at 153.

6. *Stmnt. by Victoria Nuland, Spokesperson of the U.S. Dept. of St., on the ASEAN Hum. Rts. Dec.*, 20 Nov. 2012, in id. annex 43, at 152.

7. In *Griswold v. Connecticut*, 381 U.S. 479, 484–485 (1965) the United States Supreme Court argued that the specific guarantees of the Bill of Rights of the Constitution

As in a game of billiards, ASEAN may be understood to have shot their own cultural and regional rights and national sovereignty into the stream of human rights in order to knock out of that stream Western/Northern cultural and regional rights to abortion and homosexual sodomy.[8] Persons self-identifying as Lesbian, Gay, Bisexual, Transgender, Intersexed, and Queer (LGBTIQ) activists criticized the ADHR for diverging from the universal and indivisible nature of human rights in the name of regional particularities, common values, and public morality, thereby hampering their project to deconstruct natural marriage.[9] The ASEAN LGBTIQ Caucus deplored the violation of the "principle of non-discrimination" in the ADHR which they interpret as including a right to homosexual sodomy:

> "All 10-members countries of ASEAN have ratified (. . .) (CEDAW=Convention on the Elimination of all Forms of Discrimination Against Women) and the (. . .) (CRC=Convention of the Rights of the Child), which have specific provisions of non-discrimination on the basis of sexual orientation and gender identity, and are therefore, obliged to protect and promote the rights of LGBTIQ people in the ASEAN region."[10]

The International Women's Rights Action Watch Asia Pacific warned that the ADHR would provide ASEAN member states with a pretense to "negatively impact women's human rights" while concealing this attack against women's liberty "under the protective shroud of culture and

---

of the United States were merely iterations of broader and more general rights. The right to privacy was one such broader more general right and that other specific iterations of this general right to privacy, such as the right of married couples to use contraceptive devices, were to be found within the penumbra of that general right and that the Supreme Court was charged to articulate these new iterations from time to time according to the changing needs of society. Also see *Roe v. Wade*, 410 U.S. 113, 152 (1973).

8. See Scarnecchia, "Human Rights in ASEAN," 62–85.

9. One LBGTIQ activist said, "Now, as I understand from a human rights perspective, particularism is not really welcome. Rights are universal. But now all these ASEAN common values are coming into the discussion, and they go against the concept of universality. And as someone who has actually studied language and culture in my country in Southeast Asia, I always question these common values. Whose common values are the [sic]? The common values are usually those of the leaders, of the politicians, of the religious leaders. But they are not the common values of the prostitutes, of the lesbian, gay, bisexual, transgender, intersex, or queer ("LGBTIQ") riff raff near the riverbanks. These ASEAN common values make me nervous because they are embedded in the text of the . . . Declaration" (Oetomo, "New Kids on the Block," 120).

10. Forum-Asia, *Still Window-Dressing*, annex 31, supra note 7, at 124.

traditions of the region which are patriarchal and anachronistic standards."[11] The ASEAN LGBTIQ Caucus was outraged for similar reasons: "This AHRD not only shows a lack of respect to LGBTIQ people but also makes a mockery of the international human rights[,] values[,] and principles that all nations and citizens abide by and are held accountable to."[12] International Women's Rights Action Watch Asia Pacific was also chagrined over the insertion of the public morality clause: "[H]istorically the notion of public morality has been used to deny and violate women's human rights to sexual autonomy and bodily integrity."[13] The Southeast Asian Woman's Caucus on ASEAN decried ASEAN's promotion of the natural family[14] which they claim represses women's autonomy and only serves to "reinforce women in their gendered roles as wives and mothers in a dichotomized world of 'private' and 'public' life."[15] They also criticized the ASEAN Declaration (1967) and the ASEAN Charter (2007) for adopting gender-neutral language, which failed to address women specifically or to include women for special consideration under the principles of non-discrimination and equality.[16] Moreover, the Caucus rejected ASEAN's characterization of women as simple "stereotyping"[17] that reflects patriarchal values and practices, rooted in religious and cultural norms, which discriminate against women.[18]

Good Use of the Sovereignty Clause

The International Commission of Jurists correctly pointed out that the broad and all-encompassing limitations of the sovereignty clause provision in General Principle 8 of the ADHR can quite easily be converted into a tool for political repression.[19] However, while the ADHR's cultural and regional

11. Forum-Asia, *Still Window-Dressing*, supra note 7, annex 35, at 133.

12. ASEAN LGBTIQ Caucus, "68 LGBT Groups and NGOs" para. 1. See also, Forum-Asia, *Still Window-Dressing*, annex 31, at 124.

13. Forum-Asia, *IWRAW-AP Statement on the AHRD* 21 November 2012, in Window Dressing, annex 35, supra note 7, at 134.

14. International Center for Not-for-Profit Law, "1997 ASEAN VISION 2020," under the heading "A Community of Caring Societies," 5. See also art. 19 of the ADHR, under "Civil and Political Right" affirms that the "family[,] as the natural and fundamental unit of society[,] is entitled to protection by society and each ASEAN Member State."

15. Prasertsri, *ASEAN Handbook for Women Rights Activities*, 44, [hereinafter ASEAN Handbook], supra n. 18, at 13.

16. Ibid., 17.

17. Ibid., 15.

18. Ibid., 46.

19. "The ASEAN Declaration extends the possibility of imposing limitations to

values provisions may provide cover for egregious human rights violations, they may also serve to protect authentic human rights.

Non-governmental organizations (NGOs) of Catholic inspiration routinely lobby UN delegates to include sovereignty clauses as a last line of defense when they have been unsuccessful in preventing language endorsing abortion and homosexual activity under the guise of sexual and reproductive rights or gender mainstreaming from being included in hard and soft law documents. For instance, Stefano Gennarini, Director of Legal Studies at Catholic Family and Human Rights Organization (C-Fam), said, "We do this every single time it comes up."[20] Sharron Slater, from Family Watch International and Stand for the Family, said: "We have worked very hard over the past years at [the Convention on Population and Development] CPD negotiations to get a paragraph adopted that recognizes national sovereignty and calls for respect of religious cultural values in implementing the CPD document[,] and have found success in several CPD sessions."[21] Doug Clark, from Family Policy Center, also confirmed the frequent use of this tactic when he states: "See paragraph 37 of the Children's Summit outcome ("A World Fit for Children") (. . . .) The language of paragraph 37 came after a long and protracted battle in which John Klink and Mike Dennis refused to give up."[22] Finally, Laura Miranda-Flefil from Alliance Defending Freedom, wrote: "It's been pushed by Malta for over 5 years and has been included every time."[23]

---

all rights, even those that are absolute under international law, such as freedom from torture and cruel, inhuman[,] and degrading treatment and punishment. Rather than applying a condition of strict necessity, General Principle 8 merely says that limitations have to be imposed for the purpose of meeting the 'just requirements' of national security and other purposes. The ASEAN Declaration, unlike the ICCPR, allows for limitation on the bases of 'general welfares of peoples in a democratic society.' This category is so broad that it could be interpreted to encompass almost all State activity." International Commission of Jurists. "ASEAN Human Rights Declaration," 8.

20. E-mail from Stefano Gennarini, director of legal studies, Catholic Family and Human Rights Organization (on file with author).

21. E-mail from Sharron Slater, President, Family Watch International and Stand for the Family (on file with author).

22. E-mail from Doug Clark, President, Family Policy Center (Feb. 14, 2015, 8:22 p.m. EST) (on file with author) referencing the following—"To achieve these goals and targets, taking into account the best interest of the child, consistent with national laws, religious and ethical values and cultural backgrounds of the people . . . " in G.A. Res. S-27/2, annex, *A World Fit for Children* para. 37 (May 10, 2002), http://www.un.org/en/ga/search/view_doc.asp?symbol=A/RES/S-27/2 .

23. E-mail from Miranda-Flefil, staff attorney, Alliance Defending Freedom (on file with author).

The sovereignty clause strategy of the pro-life and family coalition at the UN seems to be working. For instance, the Southeast Asia Women's Caucus on ASEAN lamented the inclusion of sovereignty clauses that will hinder women's rights in ASEAN:

> "Much disappointment has been expressed by civil society over the inclusion of the principles of sovereignty and non-interference in AICHR's TOR [ASEAN's Intgovn'tl Comm'n on Hum. Rts., Terms of Reference.]. These principles are often used by member states as an excuse or defense to avoid fulfilling their human rights obligations, which is detrimental to the promotion and protection of (. . .) women's rights."[24]

The experience of NGOs of Catholic inspiration and their opponents confirms that the insertion of sovereignty clauses in international hard-law and soft-law documents has been effective in blunting the advance of postmodern disvalues. It has helped protect the Developing World from the Developed World's big push to insert their own cultural and regional values, namely, sexual and reproductive rights and gender mainstreaming, into the main stream of universal human rights.

Conflicts of Law

All ten ASEAN member states have signed CEDAW, CRC and the CRPD (Convention on the Rights of Persons with Disabilities).[25] The American Bar Association Rule of Law Initiative strongly criticized the ADHR and insists that the Vienna Declaration and Program of Action (VDPA) obligates the states, as members of ASEAN, to uphold their treaty commitments, regardless of conflicting cultural values and customs.[26] They cite the Vienna Declaration and Program of Action in support:

> "All human rights are universal, indivisible, and interdependent and interrelated (. . . .) While the significance of national and regional particularities and various historical, cultural, and religious backgrounds must be borne in mind, it is the duty of States, regardless of their political, economic, and cultural systems, to promote and protect all human rights and fundamental freedoms."[27]

---

24. Prasertsri et al., *ASEAN Handbook for Women Rights Activities*, 44.

25. See Davies, "States of Compliance?," 419.

26. A.B.A. Rule of Law Initiative, The ASEAN Human Rights Declaration: A Legal Analysis 18 (2014) [hereinafter ASEAN Human Rights].

27. World Conference on Human Rights, "Vienna Declaration and Program of

Moreover, the ABA Rule of Law Institute argues that national laws cannot be used to shield states from their treaty obligations, citing the Vienna Convention Law of Treaties.[28] "CEDAW and the CRC particularly emphasize that states' parties have an overriding obligation to uphold the principles of non-discrimination and equality and protect the rights of women and children even in the face of contrary traditional attitudes . . . "[29]

Nevertheless, the International Commission of Jurists laments that the state members of ASEAN may treat the ADHR as their "primary standard" and so, "it is possible that they may disregard the universal standards, including hard legal obligations, when formulating their domestic law, policies and practices."[30] The recommendations offered below are made in the hope that the states members and peoples of ASEAN may better disregard First World cultural and regional dis-values while honouring authentic human rights.

First Recommendation—Sub-Regional Declarations

For ASEAN to take official action, all (ten) Member States must agree to act. In order to break a stalemate, sometimes two or more member states will form special agreements, usually for economic benefit, between themselves. "ASEAN-5" provides a good example.[31] On other occasions, all the nations of ASEAN will join with other non-ASEAN countries for cultural or trade purposes as in the case of "ASEAN + China, Japan and ROK" (aka ASEAN+3).[32]

Those nations that have inserted sovereignty clauses into UN outcome documents or as reservations in multilateral treaties might agree to reaffirm their reservations in a stand-alone sub-regional declaration similar to the ASEAN-5 or ASEAN+ 3 in order to safeguard their longstanding traditions and cultural values not inconsistent with the UDHR. In this way, they may more effectively defeat the cultural imperialism of

---

Action," para. 5.

28. Association of Southeast Asia Nations, "ASEAN Declaration on Human Rights," supra note 30, at 18, citing VCLT, art. 27.

29. Ibid., 18.

30. International Commission of Jurists, "ASEAN Human Rights Declaration," 10.

31. See Song, "Why 5 ASEAN Countries Combined," *Investing.com*, 5 March 2014; See also Fadillah, "RI Investment the Highest in ASEAN-5 Countries," *The Jakarta Post*, 2 March 2011.

32. See H. E. Li Keqiang, Premier of the State Council of the People's Republic of China, *Remarks at the 17th ASEAN Plus China, Japan and ROK Summit*, Nay Pyi Taw, Myanmar, 13 November 2014.

the post-modern West. Taking the UDHR as their standard, they would ensure that any human rights added to the core provisions annunciated in the UDHR would be truly "value plus" in that they are 1) consistent with the UDHR as those terms were understood at the time it was drafted and 2) are also consistent with the long-standing traditions of their people that are not incompatible with the UDHR. (*See* Annex 1—Manifesto of Core Political and Cultural Rights).

Second Recommendation—Public Trust Litigation

NGOs of Catholic inspiration might borrow from precedents in natural resource law and use the Public Trust Doctrine (PTD) to promote authentic human rights and exclude Western/Northern post-modern cultural and regional disvalues as toxic to human ecology within the nations of ASEAN.

The public trust doctrine applies trust law principles to the natural and human ecosystems:

> The concept of the public trust doctrine is simple: certain natural resources—such as air, water and the sea—that are essential for all humans are held in trust by government for the benefit of all people, including future generations. Government is the trustee for these resources, the trust *res*, and has a fiduciary duty to protect the resources for the beneficiaries of the trust—present and future generations.[33]
>
> Importantly, government does not hold these natural resources in fee simple, but rather holds them in trust for the people and only for purposes that benefit the public interest. Government is a usufructuary rights-holder and cannot allow waste (permanent damage) to the trust resources.[34]

The PTD provides for the wise stewardship of common property held in trust for the benefit of all people. It demands that public authorities exercise their fiduciary duty to both conserve and provide public access to the trust resources. Originally, the PTD was bound to lands subject to tidal waters under English and American common law. "At common law, the title and dominion in lands flowed by the tide water were in the King for the benefit of the nation . . . . Upon the American Revolution, these rights . . . were vested in the original States . . . "[35] Today the scope of the PTD

---

33. Torres and Bellinger, "Public Trust," 281, 283.
34. Ibid., 286.
35. *Shively v. Bowlby*, 152 U.S. 1, 14-15 (1894).

has been expanded and it has been adopted by many nations, especially in the Developing World, to protect all natural resources.[36] Moreover, the PTD has been recommended as perhaps the most effective way to realize the goals of Rio + 20 since "the PTD converts stewardship principles to substantive stewardship requirements."[37] The PTD is analogous to the Common Heritage of Humanity (CHH) provisions already included in both hard and soft international law.[38]

The Supreme Court of the Philippines, for instance, declared all natural resources are held in trust by the government for the benefit of the Filipino people.[39] Hard natural resources with easily recognizable economic value have been included in the corpus or *res* of the public trust as well as whole ecosystems and their less quantifiable natural capital.[40] Already, scholars in the Catholic tradition have compared ecosystem services and natural capital to human ecosystem services and human capital to show the utility of natural marriage and the naturally procreative family to the integral and sustainable development of the society and a just social order.[41]

Pope Francis—Linking Natural and Human Ecology

Pope Francis in *Laudato Si'* challenged the international community of nations to be responsible stewards and "'safeguard the moral conditions for an authentic *human ecology*."[42] He made clear that there is link and unity between the natural and social environment: "'[T]he book of nature is one

36. See Blumm and Guthrie, *Internationalizing the Public Trust Doctrine*, 760–800, noting that in India, Pakistan, Philippines, Uganda, Kenya, Nigeria, South Africa, Brazil, and Ecuador, all natural resources are held in public trust.

37. See Turnipseed et al., "Public Trust Doctrine and Rio," 3.

38. See Feris, "Public Trust Doctrine and Liability," noting that CHH terms are included in several multilateral treaties including the *Convention Concerning the Protection of the World Cultural and Natural Heritage*, Paris, 16 Nov. 1972, 1037 UNTS 151, the *Agreement Governing the Activities of States on the Moon and Other Celestial Bodies*, New York, 5 Dec. 1979, 1363 UNTS 3, art 5,7, 11, the *Antarctic Treaty*, Washington, 1 Dec. 1959, 402 UNTS 71, preamble, the *Protocol on Environmental Protections to the Arctic Treaty*, Madrid, 4 Oct. 1991, 30ILM 1455 (1991), and the *UN Law of the Sea Convention*, Montego Bay, 10 Dec 1982, 1833 UNTS 3).

39. *Oposa v. Factoram*, G.R. No. 101083, 224 S.C.R.A. 792, 797-98 (Aug. 9, 1993).

40. Salzman and Ruhl, "Ecosystem Services," 15.1 Se. Envtl. L.J, 224 (2006).

41. See generally, The Witherspoon Institute, *Marriage and the Public Good*. Although the authors focus on the utility of natural marriage as opposed to so-called same-sex marriage, they also include a subsection on the innate value of natural marriage as an end in itself, conducive to human flourishing.

42. Francis, *Laudato Si*, #5, citing John Paul II, *Centesimus Annus*, #38.

and indivisible,' and includes the environment, life, sexuality, the family, and social relations and so forth."[43] It follows that 'the deterioration of nature is closely connected to the culture which shapes human coexistence,'" he said.[44] Pope Francis proposed St. Francis of Assisi as "the example par excellence of care for the vulnerable and of an integral ecology . . . "[45] and noted that we are facing an "urgent challenge to protect our common home" that includes seeking "sustainable and integral development . . . ."[46]

Pope Francis explained that real solutions concerning harms to the natural environment are linked to those of the social environment: "[W]e cannot adequately combat environmental degradation unless we attend to causes related to human and social degradation"[47] because "environmental deterioration and human and ethical degradation are closely linked."[48] Ethical degradation is found when men and women attempt to exercise absolute dominion over the earth by imposing their own laws and interests on reality.[49] This inclines us to "tolerate that some consider themselves more human than others, as if they had been born with greater rights."[50] Those who believe they have greater rights, Pope Francis says, make use of a "technological paradigm" that has the "power to globalize and make us all the same" by seizing "hold of the naked elements of both nature and human nature."[51]

Pope Francis challenged us to cast off this "Promethean vision of mastery over the world."[52] We must learn to "respect the natural and moral structure with which [we have] been endowed."[53] He warned that we disregard the "message contained in the structures of nature itself," when we disregard the "worth of a poor person, a human embryo, a person with disabilities."[54] Moreover, he emphatically stated that concern for nature is

---

43. Francis, *Laudato Si*, #6.
44. Ibid., citing Pope Benedict XVI, *Caritas in Veritate* #51.
45. Francis, *Laudato Si*, #10.
46. Ibid., #12.
47. Ibid., #48.
48. Ibid., #56.
49. Ibid., #75.
50. Ibid., #90.
51. Ibid., #108, citing Guardini, *End of the Modern World*, 64. See also, Tomasi, *Intervention by the Holy See* (noting the importance of "international protection of genetic resources, traditional knowledge, folklore and cultural expression"), cited in http://www.vhi.st-edmunds.cam.ac.uk/publications-folder/fciv-wp3.
52. Francis, *Laudato Si*, #116.
53. Ibid., #115, citing John Paul II, *Centesimus Annus* #38).
54. Francis, *Laudato Si*, #117.

"incompatible with the justification of abortion."⁵⁵ Pope Francis stressed that a genuinely human ecology must respect the relationship "between human life and the moral law" inscribed in our nature in the complimentary of the sexes, male and female.

> "Learning to accept our body, to care for it and to respect its fullest meaning, is an essential element of any genuine human ecology. Also, valuing one's own body in its femininity or masculinity is necessary if I am going to be able to recognize myself in an encounter with someone who is different (. . . .) It is not a healthy attitude, which would seek 'to cancel out sexual difference because it no longer knows how to confront it.'"⁵⁶

Therefore, in order to halt the degradation of the natural and moral environment, Pope Francis tells us that there is "an urgent need of a true world political authority."⁵⁷ To that end, humanity must devise stronger international organizations and confer upon them the police power and discretion to impose sanctions and ensure compliance. In the meantime, due to political stalemate, a "myopia of power politics delays,"⁵⁸ and corruption, non-governmental organizations and intermediate groups "must put pressure on governments to develop more rigorous regulations, procedures and controls."⁵⁹ Pope Francis recommendations appear compatible with the general thrust of the *Millennium Development Goals,* Goal 8—Develop a Global Partnership for Development—and *Sustainable Developments Goals,* Goal 17—Revitalizing the Global Partnership for Sustainable Development—in so far as "what is needed . . . is an agreement on systems of governance for the whole range of so-called '*global commons.*'" ⁶⁰

Pope Francis's analysis, now part of the patrimony of Catholic social thought,⁶¹ affirms the fact that there is an inseparable link between the natural, social, and ethical environments in a "global commons" and he describes how special interests thwart effective political or legislative remedy.

---

55. Ibid., #119.
56. Ibid., #155, citing Catechesis (April 15, 2015); *L'Osservatore Romano,* 8 (April 16, 2015).
57. Francis, *Laudato Si,* #175.
58. Ibid., #178.
59. Ibid., #179.
60. Ibid., #174.
61. Ibid., #15.

The Public Trust Doctrine Applied to Human Ecology

In order to circumvent the legislative roadblocks created by Western/Northern special interests, climate change activists have turned to the courts.[62] Their most potent weapon to prevent trespass upon the "commons"—land, sea and air—is the Public Trust Doctrine (PTD). From humble beginnings in English and American common law, the PTD has become a revolutionary legal stratagem.[63] Some describe the PTD as an inalienable indicia of sovereignty,[64] others think of it as "the law's DNA," or the "chalkboard" upon which constitutions are written.[65] Others have advanced the PTD as an effective means to implement the Sustainable Development Goals (SDGs).[66]

Already, many countries in the Developing World have incorporated the PTD into their legal systems.[67] The Supreme Court of India declared that *all* natural resources are held in trust by the government for the benefit of the people.[68] The Supreme Court of the Philippines declared that the public trust doctrine is grounded in natural law and exists independently of its constitutional or statutory recognition. The right to "a balanced and healthful ecology" is fundamental.

> "[It] belongs to a different category of rights altogether for it concerns nothing less than self-preservation and self-perpetuation . . . the advancement of which may even be said to predate all governments and constitutions. As a matter of fact, these basic rights need not even be written in the Constitution for they are assumed to exist from the inception of humankind. If they are now explicitly mentioned in the fundamental charter, it is because of the well-founded fear of its framers that unless the rights to a balanced and healthful ecology and to health are mandated as state policies by the Constitution itself, thereby highlighting their continuing importance and imposing upon

---

62. See Blumm and Wood, *Public Trust Doctrine*.

63. Ibid. For the first reformulation of the Public Trust Doctrine into a revolutionary legal strategy, see Sax, "Public Trust Doctrine," 471–566.

64. Blumm and Wood, *2014 Teacher's Manual*, 7.

65. Torres and Bellinger, "Public Trust," 283.

66. Turnipseed et al., "Public Trust Doctrine and Rio."

67. Developing countries that conceive all natural resources as held in public trust include India, Pakistan, the Philippines, Uganda, Kenya, Nigeria, South Africa, Brazil, and Ecuador. See Blumm and Guthrie, *Internationalizing the Public Trust Doctrine*, 760–800.

68. Ibid., 760, citing *M.C.Mehta v. Kamal Nath* (1997) 1 S. C.C. 388 (1996)(India); at 771 citing *Oposa v. Factoram*, G.R. No. 101083, 224 S.C.R.A. 792, 797-98 (Aug. 9, 1993).

the state a solemn obligation to preserve the first and protect and advance the second, the day would not be too far when all else would be lost not only for the present generation, but also for those to come — generations which stand to inherit nothing but parched earth incapable of sustaining life."[69]

The PTD's "Natural Use Principle"

Under the "Natural Use Principle," a corollary of the PTD, all un-natural development in an ecosystem should be enjoined. As a matter of principle "there is no property right in the first place to develop the land to change its natural character"[70] to "non-indigenous property uses that might harm the public."[71] Why? "Because a landowner is only entitled to reasonable expectations of what can be done to the land given "the natural character of the property and nature's laws."[72] To do otherwise would destroy trust property, thereby depleting the natural wealth of the trust much like "where a banker depletes monetary assets from a financial trust."[73]

For example, even though the state acting through developers and financial investors have the money and technology to drain marshes and wetlands in order to build airfields, gated communities and casinos they would destroy its natural ecosystem to do so. Since developers can have no *reasonable* expectation that a wetland ecosystem can be adapted to such un-natural and non-indigenous uses and still survive, they should be enjoined.

The PTD's "Precautionary Principle"

Plaintiffs defending the public trust enjoy the benefit of the burden-of-proof-shifting precautionary principle.[74] "[W]hen an activity raises threats of harm

---

69. *Oposa v. Factoran* 224 S.C.R.A. 792, available at http://www.lawphil.net/judjuris/juri1993/jul1993/gr_101083_1993.html. See Blumm and Guthrie, *Internationalizing the Public Trust Doctrine*, 773: "Thus, although the primary basis of the Filipino public trust doctrine jurisprudence lies in the constitutional right [to a] balanced and healthful ecology, the Court has ruled that the constitutional right merely reflects the public trust doctrine. The doctrine in turn is part of natural law rights to self-preservation and self-perpetuation that have existed from time immemorial."

70. Blumm and Wood, *2014 Teacher's Manual*, 55.

71. Ibid., 50.

72. Ibid., 50.

73. Ibid., 51.

74. Ibid., 766. ("Embracing the precautionary principle, the [Supreme] Court [of

to human health or the environment, precautionary measures should be taken even if some cause and effect relationships are not fully established scientifically."[75] The four central components of the principle are: taking preventative action in the face of uncertainty; shifting the burden of proof to the proponent of a risky activity; exploring a wide range of alternatives to possibly harmful actions; and increasing participation in decision making."[76]

Trustees have an affirmative fiduciary duty under the PTD to be proactive and protect trust assets before it is too late. The law should and must enable them to challenge effectively threats to public trust assets. "Many environmental conflicts result in degradation because there is not adequate scientific evidence to support regulation."[77] The precautionary principle essentially shifts the burden of proof to those who propose activity which threatens harm to an ecosystem. "Note that the precautionary approach dismantles the general argument of industry that it should not be regulated until the agency has proven harm from the industry practice."[78] Pope Francis endorsed the precautionary principle: "This precautionary principle makes it possible to protect those who are most vulnerable and whose ability to defend their interests and to assemble incontrovertible evidence is limited. If objective information suggests that serious and irreversible damage may result, a project should be halted or modified, even in the absence of indisputable proof. Here the burden of proof is effectively reversed . . ."[79]

Application of the PTD's Natural Use and Precautionary Principles

Given favorable precedents in the Developing World that have incorporated the PTD into domestic law, it would seem opportune to file suit in those domestic courts in order to protect the genetic heritage and biodiversity of their native people and cultural ecosystem.[80] According to the Natural Use Prin-

---

Pakistan] directed the government to conduct research on the potential harmful effects of electromagnetic energy . . . .") See also Paul, "Public Trust Doctrine."

75. Bento, "Searching for Intergenerational Green Solutions," 7.
76. Ibid.
77. Blumm and Wood, 2014 *Teacher's Manual*, 68.
78. Ibid., 70.
79. Francis, *Laudato Si*, #186.
80. See Nebel and Marenghi, "Emergence of IP Regimes," 115–16. See also, Bovenberg, "DNA as Universal Property," 35–73. However, anyone utilizing public trust litigation in order to protect the human genome would have to carefully distinguish *who* was the settlor of the *res* of the trust. Who has placed the human genome in the corpus of universal goods a trust asset for the benefit of all people? For NGOs of Catholic

ciple, those who introduce regional and cultural disvalues and misbehavior, such as elective abortion and same-sex marriage, threaten the natural fecundity of the native population and endanger their cultural ecosystem. LGBTIQ partners can form no reasonable expectation that anyone other than a man and a woman can be *naturally* fecund according to the "natural character" of their bodies and "nature's laws." Therefore, they have no right to change the natural reproductive environment of marriage and the family through force of law (under the guise of "equality" and "non-discrimination") and through technological prowess (IVF, surrogacy, hormonal treatment and same sex adoption, etc.). For the government to allow homosexual activists to drain the natural marriage ecosystem of its vitality and destroy the human ecological services it provides in order to satisfy unnatural uses amounts to gross mismanagement of public trust resources.[81]

Strategic lawsuits would also invoke the Precautionary Principle and call for a halt to the legalization of same-sex marriage in light of substantial evidence from the social sciences that it is not in the best interests of children to be raised by same sex parents.[82] These public and private actors have failed to meet their burden of proof—to show with clear and convincing evidence that a host of social ills will not follow upon violations of the rights safeguarded in "Model Declaration on the Rights of the Family."[83] The domestic courts that have applied the PTD to natural resources cannot ignore that the anti-natal practices recommended by LGBTIQ activists collectively and disproportionately affect the poor whose posterity are diminished. An agreement on systems of governance for the whole range of so-called *global*

---

inspiration, the settlor of the public trust *res* can only be God, the creator and sustainer of all creation. Therefore, there can be no private or public fee simple ownership of the human genome. It is already patented, if you will, by the *Imago Dei* found in the spiritual/non-material human soul it uniquely knits together to embody. See Francis, *Laudato Si*, #67 in general ("The earth is the Lord's" [Ps 24:1]) and more specifically #108 wherein Pope Francis warns of a dominant "technological paradigm" with a power to "globalize and make us all the same" by seizing "hold of the naked elements of both nature and human nature," citing Guardini, 64 (*End of the Modern World*, 56).

81. See footnote 40; also see "Brief of Amici Curiae," in *Obergefell v. Hodges*, Supreme Court of the United States, http://www.supremecourt.gov/ObergefellHodges/AmicusBriefs/14-556_100_Scholars_of_Marriage.pdf.

82. See Sullins, "Emotional Problems among Children," 99–120.

83. International Center on Law, Life, Faith, and Family (ICOLF), "Model Declaration on the Rights," Article 2; also see The Witherspoon Institute, *Marriage and the Public Good*, (evidence from the social sciences showing the benefits that accrue to society from natural marriage and the procreative family). "Brief of Amici Curiae," *Obergefell v. Hodges*, available at http://www.supremecourt.gov/ObergefellHodges/AmicusBriefs/14-556_100_Scholars_of_Marriage.pdf (arguing the natural procreative family is a delicate ecosystem with inherent laws for human flourishing).

commons cannot rest upon such injustice and invidious discrimination against the poor.

Conclusion

The international community is skeptical, rightfully so, of the inclusion of those articles in the ADHR that stress its regional and cultural values and national sovereignty lest these serve as a shield for the repression of politically inexpedient views. However, NGOs of Catholic inspiration have consistently encouraged the insertion of national sovereignty clauses in UN outcome documents as an effective means to block the inclusion of so-called rights of abortion and same-sex marriage into the domestic laws of various Developing Nations.

In order to assure that cultural and regional values and assertions of national sovereignty are used only for good, this paper recommends that those Member States of ASEAN that have asserted national sovereignty to block abortion and sodomy rights should sign a common declaration based on the model of ASEAN-5 or ASEAN+3. Their declaration would reaffirm the human rights articulated in the UDHR as they were understood at the time it was originally ratified. This would serve to block the recognition of specific Western/Northern cultural and regional disvalues (such as abortion and same-sex marriage supposedly lurking in the penumbras of the "non-discrimination" and "equality" clauses of the UDHR and other international treaties) as international customary law.

This paper also recommends that the public trust doctrine should be expanded in scope to include the whole ecological *res*, both natural and human, along the lines Pope Francis points out in *Laudato Si'* so that we protect "our common home"—a united healthful natural and human ecosystem.[84] The people of ASEAN need help to preserve their land and natural resources and, even more, their cultural values, traditional knowledge, folklore, genetic heritage and their natural fecundity through "systems of governance for the whole range of so-called 'global commons.'"[85] Therefore people of good will and NGOs of Catholic inspiration ought to take the offensive and file strategic lawsuits to protect integral human ecology in venues where the public trust doctrine has already been recognized in environmental and natural resource law. No less than climate change, a demographic winter threatens our planet as human population plummets worldwide.[86]

84. Francis, *Laudato Si*, #12.
85. Ibid., #174.
86. See Stout, *Demographic Winter*: www.demographicwinter.com.

As the age old saying goes, "One fool throws a stone into a river and a thousand wise men can't get it out." NGO's of Catholic inspiration and the poor and powerless people of the Developing World that they represent are locked in a life and death demographic struggle against powerful Western/Northern cultural and regional interests. It is good to recall that David defeated Goliath with a stone and God's help. National sovereignty and the public trust doctrine are legal stones, if you will, that if flung with grace may help to dislodge abortion and same-sex marriage from the stream of international human rights.

Annex 1: Draft Manifesto of Core Political and Cultural Rights of ASEAN Culture-3

We, ASEAN Culture-3 agree to the following human rights and fundamental freedoms, notwithstanding any developments in international customary law or interpretation given international treaties by special rapporteurs or treaty monitoring bodies;

Resolved the Universal Declaration of Human Rights (UDHR) reflects and articulates the long standing traditions of the people and nations of ASEAN Culture-3 and shall not be subject to regional or national particularities that undermine its recognition of human rights and fundamental freedoms as these were understood at the time the UDHR was drafted.

Resolved that all provisions of international treaties and customary international law signed or ratified by the states members of ASEAN Culture-3 as interpreted by special rapporteurs or treaty monitoring bodies shall be disregarded if inconsistent with the human rights and fundamental freedoms of the UDHR as these were understood at the time the UDHR was drafted.

Resolved that in order to add value to the human rights and fundamental freedoms of the UDHR, each state member of ASEAN Culture-3 shall subject all future developments to the long standing traditions of the people of ASEAN Culture-3 to the extent these are not inconsistent with the human rights and fundamental freedoms guaranteed in the UDHR as these were understood at the time it was drafted.

Annex 2: ASEAN Declaration of Human Rights

We, the Heads of State/Government of the Member States of the Association of Southeast Asian Nations (hereinafter referred to as "ASEAN"), namely Brunei Darussalam, the Kingdom of Cambodia, the Republic of Indonesia, the Lao People's Democratic Republic, Malaysia, the Republic of the Union of Myanmar, the Republic of the Philippines, the Republic of Singapore, the Kingdom of Thailand and the Socialist Republic of Viet Nam, on the occasion of the 21st ASEAN Summit in Phnom Penh, Cambodia.

Reaffirming our adherence to the purposes and principles of ASEAN as enshrined in the ASEAN Charter, in particular the respect for and promotion and protection of human rights and fundamental freedoms, as well as the principles of democracy, the rule of law and good governance;

Reaffirming Further our commitment to the Universal Declaration of Human Rights, the Charter of the United Nations, the Vienna Declaration and Programme of Action, and other international human rights instruments to which ASEAN Member States are parties;

Reaffirming Also the importance of ASEAN's efforts in promoting human rights, including the Declaration of the Advancement of Women in the ASEAN Region and the Declaration on the Elimination of Violence against Women in the ASEAN Region;

Convinced that this Declaration will help establish a framework for human rights cooperation in the region and contribute to the ASEAN community building process;

Hereby Declare As Follows:

General Principles

1. All persons are born free and equal in dignity and rights. They are endowed with reason and conscience and should act towards one another in a spirit of humanity.
2. Every person is entitled to the rights and freedoms set forth herein, without distinction of any kind, such as race, gender, age, language, religion, political or other opinion, national or social origin, economic status, birth, disability or other status.

3. Every person has the right of recognition everywhere as a person before the law. Every person is equal before the law. Every person is entitled without discrimination to equal protection of the law.

4. The rights of women, children, the elderly, persons with disabilities, migrant workers, and vulnerable and marginalised groups are an inalienable, integral and indivisible part of human rights and fundamental freedoms.

5. Every person has the right to an effective and enforceable remedy, to be determined by a court or other competent authorities, for acts violating the rights granted to that person by the constitution or by law.

6. The enjoyment of human rights and fundamental freedoms must be balanced with the performance of corresponding duties as every person has responsibilities to all other individuals, the community and the society where one lives. It is ultimately the primary responsibility of all ASEAN Member States to promote and protect all human rights and fundamental freedoms.

7. All human rights are universal, indivisible, interdependent and interrelated. All human rights and fundamental freedoms in this Declaration must be treated in a fair and equal manner, on the same footing and with the same emphasis. At the same time, the realisation of human rights must be considered in the regional and national context bearing in mind different political, economic, legal, social, cultural, historical and religious backgrounds.

8. The human rights and fundamental freedoms of every person shall be exercised with due regard to the human rights and fundamental freedoms of others. The exercise of human rights and fundamental freedoms shall be subject only to such limitations as are determined by law solely for the purpose of securing due recognition for the human rights and fundamental freedoms of others, and to meet the just requirements of national security, public order, public health, public safety, public morality, as well as the general welfare of the peoples in a democratic society.

9. In the realisation of the human rights and freedoms contained in this Declaration, the principles of impartiality, objectivity, non-selectivity, non-discrimination, non-confrontation and avoidance of double standards and politicisation, should always be upheld. The process of such realisation shall take into account peoples' participation, inclusivity and the need for accountability.

Civil And Political Rights

10. ASEAN Member States affirm all the civil and political rights in the Universal Declaration of Human Rights. Specifically, ASEAN Member States affirm the following rights and fundamental freedoms:

11. Every person has an inherent right to life, which shall be protected by law. No person shall be deprived of life save in accordance with law.

12. Every person has the right to personal liberty and security. No person shall be subject to arbitrary arrest, search, detention, abduction or any other form of deprivation of liberty.

13. No person shall be held in servitude or slavery in any of its forms, or be subject to human smuggling or trafficking in persons, including for the purpose of trafficking in human organs.

14. No person shall be subject to torture or to cruel, inhuman or degrading treatment or punishment.

15. Every person has the right to freedom of movement and residence within the borders of each State. Every person has the right to leave any country including his or her own, and to return to his or her country.

16. Every person has the right to seek and receive asylum in another State in accordance with the laws of such State and applicable international agreements.

17. Every person has the right to own, use, dispose of and give that person's lawfully acquired possessions alone or in association with others. No person shall be arbitrarily deprived of such property.

18. Every person has the right to a nationality as prescribed by law. No person shall be arbitrarily deprived of such nationality nor denied the right to change that nationality.

19. The family as the natural and fundamental unit of society is entitled to protection by society and each ASEAN Member State. Men and women of full age have the right to marry on the basis of their free and full consent, to found a family and to dissolve a marriage, as prescribed by law.

20. (1) Every person charged with a criminal offence shall be presumed innocent until proved guilty according to law in a fair and public trial, by a competent, independent and impartial tribunal, at which the accused is guaranteed the right to defence.

(2) No person shall be held guilty of any criminal offence on account of any act or omission which did not constitute a criminal offence, under national or international law, at the time when it was committed and no person shall suffer greater punishment for an offence than was prescribed by law at the time it was committed.

(3) No person shall be liable to be tried or punished again for an offence for which he or she has already been finally convicted or acquitted in accordance with the law and penal procedure of each ASEAN Member State.

21. Every person has the right to be free from arbitrary interference with his or her privacy, family, home or correspondence including personal data, or to attacks upon that person's honour and reputation. Every person has the right to the protection of the law against such interference or attacks.

22. Every person has the right to freedom of thought, conscience and religion. All forms of intolerance, discrimination and incitement of hatred based on religion and beliefs shall be eliminated.

23. Every person has the right to freedom of opinion and expression, including freedom to hold opinions without interference and to seek, receive and impart information, whether orally, in writing or through any other medium of that person's choice.

24. Every person has the right to freedom of peaceful assembly.

25. (1) Every person who is a citizen of his or her country has the right to participate in the government of his or her country, either directly or indirectly through democratically elected representatives, in accordance with national law.

    (2) Every citizen has the right to vote in periodic and genuine elections, which should be by universal and equal suffrage and by secret ballot, guaranteeing the free expression of the will of the electors, in accordance with national law.

Economic, Social, and Cultural Rights

26. ASEAN Member States affirm all the economic, social and cultural rights in the Universal Declaration of Human Rights. Specifically, ASEAN Member States affirm the following:

27. (1) Every person has the right to work, to the free choice of employment, to enjoy just, decent and favourable conditions of work and to have access to assistance schemes for the unemployed.

(2) Every person has the right to form trade unions and join the trade union of his or her choice for the protection of his or her interests, in accordance with national laws and regulations.

(3) No child or any young person shall be subjected to economic and social exploitation. Those who employ children and young people in work harmful to their morals or health, dangerous to life, or likely to hamper their normal development, including their education should be punished by law. ASEAN Member States should also set age limits below which the paid employment of child labour should be prohibited and punished by law.

28. Every person has the right to an adequate standard of living for himself or herself and his or her family including:
    a. The right to adequate and affordable food, freedom from hunger and access to safe and nutritious food;
    b. The right to clothing;
    c. The right to adequate and affordable housing;
    d. The right to medical care and necessary social services;
    e. The right to safe drinking water and sanitation;
    f. The right to a safe, clean and sustainable environment.

29. (1) Every person has the right to the enjoyment of the highest attainable standard of physical, mental and reproductive health, to basic and affordable health-care services, and to have access to medical facilities.

(2) The ASEAN Member States shall create a positive environment in overcoming stigma, silence, denial and discrimination in the prevention, treatment, care and support of people suffering from communicable diseases, including HIV/AIDS.

30. (1) Every person shall have the right to social security, including social insurance where available, which assists him or her to secure the means for a dignified and decent existence.

(2) Special protection should be accorded to mothers during a reasonable period as determined by national laws and regulations before and after childbirth. During such period, working mothers should be accorded paid leave or leave with adequate social security benefits.

(3) Motherhood and childhood are entitled to special care and assistance. Every child, whether born in or out of wedlock, shall enjoy the same social protection.

31. (1) Every person has the right to education.

    (2) Primary education shall be compulsory and made available free to all. Secondary education in its different forms shall be available and accessible to all through every appropriate means. Technical and vocational education shall be made generally available. Higher education shall be equally accessible to all on the basis of merit.

    (3) Education shall be directed to the full development of the human personality and the sense of his or her dignity. Education shall strengthen the respect for human rights and fundamental freedoms in ASEAN Member States. Furthermore, education shall enable all persons to participate effectively in their respective societies, promote understanding, tolerance and friendship among all nations, racial and religious groups, and enhance the activities of ASEAN for the maintenance of peace.

32. Every person has the right, individually or in association with others, to freely take part in cultural life, to enjoy the arts and the benefits of scientific progress and its applications and to benefit from the protection of the moral and material interests resulting from any scientific, literary or appropriate artistic production of which one is the author.

33. ASEAN Member States should take steps, individually and through regional and international assistance and cooperation, especially economic and technical, to the maximum of its available resources, with a view to achieving progressively the full realisation of economic, social and cultural rights recognised in this Declaration.

34. ASEAN Member States may determine the extent to which they would guarantee the economic and social rights found in this Declaration to non-nationals, with due regard to human rights and the organisation and resources of their respective national economies.

Right to Development

35. The right to development is an inalienable human right by virtue of which every human person and the peoples of ASEAN are entitled to participate in, contribute to, enjoy and benefit equitably and sustainably from economic, social, cultural and political development. The

right to development should be fulfilled so as to meet equitably the developmental and environmental needs of present and future generations. While development facilitates and is necessary for the enjoyment of all human rights, the lack of development may not be invoked to justify the violations of internationally recognised human rights.

36. ASEAN Member States should adopt meaningful people-oriented and gender responsive development programmes aimed at poverty alleviation, the creation of conditions including the protection and sustainability of the environment for the peoples of ASEAN to enjoy all human rights recognised in this Declaration on an equitable basis, and the progressive narrowing of the development gap within ASEAN.

37. ASEAN Member States recognise that the implementation of the right to development requires effective development policies at the national level as well as equitable economic relations, international cooperation and a favourable international economic environment. ASEAN Member States should mainstream the multidimensional aspects of the right to development into the relevant areas of ASEAN community building and beyond, and shall work with the international community to promote equitable and sustainable development, fair trade practices and effective international cooperation.

Right to Peace

38. Every person and the peoples of ASEAN have the right to enjoy peace within an ASEAN framework of security and stability, neutrality and freedom, such that the rights set forth in this Declaration can be fully realised. To this end, ASEAN Member States should continue to enhance friendship and cooperation in the furtherance of peace, harmony and stability in the region.

Cooperation in the Promotion and Protection of Human Rights

39. ASEAN Member States share a common interest in and commitment to the promotion and protection of human rights and fundamental freedoms which shall be achieved through, inter alia, cooperation with one another as well as with relevant national, regional and international institutions/organisations, in accordance with the ASEAN Charter.

40. Nothing in this Declaration may be interpreted as implying for any State, group or person any right to perform any act aimed at undermining the purposes and principles of ASEAN, or at the destruction of any of the rights and fundamental freedoms set forth in this Declaration and international human rights instruments to which ASEAN Member States are parties.

Adopted by the Heads of State/Government of ASEAN Member States at Phnom Penh, Cambodia, this Eighteenth Day of November in the Year Two Thousand and Twelve, in one single original copy in the English Language.

Bibliography

ASEAN LGBTIQ Caucus. "68 LGBT Groups and NGOs Protest Non-inclusion of LGBTs in ASEAN Human Rights Declaration." https://www.fridae.asia/gay-news/2012/11/16/12072.68-lgbt-groups-and-ngos-protest-non-inclusion-of-lgbts-in-asean-human-rights-declaration.

Asian Forum for Human Rights and Development. *Still Window-Dressing: A Performance Report on the Third Year of the ASEAN Intergovernmental Commission on Human Rights (AICHR) 2011–2012*. Bangkok: Asian Forum for Human Rights and Development, 2013.

Association of Southeast Asia Nations. "ASEAN Declaration on Human Rights." November 9, 2012. http://www.mfa.go.th/asean/contents/files/other-20121217-165728-100439.pdf.

Bento, Lucas. "Searching for Intergenerational Green Solutions: The Relevance of the PTD to Environmental Protection." *The Common Law Review* 11 (2009) 7–13. https://papers.ssrn.com/sol3/papers.cfm?abstract_id=1709104.

Blumm, Michael C., and Mary C. Wood. *The Public Trust Doctrine in Environmental and Natural Resources Law*. Durham, NC: Carolina Academic Press, 2013.

———. *2014 Teacher's Manual: The Public Trust Doctrine: In Environmental and Natural Resource Law*. Durham, NC: Carolina Academic Press, 2014.

Blumm, Michael C., and Rachel D. Guthrie. *Internationalizing the Public Trust Doctrine: Natural Law and Constitutional and Statutory Approaches to Fulfilling the Saxion Vision*. 45 U.C. Davis L. Rev. 741, 760–800.

Bovenberg, Jaspar A. "DNA as Universal Property." In *Property Rights in Blood, Genes and Data: Naturally Yours?*, edited by Jaspar A. Bovenberg, 35–73. Leiden: Brill-Nijhoff, 2005.

"Brief of Amici Curiae, 76 Scholars of Marriage." In *Obergefell v. Hodges. Supreme Court of the United States*. (Dec. 15, 2014) i–27. http://sblog.s3.amazonaws.com/wp-content/uploads/2014/12/ac76ScholarsOfMarriageOkToPrint.pdf.

"Brief of Amici Curiae, 100 Scholars of Marriage in Support of Respondents." In *Obergefell v. Hodges. Supreme Court of the United States*. http://www.supremecourt.gov/ObergefellHodges/AmicusBriefs/14-556_100_Scholars_of_Marriage.pdf.

Davies, Matthew. "States of Compliance?: Global Human Rights Treaties and ASEAN Member States." *Journal of Human Rights* 13.4 (2014) 414–33. https://doi.org/10.1080/14754835.2014.886949.

Desierto, Diane A. "Universalizing Core Human Rights in the 'New' ASEAN: A Reassessment of Culture and Development Justifications Against the Global Rejection of Impunity." *Göttigen Journal of International Law* 1.1 (2009) 77–114.

Fadillah, Rangga D. "RI Investment the Highest in ASEAN-5 Countries." *The Jakarta Post.* 2 March 2011.

Feris, Loretta. "Public Trust Doctrine and Liability for Historic Water Pollution in South Africa." *Law, Environment and Development Journal* 8.1 (2012) 3–18. https://www.researchgate.net/publication/303686753_The_Public_Trust_Doctrine_and_Liability_for_Historic_Water_Pollution_in_South_Africa.

Francis, Pope. *Laudato Si.* http://w2.vatican.va/content/francesco/en/encyclicals/documents/papa-francesco_20150524_enciclica-laudato-si.html.

Guardini, Romano. *End of the Modern World.* Basel: Hess Verlag, 1950.

International Center for Not-for-Profit Law. "1997 ASEAN VISION 2020." http://www.icnl.org/research/library/files/Transnational/vision.pdf.

International Center on Law, Life, Faith, and Family (ICOLF). "A Model Declaration on the Rights of the Family." http://icolf.org/wp-content/uploads/ICOLF.ModelFamilyDeclaration.2017.pdf.

International Commission of Jurists. "The ASEAN Human Rights Declaration: Questions and Answers." July 30, 2013. https://www.icj.org/wp-content/uploads/2013/07/ASEAN-leaflet-240713.pdf/.

Nebel, Mathias, and Carlo Marenghi. "The Emergence of IP Regimes and the Question of the Genetic Resources at WIPO: Toward a New Legal Instrument." In *Patents of Genetic Resources?: A Catholic Perspective for the World Intellectual Property Organization*, edited by Mathias Nebel, 119–29. Geneva: The Caritas in Veritate Foundation, 2013.

Oetomo, Dédé. "New Kids on the Block: Human Rights, Sexual Orientation and Gender Identity in Southeast Asia." *Asian-Pacific Law & Policy Journal.* 14.2 (2011) 118–31.

Paul, James T. "Public Trust Doctrine: Who Has the Burden of Proof?" Paper presented at the Association of Wildlife and Fisheries Administrators, State of Hawaii, July, 1996. http://www.precaution.org/lib/paul_public_trust_who_has_burden_of_proof.pdf

Prasertsri, Dalina, et al. *ASEAN Handbook for Women Rights Activities.* Chiang Mai, Thailand: The Southeast Asia Women's Caucus on ASEAN, 2013. http://apwld.org/wp-content/uploads/2013/12/ASEAN-Handbook-for-Womens-Rights-Activists.pdf.

Salzman, James, and J. B. Ruhl. "Ecosystem Services and the Public Trust Doctrine: Working Change From Within." *Southeastern Environmental Law Journal* 15 (2006) 223–39.

Sax, Joseph L. "Public Trust Doctrine in Natural Resource Law: Effective Judicial Intervention." *Michigan Law Review* 68 (1970) 471–566.

Scarnecchia, Brian. "Human Rights in ASEAN: A Catholic Critique of the Human Rights Mechanisms in the Association of Southeast Asian Nations (ASEAN)." *Ave Maria International Law Journal* 2.2 (2013) 62–85.

Song, Sophie. "Why 5 ASEAN Countries Combined are Attracting More Investment than China." https://www.investing.com/news/economy-news/why-5-asean-countries-combined-are-attracting-more-investment-than-china-270516.

Stout, Rick, dir. *Demographic Winter: The Decline of the Human Family*. 2008; Sydney: Acuity Productions, 2008. DVD. https://www.youtube.com/watch?v=lZeyYIsGdAA.

Sullins, Donald. "Emotional Problems among Children with Same-sex Parents: Difference by Definition." *British Journal of Education, Society and Behavioural Science* 7.2 (2015) 99–120.

Tomasi, Archbishop Silvano M. *Intervention by the Holy See at the General Assembly of the World Intellectual Property Organization (WIPO)*. September 22, 2008. http://www.vatican.va/roman_curia/secretariat_state/2008/documents/rc_seg-st_20080922_wipo_en.html.

Torres, Gerald. and Nathan Bellinger. "The Public Trust: The Law's DNA." *Wake Forest Journal of Law & Policy* 4.2 (2014) 281–317.

Turnipseed, Mary, et al. "The Public Trust Doctrine and Rio + 20." February 2012. http://www3.e-joussour.net/files/The%20Public%20Trust%20Doctrine%20and%20Rio%20+20_0.pdf.

The Witherspoon Institute. *Marriage and the Public Good: Ten Principles*. Princeton, NJ: The Witherspoon Institute, 2008. http://winst.org/wp-content/uploads/WI_Marriage_and_the_Public_Good.pdf.

World Conference on Human Rights. "Vienna Declaration and Programme of Action." https://www.ohchr.org/Documents/ProfessionalInterest/vienna.pdf.

Chapter 11

Religious Freedom and Christianity in the Middle East and North Africa (MENA) in the Context of the Papal Trip to Turkey

Geoffrey Strickland

During his November 2014 in-flight press conference from Istanbul to Rome, a Turkish journalist asked Pope Francis to comment upon the neologisms (or recently coined expressions)[1] of "Islamophobia," "Christianophobia," and what more can be done to address them.[2] Leaving aside for the moment the merits of using these new terms, this paper will explore aspects of his response and related issues, and argue that both Islamophobia in the West and Christianophobia in the Middle East and North Africa (MENA) region must be integrally addressed if authentic

---

1. Neologism is "a word or phrase which is new to the language; one which is newly coined." See "Neologism" in the Oxford English Online Dictionary, available at http://www.oed.com/.

2. The full question, posed by Yasemin Taskin, of Turkish television, is as follows: "President Erdogan spoke about 'Islamophobia.' Naturally, you reflected more on the current 'Christianophobia' in the Middle East, which is affecting both Christians and minorities. Taking interreligious dialogue into consideration as well, what more can be done? That is, is interreligious dialogue enough? Can more be done? And in your opinion, what must world leaders do? As you are not only the spiritual leader of Catholics, but also a moral leader on a global scale, what can be done concretely, is it possible to go further?" (Pope Francis, In-flight Press Conference of His Holiness Pope Francis From Istanbul to Rome, November 30, 2014, http://w2.vatican.va/content/francesco/en/speeches/2014/november/documents/papa-francesco_20141130_turchia-conferenza-stampa.html.)

non-discrimination is to be achieved. To this end, this chapter will be divided into the following sections. Part one will examine the notion of Islamophobia as articulated by the Organisation of Islamic Cooperation (OIC). Part two studies the notion of Christianophobia. Part three considers the question of what more can be done to effectively address the two phenomena. Finally, a brief conclusion is offered.

Islamophobia

Pope Francis began his response by addressing the notion of Islamophobia. He stated that:

> "It's true that there has been a reaction to these acts of terrorism, not just in this region but in Africa as well: 'If this is Islam it makes me angry!'. So many Muslims feel offended, they say: 'But that is not what we are. The Quran is a prophetic book of peace. This is not Islam'. I can understand this. And I sincerely believe that we cannot say all Muslims are terrorists, just as we cannot say that all Christians are fundamentalists—we also have fundamentalists among us, all religions have these small groups […]"[3]

Pope Francis seems to say that a "small group" of "fundamentalists," specifically "fundamentalists" who carry out "acts of terrorism" in the name of Islam, perpetuate the association of Islam to violence. This linking of Islam to violence is what the Holy Father seems to indicate as a major contributor to the phenomena described as Islamophobia.

Definition of Islamophobia

The words "Islam" and "phobia" are combined to form the neologism of Islamophobia. "Islam" denotes the religion of Muslims, it literally meaning submission, resignation, or reconciliation to the will of God coming from the root "Salam," or a notion of "peace," as the fruit of this submission.[4] "Phobia" is generally understood as "an exaggerated usually inexplicable and illogical fear of a particular object, class of objects, or situation," as

---

3. Ibid., supra note 2.
4. See "سلم" and "اسلام" in the *Hans Weir Arabic English Dictionary*, 4th edition (1993).

opposed to a rational fear.[5] Literally, thus, Islamophobia indicates the irrational fear of Islam.

Regarding Islamophobia in the international arena, the Organization for Islamic Cooperation (OIC), based in Saudi Arabia, is arguably the most vocal entity in defining and advocating against it. With a membership of 57 States in the MENA region and beyond, the OIC is the second largest intergovernmental organization after the United Nations.[6] The OIC describes itself as "the collective voice of the Muslim world."[7] Through its "Islamophobia Observatory," the OIC has published yearly reports since 2008 to raise international awareness of Islamophobia "as harmful to global efforts for peaceful coexistence, harmonious and multicultural societies."[8] In its 2013–2014 Report, the OIC offers the following definition of Islamophobia:

> "Islamophobia is a contemporary form of racism and xenophobia motivated by *unfounded* fear, mistrust and hatred of Muslims and Islam. Islamophobia is also manifested through intolerance, discrimination, unequal treatment, prejudice, stereotyping, hostility and adverse public discourse. Differentiating from classical racism and xenophobia, Islamophobia is mainly based on stigmatization of a religion and its followers. As such, Islamophobia is an affront to the human rights and dignity of Muslims."[9]

The OIC concludes that the prevalent attitude in the West is that "being Muslim should be confined to the private space, as the perceived fashions or societal behavior linked to Islam are seen as a threat to the established way of being in those societies."[10] In response, the OIC dedicated special attention in its latest report "to local Muslim communities living in the West, as these are the main victims."[11]

The OIC offers various cases that illustrate Muslims as the victims of Islamophobia in the United States,[12] Canada, and European countries in

---

5. See "phobia" in the Merriam Webster Online Dictionary.

6. See Organisation of Islamic Cooperation, "About the OIC," para. 1.

7. Ibid, para. 1.

8. Organisation of Islamic Cooperation, "Seventh OIC Observatory Report on Islamophobia," 10.

9. Ibid., 10 (emphasis by author).

10. Ibid., 10.

11. Ibid., 7.

12. The University of California at Berkeley Center for Race and Gender has a special Islamophobia Research and Documentation Project that "focuses on a systematic and empirical approach to the study of Islamophobia and its impact on the American Muslim community." They offer the following definition and history of the term: "The

its latest report. Generally, according to the OIC, the report "confirms the OIC's concerns and apprehensions that in some Western societies Islam was being increasingly misperceived as a religion of intolerance."[13] The OIC noted that Western media "continued to play a key role in promoting and disseminating an anti–Muslim culture," with a "continuous focus on the issue of 'Islamic extremism'" that "steadily consolidated negative stereotyping of Muslims."[14] However, a key question is both raised and answered in the OIC report: "What accounts for this trend toward more negative views of Islam and Muslims? Surely this trend is due in part to the drumbeat of alarming news linking Muslims with violent events."[15]

As to concrete examples of Islamophobia cited in the report, the following are some incidences noted by the OIC in the United States. Regarding behavior by US Law Enforcement, the OIC highlights the "practice of pressuring Muslims to become informants in their own communities in exchange for law enforcement help," namely having their names deleted from the "No-fly list."[16] The OIC then cites the "existence of a pervasive 'Crusader' sub-culture" affiliated with the US Military, illustrated by the existence of items or tattoos bearing the words "Kafir" and "Infidel."[17] Legislation is then discussed in reference to the initiative of several states in the United States

---

term 'Islamophobia' was first introduced as a concept in a 1991 Runnymede Trust and defined as 'unfounded hostility towards Muslims, and therefore fear or dislike of all or most Muslims.' The term was coined in the context of Muslims in the UK in particular and Europe in general, and formulated based on the more common 'xenophobia' framework. . . . For the purposes of anchoring the current research and documentation project, we provide the following working definition: Islamophobia is a contrived fear or prejudice fomented by the existing Eurocentric and Orientalist global power structure. It is directed at a perceived or real Muslim threat through the maintenance and extension of existing disparities in economic, political, social, and cultural relations, while rationalizing the necessity to deploy violence as a tool to achieve 'civilizational rehab' of the target communities (Muslim or otherwise). Islamophobia reintroduces and reaffirms a global racial structure through which resource distribution disparities are maintained and extended." See https://www.crg.berkeley.edu/research-projects/islamophobia-research-documentation-project/.

13. Islamophobia Observatory of the Organisation of Islamic Cooperation, *Seventh OIC Observatory Report on Islamophobia*, 4.

14. Ibid., 5.

15. Ibid., 15.

16. Ibid., 16, 20–22.

17. Ibid., 17–20. "Kafir" denotes "irreligious, unbeliever, infidel, atheist, ungrateful" and is an Arabic term with derogatory connotation in the Quran associated with non Muslims. See "كافر" and "كفر" in the *Hans Weir Arabic English Dictionary*, 4th edition.

that have legislated against the inclusion of Foreign or International law within their jurisdictions.[18]

Thankfully, the number of deaths of Muslims in the West attributed to Islamophobia in the report has been low. Prior to 2015 only one death in the United States was referenced as a "possible hate crime"[19] In 2015, however, three Muslim Americans were tragically murdered in North Carolina. The alleged killer, Craig Stephen Hicks, is awaiting trial for murder and a possible hate crime.[20] It is noteworthy, however, that according to the extensive "2011 Mosque Survey," sponsored in part by the Council on American-Islamic Relations (CAIR), there are over 2000 mosques in the United States alone, present in all 50 states.[21] The survey further indicated that "the vast majority of mosque leaders do not feel that American society is hostile to Islam."[22]

Christianophobia

After briefly discussing Islamophobia, Pope Francis then turned to Christianophobia. He explained:

18. Ibid, 22–24. The report listed the following proposed legislation: Florida Senate Bill 386; Georgia's HB 895 and SR 808; Iowa's House Bill 76; Kentucky's HB 43; Missouri's SB 619; South Carolina's HB 4494, SB 60 and 81; Mississippi's HB 44; Vermont's SB 265; West Virginia's SB 2116; Washington's SB 6118 and HB 1392.

19. The full description of the incident, entitled "US: Shooting Death of Sacramento Muslim Man Eyed as Possible Hate Crime," is as follows: "On 27 March 2014, the Council of American Islamic Relations (CAIR) held a press conference for Hassan Alawsi, a Sacramento-area Muslim man shot and killed in the parking lot of Home Depot off of Florin Road on 16 March 2014. At first, the Sacramento County Sheriff's Department thought Alawsi's murder was random but information from the family of the alleged shooter, Jeffrey Michael Caylor, led them to believe it may have been racially motivated. Sheriff's Department Sergeant Jim Barnes said: 'It seems he has a dislike for what he describes as a Muslim community.' Investigators had Caylor, 44, in custody. Video of the suspect showed him stalking Alawsi in the minutes leading up to the shooting. Still, the Sheriff's Department would not confirm Alawsi's death to be a hate crime." See Ibid., 110.

20. See, for example, Katz and Perez-Pena, "Federal Inquiry Begins."

21. According to the Introduction of the survey, "The US Mosque Survey 2011 is a comprehensive study of mosques in America. The Survey consisted of (1) a count of all mosques in America and then (2) a telephone interview with a mosque leader (Imam, President or board member) from a large sample of mosques. The mosque count was conducted from February to July 2010 and the mosque leader interviews were conducted from August 2010 to November 2011. A total of 2,106 mosques were counted. From this list, a random sample of 727 mosques was selected. 524 interviews were then completed, which means that the margin of error for the Survey is within the range of +/- 5 percent." See Bagby, *American Mosque 2011*, 2–4.

22. Ibid., 2–4.

"It's true, I'm not going to soften my words, no. We Christians are being chased out of the Middle East. In some cases, as we have seen in Iraq, in the Mosul area, they have to leave or pay a tax which then makes no sense. And other times they push us out wearing white gloves. . .It's as if they wished that there were no more Christians, that nothing remain of Christianity. In that region this is happening. It's true, it's first of all a result of terrorism, but when it's done diplomatically with white gloves, it's because there's something behind it. This is not good."[23]

Essentially, the Holy Father links Christianophobia to the desire for the eradication of Christians and of Christianity and to the subsequent exodus of Christians from the region. Among the causes of this exodus of Christians alluded to by Pope Francis are terrorism, and policy decisions, or acts done "diplomatically with white gloves," with this latter category being noteworthy "because there is something behind it."

Definition of Christianophobia

The Holy See has not issued an official definition of the term Christianophobia, though both Pope Benedict and Pope Francis have spoken in reference to it.[24] The former Vatican Secretary for Relations with States, H.E. Dominique Mamberti, described Christianophobia as a phenomenon understood in three aspects: erroneous education or disinformation regarding Christians and Christianity; intolerance and discrimination against Christian citizens through legislation and administrative decrees, and actual violence and persecution.[25]

The Observatory on Intolerance and Discrimination against Christians offers a similar explanation.[26] The Observatory explains that Chris-

23. The Holy Father also links Christianophobia to the tax levied on Christians, which to him "makes no sense." This tax, known as the "jizya," is the tax Christians historically paid according to Sharia Law to live in territories under Islamic rule. Through the "jizya," the life of the Christian is spared and the Christian is allowed to remain in the Islamic territory, though the Christian is relegated to the lesser sociopolitical and theological category with rights that are restricted. The "jizya" is reportedly making a comeback, however, in Egypt, Iraq, and Syria. See Quran IX, 29; Chasmar, "Egypt's Muslim Brotherhood"; Gol, "Iraqi Christians Flee"; Kelly Phillips Erb, "Islamic State Warns Christians," *Forbes*, July 19, 2014.

24. For example, see Benedict XVI, "Address on the Occasion."

25. See Mamberti, "La protezione del diritto."

26. According to its website, "the Observatory focuses on the European Union and (potential) accession countries. The information provided is a supplement to concerns regarding the worldwide phenomenon of intolerance against Christians—by

tianophobia describes "the phenomenon of intolerance and discrimination against Christians." Consisting of the "words 'Christian' or 'Christ' and 'phobias', the term means therefore an irrational animosity towards Christ, Christians, or Christianity as a whole."[27]

Examples of Christianophobia in the MENA Region

Christianophobia in the MENA region is rampant. In the Middle East alone, the Christian population has dropped from 20 percent of the total population to 5 percent and falling.[28] In Egypt, thousands upon thousands of Coptic Christians continue to experience persecution, violence, and massacres.[29] In Iraq, countless churches have been destroyed and numerous Christians persecuted, violated, and killed, causing hundreds of thousands of Christians to flee.[30] The situation in Syria, Iran, Pakistan, among others, continues to be tragic.[31] Because Saudi Arabia is one of the more prominent members of the OIC and also the location of the permanent secretariat of the OIC (Jeddah), some examples of Christianophobia will be taken from there.[32]

In Saudi Arabia, Christianophobia is astounding. Islam is the official religion and there is no legal recognition or protection of religious freedom.[33] Despite having an estimated 1.5 million Christian guest work-

---

calling attention to the more subtle forms occurring in Europe. The focus on Europe by no means disregards or devalues the tragic persecution of Christians in other areas of the world. The Observatory is a member of the Fundamental Rights Platform of the EU-Fundamental Rights Agency." See "About Us," Intolerance Against Christians, available at http://www.intoleranceagainstchristians.eu/about/about-us.html.

27. "Terminology," Intolerance Against Christians, available at http://www.intoleranceagainstchristians.eu/about/terminology.html. The Observatory describes the history of the term in the following manner: The terms "Christophobia" or "Christianophobia" entered the public debate in 2004, in the spring at the UN, and in the fall also at the European Institutions, after the European Parliament caused the rejection of Rocco Buttiglione, a practising Catholic, as a member of the EU commission. Several politicians and diplomates argued that discrimination against Christians must not spread any further. They called on the UN to speak up against Christianophobia, as it has done on Islamophobia and anti-Semitism. The UN Human Rights Commission in Geneva now speaks of "anti-Semitism, Islamophobia and Christianophobia."

28. Allen, *Global War on Christians*, 116.
29. Ibid., 120–24.
30. Ibid., 4, 134–39.
31. Ibid., see generally chapters 3 and 5.
32. See Organisation of Islamic Cooperation, "About the OIC," supra note 6.
33. See United Department of State Bureau of Democracy, "Human Rights and Labor" (hereinafter "Freedom Report for 2013"), 1; Allen, *Global War on Christians*, supra note 28, 138–42.

ers in the Kingdom and numerous appeals from the Vatican, no Churches are allowed in the country.[34] In theory private worship is permitted within personal residences but in practice there are many abuses by the "religious police."[35] There are persistent reports of "honor killings" in Muslim families when a conversion to Christianity is discovered.[36]

Incredibly, the Saudi Grand Mufti, who is the highest religious and legal official in the country, has called for the destruction of all the Churches in the Arabian Peninsula Region.[37] Most troubling, however, is the national and international proliferation of Christianophobia by Saudi Arabia. There have been numerous and continual Christianophobic references documented in the State approved primary and secondary school textbooks.[38] These textbooks are distributed throughout the Saudi public school system, to the academies it runs in many capitals of nations throughout the world, as well to other Islamic schools globally.[39] The following are a few literal examples of the violence in the textbooks:

> "Christians are enemies of the Muslims and there is perpetual clash with them,
>
> the Crusades have not ended and the 'Crusader Threat' continues, legally the life of a Christian is worth a fraction of that of a free Muslim male, Christians are swine, and Muslims are to hate Christians."[40]

---

34. Allen, *Global War on Christians*, supra note 28, at 138; Nina Shea, "Obama and the Churches of Saudi Arabia," *New York Times*, February 13, 2015.

35. "Freedom Report for 2013," supra note 33; Allen, *Global War on Christians*, supra note 28, 138–42.

36. Allen, *Global War on Christians*, 139.

37. See, for example, Mideast Christian News, مفتى السعودية يدعو لهدم كل كنائس شبه الجزيرة, MCN, March 13, 2012, available at http://www.mcndirect.com/showsubject_ar.aspx?id=32143.

38. "Freedom Report for 2013," supra note 33. For a report reviewing some of the major textbooks on Islamic studies published by the Saudi Ministry of Education see: Freedom House's Center for Religious Freedom and the Institute for Gulf Affairs, *Saudi Arabia's Curriculum of Intolerance*.

39. Freedom House's Center for Religious Freedom and the Institute for Gulf Affairs, *Saudi Arabia's Curriculum of Intolerance*, supra note 38, 15, 17.

40. See "Freedom Report for 2013," supra note 33; and Freedom House's Center for Religious Freedom and the Institute for Gulf Affairs, *Saudi Arabia's Curriculum of Intolerance*, supra note 38 at 23–30.

What Is to Be Done?

Pope Francis suggests the following:

> "I told the President [Erdogan] that it would be good to issue a clear condemnation against these kinds of groups. All religious leaders, scholars, clerics, intellectuals and politicians should do this. This way they hear it from their leaders' mouth. There needs to be international condemnation from Muslims across the world. It must be said, "no, this is not what the Quran is about!"

> "[. . .] When the new Turkish Ambassador to the Holy See came to deliver his Letters of Credence, over a month and a half ago, I saw an exceptional man before me, a man of profound piety. The President of that office was of the same school. They said something beautiful: They said: "Right now it seems like interreligious dialogue has come to an end. We need to take a qualitative leap, so that interreligious dialogue is not merely: 'What do you think about this?' 'We [. . . .] need to take this qualitative leap, we need to bring about a dialogue between religious figures of different faiths."[41]

Apparently the Holy Father is calling for clear "international condemnation" from the International Muslim community and, in agreement with the Turkish officials, a "qualitative leap" in the realm of Christian and Islamic relations. The Holy Father's message seems clear, and in his Apostolic Exhortation *Evangelii Gaudium* he contrasts "violent fundamentalism" with "authentic Islam," which is "opposed to every form of violence."[42]

The Need for International Condemnation

In this regard the Holy Father's recent address to the Pontifical Academy of Arabic and Islamic Studies (PISAI) is poignant.[43] He noted that "One needs to pay attention to avoid falling into the snare of a *facile syncretism* which would ultimately be an empty harbinger of a *valueless totalitarianism*, as a soft and accommodating approach, 'which says 'yes' to everything in order to avoid problems ends up being 'a way of deceiving others.'"[44] The Holy Father issued the invitation to "return to the basics" of an "encounter" with

---

41. Francis, *In-flight Press Conference*, supra note 2.

42. See Organisation of Islamic Cooperation, "Observatory Report," supra note 8, 91; Francis, *Evangelii Gaudium*, paras. 252–53.

43. Francis, "Address to Participants."

44. Ibid., para. 3.

the other.⁴⁵ As such, if "one begins from the premise of the common affiliation in human nature, one can go beyond prejudices and fallacies and begin to understand the other according to a new perspective."⁴⁶

Thus, double standards in the international consideration of violence, death, and discrimination of Christians in the MENA region, particularly by the OIC and member countries as they advocate against Islamophobic tendencies in the West, are unacceptable.⁴⁷ For example, imagine if 21 Muslims had been beheaded by Christians or if the Pope called for the destruction of all the mosques in Europe? Even more absurd would be if the Holy See were to issue official educational materials which taught that the life of a Muslim was worth a fraction of that of a free Christian male or that Muslims were swine or that Christians were to hate Muslims?

The Need for a Qualitative Leap

Returning to the basics of encounter would take us to the point that, as described in the words of the Grand Mufti of Lebanon during the recent Synod for the Church in the Middle East, "when Christians are wounded, we ourselves are wounded."⁴⁸ Stated another way, in the words of Benedict XVI, "whatever damage is done to another in any one place, ends up damaging everyone."⁴⁹ It was thus that the words and ideas of that Synod were meant to be a "clarion call, addressed to all people with political or religious responsibility, to put a stop to Christianophobia; to rise up in defense of refugees and all who are suffering, and to revitalize the spirit of reconciliation."⁵⁰

This way of thinking is beneficial to all parties involved. Violence and the proliferation of violence against Christians in the MENA region perpetuates the linking of Islam to violence in the Western media. Through the strong defense of the rights of Christians in the MENA region, the OIC

45. Ibid., paras. 3–4.

46. Ibid., para. 4.

47. The Holy Father had this to say in his address to the President of Turkey, "To this end, it is essential that all citizens—Muslim, Jewish and Christian—both in the provision and practice of the law, enjoy the same rights and respect the same duties. They will then find it easier to see each other as brothers and sisters who are travelling the same path, seeking always to reject misunderstandings while promoting cooperation and concord. Freedom of religion and freedom of expression, when truly guaranteed to each person, will help friendship to flourish and thus become an eloquent sign of peace" (Francis, "Address to President," para. 5).

48. Benedict XVI, "Address on the Occasion," supra note 24.

49. Ibid., supra note 24.

50. Ibid., supra note 24.

and similar groups could make greater strides in their mission to uproot what they term as Islamophobia from Western society.[51] As Fr. Samir Khalil Samir points out, perhaps the irrational fear of Islam in the West is more accurately described as *a "fear of the aggression"* associated with Islam, as seen in countries like Saudi Arabia.[52]

Toward Renewal

It is precisely this process of questioning and discussion that is crucial to the discernment of modern modalities of coexistence, at the personal, confessional, and societal level. The diversity of responses to these questions at first blush can be disconcerting, but in this tension of encounter the other is truly met in the imperfection of his or her humanity. From our shared humanity the bonds of unity are recognized, and the common fragility of our existence is seen through the lens of our capacity to appreciate the goodness of life and ugliness of violence and death both individually and collectively. Transcending, thus, the limits of both what we had previously conceived possible in ourselves and in our conception of the other, and what we perceived to be possible in the other and their conception of us, this "qualitative leap" can occur. This leap takes us from speaking of tolerance toward a true equality and non-discrimination that sees not Christian, Jew, or Muslim, but rather, the human person.

The recent words of the Egyptian President Abdel Fattah al-Sisi are remarkable. In noting that a "religious revolution" is necessary, which "the entire world" awaits, he states:[53]

> "It's inconceivable that the thinking that we hold most sacred should cause the entire Islamic world to be a source of anxiety, danger, killing and destruction for the rest of the world. Impossible! That thinking—I am not saying 'religion' but

---

51. In this regard, Pope Francis also noted during his trip to Turkey, "Fanaticism and fundamentalism, as well as irrational fears which foster misunderstanding and discrimination, need to be countered by the solidarity of all believers. This solidarity must rest on the following pillars: respect for human life and for religious freedom, that is the freedom to worship and to live according to the moral teachings of one's religion; commitment to ensuring what each person requires for a dignified life; and care for the natural environment. The peoples and the states of the Middle East stand in urgent need of such solidarity, so that they can 'reverse the trend' and successfully advance a peace process, repudiating war and violence and pursuing dialogue, the rule of law, and justice"(Francis, "Address to President," supra note 47).

52. Pentin, "Paris Terror Attacks," para. 23.

53. See Hayward, "Egyptian President Al-Sisi," para. 9.

'thinking'—that corpus of texts and ideas that we have sacralized over the centuries, to the point that departing from them has become almost impossible, is antagonizing the entire world. It's antagonizing the entire world! Is it possible that 1.6 billion people should want to kill the rest of the world's inhabitants—that is 7 billion—so that they themselves may live? Impossible!"[54]

Within his own context, Pope Francis has espoused a notion of renewal as well in his efforts to revitalize Western Christianity, which as we all know, has its own issues that need to be resolved. The assessment, however, offered by Pope Benedict XVI in regards to those voices wishing to unify Christians and Muslims is equally applicable here: "[these] and similar voices of reason, for which we are profoundly grateful, are too weak."[55]

There is much work to be done. Research and critical analysis must support "voices of reason," in both the East and West, of both Christians and Muslims, in seeking renewal. Perhaps the International Center for Law, Life, Faith and Family can collaborate with like-minded academic institutions to further explore these and related ideas through conferences, articles, and other publications.

Conclusion

Upon hearing the question of the Turkish reporter regarding Islamophobia, Christianophobia, and what more could be done, Pope Francis exclaimed, "You've asked a book's worth of questions!"[56] This chapter was thus a very brief introduction, in the context of the Holy Father's 2014 statements, to some of the complex challenges facing the MENA region and how they echo throughout the international landscape. The essay also analyzed the notion and examples of Islamophobia as articulated by the OIC, underlining that the OIC acknowledged the linking of Islam to violence as part of the cause of what it terms "Islamophobia." It then examined the notion and examples of Christianophobia, illustrating the violence and discrimination perpetuated against Christians in the MENA region by a primary OIC member state. Finally, the question of what more can be done to effectively combat Islamophobia and Christianophobia as related phenomena was considered in arguing for a "qualitative leap" of clear "international condemnation." By pushing into the difficult question of renewal as regards both Christiano-

---

54. Ibid., paras. 6–8.
55. Benedict XVI, "Address on the Occasion," supra note 24.
56. Francis, "In-flight Press Conference," supra note 2.

phobia and Islamophobia, it is hoped that together we can move toward the day when the need for fear, phobia, and neologism will be no more in the context of equality and non-discrimination.

Bibliography

Allen, John. *The Global War on Christians, Dispatches from the Front Lines of Anti-Christian Persecution*. New York: Image, 2013.

Bagby, Ihsan. *The American Mosque 2011: Report Number 1 from the American Mosque Study 2011*. Washington, DC: CAIR, 2011.

Benedict XVI, Pope. "Address on the Occasion of Christmas Greetings to the Roman Curia" (December 20, 2010). https://w2.vatican.va/content/benedict-xvi/en/speeches/2010/december/documents/hf_ben-xvi_spe_20101220_curia-auguri.html.

Chasmar, Jessica. "Egypt's Muslim Brotherhood to Coptic Christians: Convert to Islam, or Pay Jizya Tax." *The Washington Times*, September 10, 2013. https://www.washingtontimes.com/news/2013/sep/10/egypts-muslim-brotherhood-convert-islam-or-pay-jiz/.

Erb, Kelly Phillips. "Islamic State Warns Christians: Convert, Pay Tax, Leave Or Die." *Forbes*, July 19, 2014. https://www.forbes.com/sites/kellyphillipserb/2014/07/19/islamic-state-warns-christians-convert-pay-tax-leave-or-die/#19e2498e2c25.

Francis, Pope. "Address to Participants in the Meeting Sponsored by the Pontifical Institute for Arabic and Islamic Studies on the 50th Anniversary of its Establishment in Rome (January 24, 2015). http://w2.vatican.va/content/francesco/en/speeches/2015/january/documents/papa-francesco_20150124_pisai.html.

———. "Address to President, Prime Minister and Civil Authorities During the Apostolic Journey to Turkey" (28 November 2014). https://w2.vatican.va/content/francesco/en/speeches/2014/november/documents/papa-francesco_20141128_turchia-incontro-autorita.html.

———. "In-flight Press Conference from Istanbul to Rome" (30 November 2014). https://w2.vatican.va/content/francesco/en/speeches/2014/november/documents/papa-francesco_20141130_turchia-conferenza-stampa.html.

Freedom House's Center for Religious Freedom and the Institute for Gulf Affairs. *Saudi Arabia's Curriculum of Intolerance*. Washington, DC: Center for Religious Freedom, 2006. https://freedomhouse.org/sites/default/files/CurriculumOfIntolerance.pdf.

Gol, Jiyar. "Iraqi Christians Flee After Isis Issue Mosul Ultimatum." *BBC News*, July 18, 2014. https://www.bbc.com/news/world-middle-east-28381455.

Hayward, John. "Egyptian President Al-Sisi Calls for an Islamic Reformation." *Breitbart News* (January 9, 2015). http://www.breitbart.com/national-security/2015/01/09/egyptian-president-al-sisi-calls-for-an-islamic-reformation/.

Katz, Jonathan, and Richard Perez-Pena. "Federal Inquiry Begins into Muslims' Students Killings in North Carolina." *New York Times* (February 13, 2015). https://www.nytimes.com/2015/02/14/us/fbi-inquiry-muslim-student-killings-chapel-hill-north-carolina.html?mcubz=1.

Mamberti, Dominic. "La protezione del diritto di libertà religiosa nell'azione attuale della Santa Sede." Keynote Address presented at the Conference for the Academic Celebration of the Canon Law Faculty of the Pontifical University of the Holy

Cross, Rome, Italy, 10 January 2008. http://opusdei.org/it/article/lazione-della-santa-sede-in-favore-della-liberta-religiosa.

Organisation of Islamic Cooperation. "About the OIC." https://www.oic-oci.org/page/?p_id=52&p_ref=26&lan=en.

———. "Seventh OIC Observatory Report on Islamophobia" (June 18, 2014). www.oic-oci.org/oicv3/upload/islamophobia/2014/en/reports/islamophoba_7th_report_2014.

Pentin, Edward. "Paris Terror Attacks: What They did is in the Name of Islam." *National Catholic Register* (January 13, 2015). http://www.ncregister.com/daily-news/paris-terror-attacks-what-they-did-is-in-the-name-of-islam.

United Department of State Bureau of Democracy. "Human Rights and Labor, International Religious Freedom Report for 2013, Saudi Arabia." http://www.state.gov/j/drl/rls/irf/religious freedom/index.htm?year=2013&dlid=222311.

Index of Names and Subjects

abortion: as a violation of the equal dignity of all persons,10; related to concern for the environment, 172–73; right to, 120, 164–65, 167, 178–79; right to object to, 55, 59; 67, 74n22; as a threat to the cultural ecosystem, 177
accommodation, 81, 92, 108, 117, 125, 128; attacks on the principle of, 67–68, 70–74
accommodations: living, 92, 95; public, 52–53, 57–58
ACHR. *See* Convention on Human Rights, American
adoption, 50, 89, 95, 98–99, 118, 177
adoption agencies, 44–45, 50, 56, 65
Alexander II, Pope, 6
American Bar Association Rule of Law Initiative, 168–69
American Commission of Human Rights. *See* Inter-American Commission on Human Rights
American Convention on Human Rights. *See* Convention on Human Rights, American
anti-Semitism, 96, 196n27
Aquinas, Thomas, Saint, 3–4, 29, 40

Aristotle, 3, 37
ASEAN Declaration on Human Rights (ADHR), 163–66, 168–69, 178
Association of Southeast Asian Nations (ASEAN), 163–87
Atala vs. the State of Chile, 134–42, 147, 160–61
Augustine, Saint, 40

B v. France, 122
Baggett v. Bullitt, 119
Beaman, Lori, 68, 70, 72n17, 73
behavior: consideration of in child custody cases, 136, 138–39, 141; as opposed to mere sexual orientation, 99; subject to moral evaluation, xvii, 8, 88. *See also* conduct; lifestyle
Benedict XVI, Pope, 104n1, 172n44, 195, 199, 201
bigotry, 44–46, 48, 110, 113
Boethius, 3, 4n6
Buttiglione, Rocco, 40, 196n27

Carey, George Lord (archbishop of Canterbury), 110, 113
Catechism of the Catholic Church, 3, 10

INDEX OF NAMES AND SUBJECTS

Catholic Church: clericalism within, 21–22; diversity within, 13, 18, 19n26; governance by laity, 23–25; objections to anti-discrimination laws, 84–85, 100; promoting equality, 1–7, 14–15, 17, 20, 78, 80; not promoting equality, 16, 21, 84n22; right to freedom from government interference, 97, 101; teaching on homosexual acts, 8–10, 99–100; teaching on natural law, 29–30
Catholic social teaching, 5–7, 17, 29, 76, 78–80, 171–78
CEDAW. *See* Convention on the Elimination of All Forms of Discrimination against Women
CFR. *See* Charter of Fundamental Rights of the European Union
Charter of Fundamental Rights of the European Union (CFR), 82–83, 85–87, 96–97, 100, 154
Christianity: animus toward, 68, 104–5, 115, 125–27, 195–197 (*see also* Christianophobia); decline in Europe, 121, 124; early, 13, 22; influence of, 2, 12, 14, 15n16, 25; mainstream, 44, 68, 70. *See also* Christians
Christianophobia, 190–91, 194–97, 199, 201
Christians: in conflict with persons who identify as homosexuals, 46, 67, 108–13, 116, 124; discrimination against, 127–31, 199; double standards in the treatment of, 125–26, 130–131, 199; relations with Muslims, 198, 201; violence against, 197–97, 199
Christifideles Laici, 21, 79n9
civil partnerships, same-sex, 108–9, 116n42, 119–20. *See also* homosexual unions
Civil Rights Act, 47, 52, 53
clericalism, 20–22
climate change, 174, 178

coercion, government, 44–45, 51–52, 60, 112–14, 117
COMECE, 91, 93–5
Commission of the Bishops' Conferences of the European Union [Community] (COMECE), 91, 93–5
complementarity, sexual, 8-9, 84, 173
Concepts of Equality and Non-Discrimination in Europe: A Practical Approach ("The 2009 Report"), (McCrudden and Prechal), xxvi–xxvii
conduct, 44, 47, 59, 67, 71, 117–19, 142, 158. *See also* behavior; lifestyle
Congregation for the Doctrine of the Faith, 9–10, 22n34, 100n65
conscience: coercion of Christians to violate, 44, 47, 109; development of, 30; need for narrow tailoring of anti-discrimination laws to avoid infringement on, 49, 52, 57–59; owing to man's rational nature, 6, 151n4, 180; relationship to non-discrimination, 92, 95, 108, 114, 147
Convention on Human Rights, American (ACHR), 133, 137, 140, 143, 149–61
Convention on Human Rights, European (ECHR), 82, 106, 114n33, 115n38, 149, 154; freedom of religion, 117–18, 126–27; right to marry, 120–121
Convention on Population and Development (CPD), 167
Convention on the Elimination of all forms of Discrimination against Women (CEDAW), 165, 168–69
Convention on the Rights of the Child (CRC), xxiii, 85, 90
Convention on the Rights of Persons with Disabilities (CRPD), 90, 168
Council Directives of the European Commission (EC), 81, 87n28, 91–94, 98, 101

Council of Europe, 96, 106, 114–15, 120–21
CPD. *See* Convention on Population and Development
CRPD. *See* Convention of the Rights of Persons with Disabilities
CRC. *See* Convention on the Rights of the Child

deep equality, 67–74
democracy, 97, 105, 110, 163, 181, 183; foundations of, 30; human rights not subject to, 87; judicial usurpation of 122–23, 116, 131; need for continuing limits on government power, 73n20, 118
developed nations, 168
developing nations, 168, 171, 174, 176, 178–79
disabilities, persons with, 91n46, 95, 159, 172, 181; as a category which can be objectively defined, 92; conditions under which difference in treatment of is legitimate, 47, 89, 92n47. *See also* handicapped persons
discrimination: direct, xxvi, 81, 91–92, 115; indirect, xxvi, 81, 91–92, 115, 126–28, 159; racial, 58, 79; religious, 125 (*see also* religious freedom); reverse, 84, 100, 114; sex-based, 59, 78–79, 81–82, 129; on suspect grounds, 113–16, 133-34, 137, 145, 147
dis-values, 164, 168, 170, 177, 178
diversity: in conflict with religious freedom, 115; deep, 74; functional, 17–18; genuine, 65, 67, 69, 71, 73; Holy Spirit as creator of, 13, 15, 19n26; lack of respect for, 74–75; related to equality, 14, 17, 88, 118; related to inequality, xvii, 78; religious, 69, 72, 129; sexual, 70, 71, 122; value of, 15, 123
Dworkin, Ronald, 100–101, 124

EC. *See* Council Directives of the European Commission

EChHR. *See* Charter on Fundamental Rights of the European Union
ECHR. *See* Convention on Human Rights, European
ECHR. *See* European Court of Human Rights
ecology, human, 170–71, 173–74, 178
equal protection, 64, 181; absence of in the CRC, 157; in Catholic social teaching, 79; as opposed to non-discrimination laws, 151; relative to sexual orientation, 146; reporting on required by the CCD, xxiv –xxv
Equality Act (United States), 52
Equality Act (United Kingdom), 116n42, 123
Equality and Human Rights Commission, 119–120, 123, 130–31, 196n27
ethnicity, 81–83. *See also* nationality, race
European Charter of Human Rights. *See* Charter of Fundamental Rights of the European Union
European Convention on Human Rights. *See* Convention on Human Rights, European
European Court of Human Rights: applying the "very weighty reasons" test to sexual orientation, 114–15; cases regarding clashes between religious liberty and LGBT rights, 108n13, 111; cases regarding discrimination against Christians, 128–29; cases regarding discrimination against persons who identify as LGBT, 115n39, 147; declining to consider sexual orientation in child custody cases, 141; disregarding the rule of law, 117–20
European Court of Justice, 81, 88; 93
European Union, 76–101, 106, 164, 195n26, 196n27
Evangelii Gaudium, 76, 102, 198

INDEX OF NAMES AND SUBJECTS

Eweida v. British Airways, 112n22, 125–26, 129

Francis, Pope, 5, 13, 23, 171–78, 190–201
freedom: academic, 65, 97; of association, 72, 74; from hunger, 184; of movement, 182; of peaceful assembly, 183; of speech, 95, 108, 147, 183, 199n47; of religion (*see* religious freedom); of residence, 182; from torture, 167n19; of thought, 111, 114n33, 183

Gaudium et Spes, 6, 14, 17, 22n38, 78, 79
gay. *See* homosexual, persons who identify as
gay "marriage". *See* same-sex "marriage"
gender, 72, 85, 135, 159, 180, 186; dysphoria, 56; identity, 42–46, 52, 56–57, 66, 145–46, 165; mainstreaming, 83–84, 164, 167–68; reassignment, 115–16, 120, 122–23 (*see also* sex reassignment); roles, 96, 157, 166; stereotypes, 96, 140, 157–58, 166. *See also* sex
Goodwin v. United Kingdom, 122–23
Gregory I, Pope, Saint, 6
Gregory XVI, Pope, 7
Guardini, Romano, 172n51, 177n80

Hale, Brenda (Baroness), 124
Hamalainen v. Finland, 120–22
handicapped persons, 5, 159. *See also* disabilities, persons with
harassment, 7, 83, 87, 91–93
Harmonized Guidelines on Reporting under the International Human Rights Treaties, xxiii–xxiv
hate crimes, 107, 194
hate speech, 95–96, 120
hijabs, 125–26
Holy See, xxiii, xxv, xxx, 29, 195, 198–99
homogeneity, 69, 72–73
homophobia, 72, 96, 108, 140
homosexual: activists, 45, 55, 59, 165–66, 177; desires versus actions, 51, 70–71; lobby, 60, 141; tendencies, 9; unions, 9–10, 99–100 (*see also* civil partnerships, same-sex)
homosexual, persons identifying as: adoption of children by, 56, 118; child custody cases involving, 136, 142; conflicts with the rights of Christians, 67, 110, 124; Christians forced to accommodate, 133; denial of services to, 50, 55; discrimination against, 70–71, 111, 113, 116, 124, 139; flourishing of, 49–50; irrational dislike of, 51, 110; needs of, 57–58, 60; laws to protect, 42–43, 46, 61, 85, 117, 131, 140; unfair treatment of, 43, 48–49, 116n39, 134
homosexual acts, 8, 9, 143, 165, 167; freedom to commit, 47, 59; sterility of, 177
homosexuality: Christian views on, 44, 107, 109, 129–130; social engineering to promote, 65, 139
Human Rights Campaign, 49, 52, 56–57
Human Rights Commission, 119, 120. *See also under* Equality and Human Rights Commission
humanism, 85–86, 160

IACHR. *See* Inter-American Commission on Human Rights
IACtHR. *See* Inter-American Court of Human Rights
ICCPR. *See* International Covenant on Civil and Political Rights
ICESC. *See* International Covenant on Economic, Social, and Cultural Rights
ICOLF. *See* International Center on Law, Life, Faith and Family
illegitimacy, 114, 118, 154n15, 157–58
illiberalism, 71–72
inclusion, 74, 181
Inter-American Commission on Human Rights (IACHR), 136–37, 142, 157–59, 160n28

Inter-American Court of Human Rights (IACtHR), 133–34, 137–42, 150, 152, 154–56
Inter-American System, 133–34, 147, 149–52
International Center on Law, Life, Faith and Family (ICOLF), xv, xxvi, xxxi, 177n83, 201
International Covenant on Civil and Political Rights (ICCPR), 85, 123, 149, 156n18, 167n19
International Covenant on Economic, Social, and Cultural Rights (ICESC), 85, 149
intolerance, 90n41, 183, 192–93, 195–96
Islam, 116, 125, 196–97; American attitudes toward, 194; "authentic", 198; associated with violence, 191, 200–201; as a perceived threat to Western culture, 192–93; preferential treatment by the British government versus Christianity, 108, 131. *See also* Muslims
Islamophobia, 190–94, 196, 199–202

Jews, 6, 44, 70, 199–200
Jim Crow laws, 48, 52
John XXIII, Pope, Saint, 5, 19, 29
John Paul II, Pope, Saint, 19, 21, 23, 29, 30n2, 79–80, 84
Johns v. Derby City Council, 117n44, 129–31

Ladele v. Islington LBC, 108–13, 117, 128
Laudato Si, 171–73, 177–78
law: canon, 12-25; common, 52–53, 105–7, 118, 170, 174; domestic, 106, 117, 153, 159, 169, 176; folk, 119; international, xxxi, 7, 29, 80, 90, 135, 167n19,183, 194; moral, 9, 173; national, 97, 106, 126, 145, 183; natural, 8–10, 29–41, 86, 100, 124, 174–75; of nature, 175, 177; rule of, 64, 74, 85, 105–6, 117–19, 131, 180, 200n51; soft, 95, 106, 164, 167–68
Leo XIII, Pope, 29

lesbian, persons identifying as. *See* homosexual, persons identifying as
Letter to Women (Pope John Paul II), 84–85
LGBT, persons identifying as. *See* homosexual, persons identifying as
lifestyles, 8, 98, 115–16, 131, 142. *See also* behavior; conduct
Locke, John, 69n12, 117n45
Lumen Gentium, 2, 16–19, 22n38

Maestri v. Italy, 117
Magna Carta, 106
María Eugenia Morale de Sierra vs. Guatemala, 157, 159
marriage: attacks on, 14, 44–45, 165, 177; as the basis of the family, 99; as a benefit to society, 171, 177; Christians discriminated against for their views on, 46, 108–13; coexistence of different views on, 65, 67; dissolution of, 136, 155–58, 182; equal rights of spouses in, 155n15, 156–57; legal redefinition of, 46, 59, 141, 146; natural, 12, 171, 177; nature of, 34, 67; right of Christians to act on their views of, 45–46, 50, 56, 59–60; sexual complementarity in, 12, 46, 56, 89, 99; social privileges reserved for, 98–100, 134; state's duty to protect, 99, 155n15; value of compared to same-sex relationships, 8–10, 100, 171
marriage equality, 8, 52, 65. *See also* same-sex "marriage"
Mba v. Merton LBC, 127
McFarlane v. Relate, 108–13, 117
minorities, 68–70, 82–83, 116n39, 128–29, 190n2
morality, 67, 108–9, 163–66, 181; Judeo-Christian, 105, 107, 115; judiciary ill-equipped to adjudicate issues relating to, 116; sexual, 65
multiculturalism, 69

Muslims, 44, 125, 72, 125–26, 191–94, 197–201. *See also* Islam

nationality, xxvii, 80, 82–83, 100, 114, 156, 182. *See also* ethnicity, race
Nazir-Ali, Michael (archbishop of Canterbury), 127-28
Neuberger, David Lord, 109, 111, 113
Noah v. The Wedge Hairdresser, 126
non-governmental organizations (NGOs), xxiv, 100n66, 147; Catholic, 31, 39; 167–68, 170, 176n80, 178–79
Novak, David, 73

Obergefell v. Hodges, 42, 44, 59–60
Octogesima Adveniens, 76n1, 79
Organization for Islamic Cooperation (OIC), 191–93, 196, 199, 201
Orwell, George, 63, 66, 75

Paul, Saint, 1–3, 15, 20, 40
Paul III, Pope, 7
Paul VI, Pope, Saint, 20, 29, 76n1, 79,
personhood, 4, 9n27, 149, 152, 154–55, 161
Piechowiak, Marek, 86
pluralism, 30, 52, 71–72, 74, 86, 115
Public Trust Doctrine, 170–71, 174–79
prejudice, xxv, 79, 89–91, 123, 192–93, 199. *See also* racism
proportionality test, 89, 114, 154

race: as a category that can be objectively defined, 91n46; as a comparator in discrimination law, 113; discrimination based on, xxvii, 180; discrimination based on condemned by the Catholic Church, 8, 78–79; discrimination based on prohibited by international treaties/human rights instruments, 81–83, 137, 151, 156; discrimination based on prohibited by law, 115, 116n42; dissimilarity to religion as a basis for rights, 67; dissimilarity of to sexual orientation/gender identity as a basis for rights, 45–47, 49, 52–53; dissimilarity of to sex/gender as a basis for rights, 54, 58; irrational prejudice regarding, 89; reverse discrimination based on, 101n67. *See also* ethnicity, nationality

racism, 1, 10, 96, 192; dissimilarity to discrimination based on sexual orientation/gender identity, 46–49, 57–58. *See also* prejudice
Ratzinger, Joseph Cardinal, 22n34, 30, 34
Reasonable Accommodation: Managing Religious Diversity (Beaman), 67–73
religion: as a comparator in discrimination law, 113; cultural animus toward, 105–7; discrimination based on condemned by the Catholic Church, 5, 7–8, 78–79; discrimination based on condemned by international treaties/ human rights instruments, 81–83, 98, 101n68, 137, 151, 156, 164; discrimination laws inadequate to protect, 67, 116; diversity of beliefs within, 129; freedom of (*see under* religious freedom); need for anti-discrimination laws to avoid burdening freedom of, 49, 51, 57–58, 61; as a suspect category, 114; threats to from anti-discrimination laws, 73, 92, 115
religious freedom, 45, 97–98, 106; as a basis for exemption from anti-discrimination laws, 114, 52, 57–58; compromising with LGBT rights, 42, 48, 59; in conflict with LGBT rights, 140; difference between anti-discrimination laws and, 44–45, 116, 125; infringement upon by anti-discrimination laws, 43, 52, 108–12, 115, 147; infringement

upon by the state, 107, 196; lack of state support for, 120n58; as a natural curb to state overreach, 74n20; relationship to non-discrimination rights, 95, 101, 105, 200n51

religious liberty. *See* religious freedom

rights: ancillary, 113-114; civil, 44, 47, 49, 52, 69n12, 182; of the family, 95, 139, 150, 155, 177; to life, 4, 156, 161, 182; to marry, 90, 95, 120-22, 155-56, 182; to privacy, 136-37, 139, 142, 156, 161, 165n7, 183; reproductive, 115, 120, 164-65, 167-68, 178-79; substantive, 114; of women, 89, 160, 165-66, 168-69, 181

Rule of Law Initiative, 168-69

same-sex "marriage": coercion of Christians to participate in, 46, 50-51, 56, 108, 113; coercion by international bodies to legalize, 136-137, 139, 177-78; legal recognition of, 44, 70-71, 177; legal recognition of in American countries, 133-34, 144; legal recognition of in European countries, 121; not in best interests of children, 56, 177; promotion by the judiciary, 65, 120-21, 140, 144; promotion by the State, 120, 124, 135; right of Christians to object to, 65, 74n22, 109, 113; social pressure to support, 125; sterility of, 177; value of compared to heterosexual marriage, 8-10, 99, 171n41

Scruton, Roger, 88-89

secularism, 104-5, 107

security, national, 163-64, 167n19, 181

sex (gender), 57; in the ACHR, 156; as a biological reality, 44; as a category that can be objectively defined, 91n46; difference of required for marriage, 99, 156; discrimination based on, xxvii, 59, 113; discrimination condemned by the Catholic Church, 8, 78-79; discrimination prohibited by law, 116, 145; discrimination prohibited by international treaties/human rights instruments, 81-84, 93, 137, 151; dissimilarity to race as a basis for rights, 58; dissimilarity to religion as a basis for rights, 129; dissimilarity to sexual orientation or gender identity as a basis for rights, 46-47, 49, 115; legitimate polices that consider, 55, 58, 66, 89; social pressure and economic incentives sufficient to preclude discrimination based on, 53, 58; social pressure and economic incentives not sufficient to preclude discrimination based on, 54; in the TFEU, 83. *See also* gender

sex reassignment, 46, 56, 116n42. *See also* gender reassignment

sexism, 46-47, 49, 58

sexual acts, 50, 67, 139, 143

sexual orientation: anti-discrimination laws in conflict with freedom of religion, 43, 67, 99, 108; consideration of in child custody cases, 135-39, 142, 161; cultural acceptance of, 49; differentiated from gender identity, 120; differentiated from sexual acts, 51, 56, 71; dissimilarity to race or gender, 46; elevation to a suspect category for discrimination, 114-16, 133-34, 137, 147; legally equivalent to race, 45, 52; mistreatment of persons based on, 43, 50-51, 145; prioritized above freedom of religion, 45-47, 110, 116, 124; promoted by IACHR/IACtHR, 136, 141, 143-44; as a protected class under the law, 67, 81-83, 138, 145-46, 165

sexuality, human, 39, 45-47, 65, 72, 172

Shipley, Heather, 70–73
Sikhs, 125–26
sincerity test, 109n14
slavery, 156, 182; Christianity as a social force against, 3, 7, 10; 14, 15n16; anti-discrimination laws as a response to the legacy of, 1, 48, 52
Śledzińska-Simon, Anna, 81–84, 94–95, 99
sodomy, 133, 164–65, 178
Suárez, Francisco, 7
Supreme Court, U.S., 2, 42, 54, 59
Sztompka, Piotr, 90
terrorism, 191, 195

TFEU. *See* Treaty on the Functioning of the European Union
tolerance, 67–68, 70, 72–73, 185
totalism, civic, 71, 73–74
transgender, 56–57. *See also* transsexual
transsexual, 122–23. *See also* transgender
Treaty of Amsterdam, 81–82, 85, 100
Treaty of Lisbon, 82–83
Treaty of Maastricht, 81–82
Treaty of Rome, 80, 106
Treaty on the Functioning of the European Union (TFEU), 80–85, 87, 97

UDHR. *See* Universal Declaration of Human Rights
unborn persons, 1, 4–5, 55, 57, 149–50, 161, 179

United Nations, 168, 192, 196n27; human rights treaties, 164; outcome documents, 167, 169, 178; reporting guidelines for states' reports, xxiii–xxvii; soft law of, 106, 167; treatment of equality, xxxi, 85
Universal Declaration of Human Rights (UDHR): 80n12, 85, 99, 180, 182–83; acknowledgment of the need to treat people differently based on certain differences, 90; contrasted with the ACHR, 149, 152, 155–56; corruption of core principles, 164–65; maintaining consistency with the original meaning of, 169–70, 178–79; nondiscrimination clauses in, 151

Vatican II, 6, 16–17, 19–22, 78
victimization, 91n46
Vienna Declaration and Program of Action (VDPA), 168, 180
Vitoria, Francisco de, 7
Vladimiri, Paulus, 6

W v. Registrar of Marriages, 122–23
Weber, Max, 86
weighty reasons test, 66, 114–15, 138
Westen, Peter, 66–67

xenophobia, 96, 192–93

Scripture Index

Genesis
1:26–27	1, 3, 12, 77
2:19–20	77
2:24	12

Psalms
4:7	4
24:1	177n80

Matthew
20:28	22
22:21	13, 16
28:19	2

Mark
5:13-16	19
10:42	2
10:45	3, 22
12:17	13, 16

Luke
20:25	13, 16

John
13:34	18

Acts
2:4	2
17:26	1
17:27	2

Romans
2:14	40
4:35	18
8:21	18
12:4–5	15

1 Corinthians
4:1	2
10:17	15
12:11	19
12:12–19	15
12:27–31	15

Galatians
3:27–28	77

Ephesians

5:25	2
5:28	2
6:5–9	15

Colossians

3:4	18
3:22–24	15

Titus

2:9–10	15

Philemon

1:10	3
1:17	3, 15

Hebrews

5:1	13
5:4	13

1 Peter

2:9	16
2:18–19	15

2 Peter

1:1	19
1:4	13

www.ingramcontent.com/pod-product-compliance
Lightning Source LLC
Chambersburg PA
CBHW051055230426
43667CB00013B/2299